OPEN SOURCE MODERN HORARY ASTROLOGY

Tips, Techniques & Best Practices

for a 21st Century Approach

R.K. Alexander

ALCA Publishing • Oregon, USA

Open Source Modern Horary Astrology

Copyright © 2011 by R.K. Alexander. All rights reserved.

No part of this book may be reproduced or transmitted in any form or by any means, electronic or mechanical, including photocopying, recording or by any information storage and retrieval system, without written permission from the author, except for the inclusion of brief quotations in a review.

All chart wheels courtesy of Astrodienst (www.astrodienst.ch or astro.com). Midpoint tree in Chapter 5 copyright © 2006 Matrix Software, Inc., Big Rapids, Michigan (www.astrologysoftware.com).

Cover photo: NASA/JPL-Caltech, PIA 03153. Cover design by http://www.cgvcreative.com

ALCA Publishing, Oregon, USA
International Standard Book Number/ISBN-13: 978-0615511535
ISBN-10: 0615511538
Produced and distributed in the United States of America

Library of Congress Control Number: 2011911886
Alexander, R.K.
Open Source Modern Horary Astrology/by R.K. Alexander. Includes bibliographical references.
ISBN: (Book) 978-0615511535
1. Horary Astrology. 2. Horary Astrology-Case Studies. 3. Divination.
I. Title.
ILMP59HLHC70.v1

First Edition/Version 1.0.2: 11/2011

Update codes: 77266, 2259, 135931, 117, 52, 22, 4, 11726, 81940M, ZTX564541, 813541, 65983677412 LU749RT83902, MM03882ID45920IEL, 1988M

Warning Disclaimer:
The purpose of this book is to educate and entertain and provide accurate information with regard to the subject matter covered. However, the author and publisher accept no responsibility or liability for inaccuracies or omissions. The author and the publisher specifically disclaim any liability, loss, or risk, whether personal, financial or otherwise, that is incurred as a consequence, directly or indirectly, from the use and/or application of any of the contents of this book.

This book was composed using the open source productivity suite OpenOffice.org version 3.2.0
This book uses material from Wikipedia, under the terms of its Creative Commons Attribution-Share-Alike License 3.0 <http://creativecommons.org/licenses/by-sa/3.0/> and <http://en.wikipedia.org/wiki/Wikipedia:CCBYSA>

modernhoraryastrology@gmail.com

For
Debra Sanchez Pasquotto

OPEN SOURCE MODERN HORARY ASTROLOGY

Table of Contents

FOREWARD i
INTRODUCTION 1
1 HORARY BUILDS ON NATAL ASTROLOGY'S FOUNDATION 5
    Horary Astrology's Source Code 7
2 ASTROLOGY & ASTRONOMY REUNITE FROM PLUTO'S ASHES 9
    Good News: Pluto Is Now a Dwarf Planet! 10
    Solar System 2.0 for Astrologers 12
    Clarity & Confirmation, Not Clutter 15
3 PHILOSOPHICAL DIFFERENCES BETWEEN MODERN & TRADITIONAL HORARY ... 19
    Factions and Dogmas 20
    The Advantages of Modern Horary 24
    The Proof Is In the Accuracy 26
4 TECHNICAL DIFFERENCES BETWEEN MODERN & TRADITIONAL HORARY 29
    Traditional Myths About Outer Planets Debunked 32
    Modern Horary Rulerships 38
    Finding Your Own Way 39
5 THE MODERN HORARY TOOLBOX 41
    Aspects 42
    Asteroids & Lilith 43
    Astromaps 46
    Co-significators 47
    Combust the Sun 47
    Critical Degrees 47
    Derived or Derivative Houses 48
    Dispositors 49
    Early or Late Degrees 49
    Fixed Stars 49
    House Systems 51
    Houses 51
    Interceptions 51
    Interference/Prohibition, Frustration, and Hinderance/Impedition 52
    Malefics and Benefics 52
    Midpoints 53
    The Moon 56
        Eclipses and Occultations 57
    Mutual Reception 57

North and South Nodes	58
Part of Fortune	59
Planetary Rulership (Dignity & Debility)	59
Querent & Quesited	60
Reception	60
Refranation	61
Retrogrades (Rx)	61
Significators	63
Strictures Against Judgment	63
Timing	64
Trans-Neptunian Objects (TNOs)	68
Via Combust: The Burning or Fiery Way	68
Void-of-Course (VOC)	69

6 MODERN HORARY INTERPRETATION, STEP-BY-STEP 71
- I. HEADLINES – Nouns & Overview 73
- II. DETAILS – Verbs & Action 74
- III. CONCLUSIONS – Synthesis & Confirmation 76

7 ELECTIONAL ASTROLOGY & EVENT CHARTS 79
- Guidelines for Electional Charts 81
  - Travel 82
  - Job Interviews 82
  - Business Startups 82
  - Real Estate 83
  - Marriage 83
  - Surgery 84
  - Lawsuits 84
- Electing for a Sales Agreement 85
- Electing for Divorce 87
- A Job Interview Event Chart 90
- Worst Travel Event Charts Ever 92

8 MODERN HORARY IN ACTION 95
- An Office Space Question: The Astrologer Sees the Red Flags 95
- A Moving or Relocation Question: Pluto *IS* Personal and Knows How to Force the Issue 97
- A Foreclosure Question: You, Too, Can Overcome Debility and Combustion 99
- Practice Charts 102

9 BEST PRACTICES 107
- When the Astrologer Gets in the Way 108
- You Will Be Wrong 110
- You Will Be Right 110
- You Will Be Right, But for the Wrong Reasons 111
- Common Horary Myths 111

Staying on Track..113
10 TOP TEN HORARY MISTAKES & HOW TO AVOID THEM....................................115
11 RELATIONSHIP-ORIENTED HORARY QUESTIONS..121
A Typical "Will We Get Together?" Chart...126
The Ultimate Breakup Chart..128
12 AN EVOLVING BODY OF WORK...133
What's in a Name? 133
TNOs: A New Astrological Way of Thinking...134
Using TNOs in Horary..137
Light Years Away: The Future of Horary & Astrology...150
EPILOGUE - Beyond Astrology..153
APPENDIX A – Modern Horary's Public Body of Evidence..155
PART I - Books on Symbolism & Meanings of the Outer Planets 155
PART II - Books About Modern Horary..156
PART III - Modern Horary Case Studies...157
Case Study #1: Regulus & Spica can't overcome an opposition to Neptune...............160
Case Study #2: Saturn in the 7th isn't a stricture against judgment in a relationship question—it's a wealth of information..163
Case Study #3: Pluto knows a shady car deal when it sees one.....................................166
Case Study #4: Self-delusion over a bad living situation is narrowly averted by a Uranus-Neptune mutual reception..169
Case Study #5: A retrograde significator and outer planet T-square delay retirement...............174
Case Study #6: A late degree ASC & Moon conjunct Uranus Rx causes high anxiety, but points to staying the course 176
Case Study #7: Use reality and geography when applying significators to a relocation chart...179
Case Study #8: Debilitated Venus opposing Sedna leaves a very bitter aftertaste in a long-dead relationship 182
Case Study #9: Career woes under the regime..186
Case Study #10: Pluto kills a business, while Venus brings a new opportunity.........188
Case Study #11: When the astrologer totally and completely gets it WRONG!..........190
Case Study #12: The outer planets collude extensively to foil a house sale over the course of several months..193
Case Study #13: A big change looms at 29 degrees..206
APPENDIX B – Horary Cheat Sheets..213
APPENDIX C – Practice Chart Answers..221
APPENDIX D – Sources Used for Planetary Names...225
APPENDIX E – IAU Resolutions B5 & B6..237
APPENDIX F – Astronomica..239
Part I - Sedna Discovery White Paper..239
Part II - History of the Asteroids as Minor Planets..239
Part III - The New Horizons Mission 2015-2020...239

APPENDIX G – TNOs for Recovery Data & Further Study..241
    Part I - How to Recover Newly Discovered Astronomical Objects in Horary Charts 242
    Part II - How to Generate Charts for Object Recovery..242
    Part III - The Triangle Shirtwaist Factory Fire: Recovering Pluto, Chiron, Sedna & Eris...............243
APPENDIX H – The Future of Astrology as Mirrored in Astronomy...247
BIBLIOGRAPHY..249
ACKNOWLEDGEMENTS...251

OPEN SOURCE MODERN HORARY ASTROLOGY

Table of Figures

Figure No.	Name	Page
2.1	Solar System within the Oort Cloud	12
2.2	The Four Zones of the Solar System	14
2.3	Traditional Planets Only & Whole Solar System	17
5.1	Astromap	46
5.2	Midpoint Tree	55
5.3	Lease Signing Depicting Lunar Timing	65
5.4	Relationship Chart for Significator Progression Timing	67
7.1	Sales Agreement Election Chart	86
7.2	Divorce Election Chart	88
7.3	Job Interview Event Chart	90
7.4	Andes Plane Crash - Itinerary Departure	93
7.5	Andes Plane Crash - Air Traffic Control Data	94
8.1	Should the Querent Rent the Massage Space?	96
8.2	Querent Stay at Current Residence or Move in with Friend?	98
8.3	Can My Friend Defeat the Foreclosure He's Facing?	100
Practice Chart 1:	Should the Querent Move Her Residence to City X?	103
Practice Chart 2:	Should the Querent Pursue Screenwriting?	104
Practice Chart 3:	Will the Querent Get the Job with the Evil Megacorporation?	105
Practice Chart 4:	Should Querent Rent 4th of July Craft Booth?	106
11.1	Will the Querent Get Together with Co-Worker?	127
11.2	The Ultimate Breakup Chart	129
12.1	Trans-Neptunian Objects	135
12.2	Large Kuiper Belt Objects	138
12.3	Largest Known Trans-Neptunian Objects (TNOs)	140
12.4	Orbit of Sedna	143
12.5	Orbits of Orcus and Pluto as of April 2006	145
Apdx A/Pt. III - Case Study #1:	Regulus & Spica Can't Overcome an Opposition to Neptune	160
Apdx A/Pt. III - Case Study #2:	Saturn in the 7th isn't a Stricture Against Judgment	163
Apdx A/Pt. III - Case Study #3:	Pluto Knows a Shady Car Deal When It Sees One	166
Apdx A/Pt. III - Case Study #4:	Self-delusion Over a Bad Living Situation	169
Apdx A/Pt. III - Case Study #5:	An Rx Significator & Outer Planet T-Square Delay Retirement	174

Apdx A/Pt. III - Case Study #6: Late Degree ASC & Moon Conj. Uranus Rx Causes High Anxiety..........176

Apdx A/Pt. III - Case Study #7: Use Reality & Geography When Applying Significators to a Relocation Chart..........179

Apdx A/Pt. III - Case Study #8: Debilitated Venus Opposing Sedna Leaves a Very Bitter Aftertaste..........182

Apdx A/Pt. III - Case Study #9: Career Woes Under the Regime..........186

Apdx A/Pt. III - Case Study #10: Pluto Kills a Business, While Venus Brings a New Opportunity..........188

Apdx A/Pt. III - Case Study #11: When the Astrologer Totally & Completely Gets It Wrong..........190

Apdx A/Pt. III - Case Study #12: Outer Planets Collude Extensively to Foil a House Sale..........193

Apdx A/Pt. III: Case Study #12 - Part II..........197

Apdx A/Pt. III: Case Study #12 - Part III..........202

Apdx A/Pt. III: Case Study #13: A Big Change Looms at 29 Degrees..........206

Apdx G - Pt. 3: Triangle Shirtwaist Factory Fire..........244

Apdx H: The Future of Astrology as Mirrored in Astronomy..........247

FOREWARD

This blog entry by Caltech astronomy professor Mike Brown is reprinted in its entirety, and used with his permission. It in NO WAY, SHAPE or FORM constitutes ANY kind of endorsement by Dr. Brown of this book, the author, or of the material within. He's just a very generous scientist who likes astrologers, and knows us better than we know ourselves. Read on.

I ♥Astrologers

by Dr. Mike E. Brown. Reprinted with permission.[1]

Please don't tell any of my fellow astronomers, but I love astrologers. Really I do.

Don't get me wrong. I have absolutely no belief whatsoever in the proposition that the positions of planets or stars or moons or anything else that is moving across the sky has or ever has had any sort of control over your life, your actions, or your choices. Zero. Really.

So if I don't believe in what I must assume would have to be considered a central precept of astrology, how can I possibly claim to love the practitioners? Let me count the ways.

Astrologers care about the sky and the positions of the stars and the moon. I care about the sky and the positions of the stars and the moon. Astrologers try to understand patterns in the orbits and motions of the planets and determine their meaning. I try to understand patterns in the orbits and motions of the planets and determine their meaning. In a broad sense, we do many of the same things; it's just that our methods are different.

Astrology and astronomy are brothers with roots deeper than just the first five letters. Until perhaps the Enlightenment they were inseparable. Copernicus, who made one of the greatest conceptual leaps in human history, pulling the Earth out of the center of the universe and replacing it with the Sun, was a dedicated astrologer, calculating astrological charts with as much fervor as trying to understand the paths of the planets. It's not hard to understand why he would feel that some connection should be there. I don't think anyone can watch the rhythms and pulses of the movements of the planets and Sun and Moon and not somehow get a gut feeling that there is somehow meaning in all of that beauty, precision, and symmetry.

But from their common upbringing, the brothers split in adulthood. They each retained their common interest in the sky, but with thoroughly different ways of looking at it. Astronomy moved to the purely objective realm of descriptive and predictive reality. It moved to science. And a wondrous science it is. I can go outside tonight and look up to see the bright glowing star Betelgeuse, the red orb in the upper corner of constellation Orion, and then I can tell you a pretty good version of the entire story of its birth in a cloud of gas and dust, its long existence as a smaller and cooler star with hydrogen atoms fusing together in the deep interior, and its recent expansion to form a ball of gas the size of the orbit of Mars. That we have been able to determine this story at all, simply from looking at the feeble light from these little points in the sky, is as improbable as it is incredible. When I see Betelgeuse at night and stop to think these thoughts I am left in awe.

So what can astrology offer that can even come close to matching? It can't tell me anything, I don't think, about my history or my future or my personality or my pitfalls. Or about anyone else's. Isn't it therefore worthless, or even potentially dangerous? I don't think so. Astrology is the brother who kept the fascination with the sky but rather than growing an interest in science, kept its interest in humanity. Scientific astronomy, for all of its awe-inspiring, mind expanding, and just simply amazing discoveries, leaves people and their consciousness out of the picture. Astronomy involves people looking up at the heavens, but the heavens are never looking back. Astrology, in contrast, never removed that connection between the sky and the people.

But but but, you protest, there is no connection between the sky and the people. The heavens do not, in fact, look back. And, while you are scientifically correct, you are culturally incorrect. You are thinking literally, but you need to think literarily. Good astrology can be like good literature. Good literature builds a world that is not the real world but teaches us more about ourselves than we would ever learn by simply staring in the mirror. No real King Lear ever had a trio of daughters to split his kingdom amongst nor wandered insane on the heath, but do we disdain Shakespeare for writing about it? No, we read, and we think about children and parents, we think about truth and loyalty, and scheming, and we learn more about ourselves and our world. We're left enriched by stories that are not true.

Again, I have to plead: don't get me wrong. I'm certainly not saying that all astrology is equivalent to Shakespeare, but neither is all of the rest of the fiction writing out there. The in-flight magazine that I currently have in front of me has both a short story and an astrology page. I would rate them equal quality examples of their genres.

Here's a snippet of my in-flight horoscope (I'm a Gemini, perhaps explaining my ability to accept the dual nature of astronomy/astrology) for the month of January:

> As your attention is consumed by an array of projects, you may spread yourself too thin. Remember to stop and take a breath, if for no other reason than to garner some perspective.

OK. I don't need an astrologer to tell me that, but it's hard not to read it and, why, yes, stop and take a breath and garner a little perspective. It's not such a bad idea. A quick perusal of the short story, a few pages earlier, gives a remarkably similar take home message, spread out, instead, over about three pages. After reading both of these I am now convinced: I think I will stop and garner some perspective, at least if I can finish a few of these other projects first.

So where are the Shakespeares of astrology? I will admit to not knowing if they exist at all. My astrological reading is only passive; occasionally someone will send me something and in a spare moment I will pick it up and I just might find it a bit intriguing. Here, for example, are some thoughts about Eris by Henry Seltzer, writing in *The Mountain Astrologer*:

> The astrology of Eris seems to be related to the no-holds-barred fight for continued existence that is fundamental in all natural processes, and to taking a stand for what one believes, even if violence is involved. As the sister of Mars, the God of War, Eris willingly sought the battle. There is a side of nature that is quite harsh, a struggle for survival; this struggle is an essential part of the human condition as well, for we are still half animal. Nature can be viewed in a rosy light, as it was in the hippie era of the Sixties, Bambi innocently drinking from a little stream. But underlying this beauty is the possibility of sudden death at any moment, since all of nature's children need to eat. Eris is related to this principle of violence as a natural component of existence and to the concept of the female warrior that embodies it, especially the feminist struggle for rights in a patriarchal society. [2]

As a general discussion of the national psyche circa late 2007, this passage is not at all bad. It covers the war in Iraq, global warming, and the Hilary Clinton candidacy all in the discussion of one name. It certainly does not require literal belief that the naming of an object in the sky is the actual cause of any of the things discussed.

But what is the point of astrology if you chose to read it figuratively rather than literally? Again, you could ask the same question of King Lear. You could ask the same question of the Bible. And you wouldn't. To ask it is to miss the point entirely.

Here's a question you should ask though: why tolerate the existence of astrology, with the danger that people might actually take it literally, with the danger that it might confuse and distort science, with the fear that real cause and effect will become confused, when real literature abounds? Why read pithy but relatively generic snippets of advice and pretend they are somehow connected to a particular constellation along the zodiac? Why read more extended essays purporting to be an in-depth analysis of how a recently discovered ball of rock and ice far from the earth affects all of humanity? The answer? There is no reason. I personally prefer my literature to be of higher quality, to make me think and feel more. Feel free to follow my lead. But if you do chose to read it, read it for the reason that I can't help but love it.

Astrology is not just figurative literature about humanity. Astrology cares about the sky. The astrologers who occasionally correspond with me love to hear about new solar system discoveries, figure out orbital relationships and patterns, and speculate about what else might be out there and how everything fits together. I do all of these things, too. I then take these thoughts and move on to think literally their scientific implications. The astrologers take these thoughts and move on to think figuratively about what these mean for humans. But we, astronomers and astrologers, start in the same spot, with an intense interest in the sky. To me, that matters.

Astronomy and astrology are brothers. Brothers don't always do the same things or make the same choices. But when they maintain their initial ties to where they came from, their connection cannot help but stay strong. What is not to love?

Dr. Mike E. Brown is the Richard and Barbara Rosenberg Professor of Astronomy at the California Institute of Technology (Caltech). By the age of 40, he had approximately 60 trans-Neptunian discoveries, including three dwarf planets, under his (Kuiper) belt—and still counting. (To give proper credit, Chad Trujillo and David Rabinowitz were co-discoverers of most of the objects with Brown.)

INTRODUCTION

> ***Open Source* (n.)** — Often referred to as a movement, open source software (or other content) is publicly shared intellectual property. Begun by computer programmers that reject secrecy and/or centralized control of creative work in favor of decentralization, transparency and unrestricted "open" sharing of information.[1]

Most people don't start learning astrology via horary. They begin with natal, transits and progressions, and eventually turn their eye toward horary's specialized branch once they have a solid astrological foundation. Horary is similar to natal astrology in many subtle ways because all astrological branches share the same source code: the symbolic meanings of the transits of the planets (and other astronomical objects) through the 12 houses of the horoscope at any given point in time.

After an interpretation, there's no greater compliment than to hear a querent say "This makes me want to learn horary!" And then there's nothing worse than watching them attempt to learn it via the old-fashioned, antiquated, traditional methods, and seeing their initial enthusiasm yield to "Horary is so hard—there's so much to learn; it's so confusing!" They struggle, become frustrated, and eventually give up. It doesn't have to be that way.

The modern or non-traditional methods used to interpret horary charts are faster to learn, easier to use, equally as accurate, and far less complicated than the archaic and cumbersome traditional horary methods. While traditional horary is a viable horary method, it is not the only one, and it's certainly not for everyone. It has its shortcomings, such as a huge learning curve due to a voluminous amount of complicated and unfamiliar rules, and an inability to grow, change and evolve. Further, centuries of scientific and astronomical advances have been woefully and deliberately ignored in favor of fictionalized technical devices devised by ancient authorities to compensate for the science they couldn't possibly know. Their contemporary disciples then perpetuate the ancient science fictions, and, strangely, declare them to be "tried and true."

Astrology by belief, philosophy and superstitious lore—whether handed down through the ages or contemporary—will never be as efficient, effective or objective as astrology based on science and astronomy, because that's what standardizes the body of work. Standardization, in turn, decreases complication and confusion, because in the 21st century, astrologers adjust to the solar system's realities, not the other way around. Modern horary astrology re-synchronizes science with the art by symbolically interpreting currently known astronomical objects (planets, asteroids, trans-Neptunian objects, etc.) within a horoscope to arrive at detailed and accurate conclusions to specific questions. Astronomy + mythological and archetypal symbolism = astrology.

There's an unfortunate amount of subjectivity in astrology in general, and horary in particular. There's a lot of "I did this, and it works for me" and "Well, I tried it and it didn't work." This is one of the major reasons horary can be so difficult to learn. By creating the right balance of objectivity via standardization, "Well, it works for me!" can be replaced with "It works, period."

The astrological source code of symbolism is primary in horary, and the technique to apply the symbolism is a far distant second. Knowing how to think about a horary chart will help you know what to look for *before* diving into the chart and applying whatever methods you wish to interpret with. This book is intended to give you a solid foundation in how to do both from a modern standpoint. It assumes the reader already possesses a fundamental understanding of astrology; that the meanings of the signs, planets, aspects and houses are already understood, so you can synthesize the astrological knowledge you already have into fast, detailed, and accurate horary interpretations.

Horary is not a perfect, sacred and revered institution whose strict orthodox rules must be obeyed or you will generate inaccurate and incorrect interpretations. If you try to practice paint-by-numbers astrology, you will end up overlooking too many important things in a chart in favor of trivialities. It's more about synthesizing subtlety and nuance. Horary is also not enslaved to any technique or ideology. No one person or school of thought has the market cornered on horary astrology, and no one ever will. Never let anyone else's beliefs or dogmas dictate what you can or can't use to interpret a horary chart. And never let another astrologer's limitations become your own.

Just as you would expect a physician to have an understanding of the various parts and systems of the human body, an astrologer's understanding of the components of the solar system the art is based on allows the charts to readily reveal their information. And just as physicians and other professionals must participate in continuing education to renew their licenses, astrologers can only benefit their querents by learning new things. The ability to say, "I don't know how I ever interpreted charts before without using X!" is a sign that you're on the right track. An exceptional craftsperson is always looking for ways to improve.

Astrology's overhaul and evolution is not for the narrow-minded or faint at heart—great change never is. Open source astrology, horary or otherwise, allows for and expects change and growth in the body of work.

A solid base from which to start is key to any successful endeavor. This book will provide you with a firm foundation in the logic, mechanics and methodology of interpreting horary charts, from which you can grow and eventually branch out. Whether traditional or modern in your horary leanings, try a slice of everyone else's cake, and then learn to bake your own. That's when you become a true professional and your work can have a tremendous and profound impact on others.

R.K. Alexander
June 2011

Note: Charts in this book are without data to protect privacy and to encourage astrologers to move out of the comfort zone of their proprietary software when interpreting charts. "Any chart, any technique, any time, anywhere," is the mark of a skilled practitioner, because all are valid. The ancients did this with sticks in the sand. Today we have computers.

Also omitted are specialized areas of horary interest, such as contest charts and finding lost objects. There are numerous publications focusing exclusively on those specific topics. Once you possess the horary basics, they will be easier to learn.

1 HORARY BUILDS ON NATAL ASTROLOGY'S FOUNDATION

"The best way to learn astrology is to live it." [1]
—*astrologer Michael Lutin*

Horary is the best form of astrology for the instant gratification crowd. Most horary questions are about immediate crises or situations, so the resolution or outcome occurs fairly quickly. Natal, transit and progression astrology, which look more toward the long run, can take years for patterns to unfold, especially when slower, outer planets are involved. Natal astrology is about cycles; horary astrology is about right now.

The key difference between natal and horary astrology is in the amplification. Natal astrology is an attempt at making sense of life, while horary attempts to make sense of a specific situation. Horary is a microscopic astrological view, whereas natal, transits and progressions are the broad view. Natal, transits and progressions may show activity in your career sector (10th house), but do you know which specific job offer would be better to accept? That's where horary comes in.

Since a horoscope is nothing more than a snapshot of planetary transits as viewed from Earth, it makes no difference whether that snapshot is going to be interpreted as a horary or natal chart. The planets do what they do and appear where they do regardless. Symbolism that is fundamental to natal astrology doesn't suddenly stop working when looking at a horary chart. The planets, houses and signs don't lose their symbolic meanings in the transition from natal, transits and progressions to horary. The chart focus changes—that's all.

With natal interpretation, you're looking at three wheels instead of one if you include progressions and transits, and tend to touch on every planet and house over the course of an in-depth interpretation. In horary, only what's relevant to the question asked is primary. Natal astrology also shows static trends: Everyone has a Saturn return at roughly 28 years old; a Uranus opposition in their early 40's; a Chiron return around the age of 50, etc. Horary, on the other hand, shows a specific microtrend within a snapshot of current transits tied to a specific question. You don't have to wait eight years for Uranus to plod its way through the 2nd house. In horary, it's there *right now*, up close and personal, providing outrageous swings of fortune in relation to the question asked. Additionally, horary by its nature rapidly builds up empirical evidence as to the correct symbolism, application and meaning of new astronomical discoveries, thereby greatly assisting natal astrologers with their integration of these objects over the long term.

There are several interpretive forms of horary astrology, including modern, traditional, Uranian and Vedic. But interpretive technique is distant and secondary because in spite of the various methods, they all yield correct answers because they all share the same source code: symbolism. The real-world meaning of Saturn in Pisces square Mercury in Gemini, for example, is the same for all astrologers, no matter what branch of astrology or school of horary thought subscribed to. Since astrology is the symbolic interpretation of astronomical objects applied to human affairs, modern horary technique, like all astrology, focuses on two specific skills: 1) How well you can interpret the symbolism and 2) How well you can translate and explain that symbolism to the querent in a complete, cohesive, and accurate narrative.

KEY DIFFERENCES BETWEEN HORARY AND NATAL ASTROLOGY

HORARY	NATAL
• Microscopic	• Broad or long-term view
• Specific question or event	• Person's life as a whole
• Immediate	• Cyclical
• Horary research of newly discovered astronomical objects is relatively quick to observe, compile, and integrate, so it can feed the slower main body of natal.	• Natal can integrate newly discovered astronomical objects over the long-term, and add more depth to the horary body of knowledge.

Modern horary gives natal practitioners a familiar frame of reference to work with—the fundamentals of a transit chart. Traditional horary astrology generally insists that you discard much of the knowledge you already use to interpret natal, transit and progressed charts, and begin anew using their ancient-based system and voluminous, antiquated, complicated and often contradictory rules. This is incredibly unnecessary—you can read a horary chart easily and accurately with the astrological knowledge you already possess. There is no need to start over, and learn to follow a proprietary technique, when you can seamlessly integrate what you already know.

Horary Astrology's Source Code

Horary is very structural and mechanical ("plug and play" as they say in the high-tech world). This is what makes it one of the easiest forms of astrology to practice. There are three main components of modern horary interpretation:

- **Science**: The astronomy and mathematics the astrology is based on: The astrophysics of planetary location and motion. The four-zone structure of the solar system, and the discovery of new objects within it. The geometry-based aspects, consisting of not-always-equal divisions of a circle. The median of midpoints, etc.

- **Symbolism**: Taking the science and math and synthesizing multiple, archetypical meanings within the "big picture" of a chart, and then specifically applying it to the question posed.

- **Structure**: The common interpretive sequence of steps inherent in horary interpretations. This generally consists of Headlines + Action + Synthesis & Confirmation, which in turn is specifically composed of Significators + Aspects + Moon + Extras = Conclusion. (Don't worry, this is all covered in detail in Chapter 6).

All of which are then applied to reality.

So the symbolic interpretation of astronomical science (the four zones of the solar system) and geometric relationships are applied to the interpretive structure of horary, which in turn is applied to reality to generate a predictive or likely outcome. No superstition, beliefs, intuition, spirituality or ancient dogmas are required. Rather than paranormal, it's far more cold and calculating, like probabilities and statistics, but certainly a lot more fun. This simple truth will give you a huge advantage over traditional horary methods, both in the learning process and in interpretative accuracy.

But the best part is this: The symbolism is really the only major variable in the equation above. The astronomical science only changes when new discoveries are made, and the structure changes when better horary methods are developed. Unfortunately, neither happens very often. So essentially, two thirds of the work is done for you before you even look at a chart. That leaves you able to focus on the most important variable of astrology: its source code, the symbolism. Look at the science-based symbolism, then plug and play it into the structure. It's really that simple.

2 ASTROLOGY & ASTRONOMY REUNITE FROM PLUTO'S ASHES

"I don't think it denigrates Pluto at all to say that it is not a planet. I think Pluto is a fascinating and interesting world, and being the largest Kuiper belt object is an honorable thing to be." [1]

— *Mike Brown, the Caltech astronomer whose discovery of Eris led to the reclassification of Pluto*

The solar system's symbolic interpretation applied to human affairs forms the foundation of the art of astrology. The planets (and other objects) are symbolically descriptive, and not influential in any way, shape or form—they are powerless to make anyone do anything. But as Dr. Brown stated in the Foreward, science and astronomy leave people and their consciousness out of the picture. Unfortunately, astrology since the Age of Reason has left science and astronomy out of the picture, with awful results. Though the art of astrology will never, ever come close to being a science, and the vast majority of astronomers will continue to loathe astrology for the foreseeable future, that doesn't mean that astronomical science should be ignored by the art. Astrology can keep its interest in humanity, and grow an interest in science, too.

Astrology and astronomy are both predictive, even if the link is tenuous. Astrology predicts events and outcomes of human affairs yet to unfold, while astronomy predicts the existence of objects yet to be discovered in the universe. The words "I don't know" are anathema to astrologers, because the whole idea of astrology is to be able to divine the future with absolute, full-bodied certainty. Astronomers, on the other hand, constantly and freely admit to not knowing the hows and whys of everything in the solar system, or the entire universe and beyond. And if astronomers, backed by science, don't know, then how much can and do astrologers *really* know?

"Most scientists would probably throw astrology in with the pseudo-science, so what do I think is the difference?" inquires Dr. Brown. "Astrology, at least as I think about it, talks about humans and their interactions and thoughts and dreams. Astrology deals with the interior rather than exterior world. While science seems to be good for understanding the physical exterior world, I think the inner world is a no-man's-land. Astrologers? Psychologists? Self-help gurus? As far as I know, astrologers understand people and their condition as well as anyone else. And I like them better, because they like stars, but I will admit a certain prejudice there."[2]

"Pseudo-science, on the other hand, does not deal with emotions and thoughts and feelings," Brown continues. "Like real science, it attempts to describe physical reality...But pseudo-science deals with objective reality more through the methods of the intuitive arts than the methods of science. And that is where it goes wrong. In the intuitive arts you are allowed—indeed required—to get a feeling that something is true and then spin a reality out of it...but it falls flat when trying to describe exterior reality."[3] Unlike actual science, modern horary astrology doesn't seek to describe exterior physical reality, as much as it endeavors to create a congruency between a querent's inner "no-man's-land" and their outer, reality-based world. So physical science and astrology can harmoniously continue to serve their vastly different, but important functions.

Astrology birthed astronomy, and while the science leaped light years ahead, astrology idled and went nowhere, flatlined a couple of times, and regressed. The pseudo-science birthed the science that outgrew and evolved far beyond its origins. Astronomers do all of the heavy lifting of painstaking research, study, observation and calculation, while astrologers have the relatively easy task of integrating the symbolic meaning of the new discoveries into their chart interpretations. By re-infusing astronomy into the art, perhaps the scientists will begrudge astrologers a little less. "[Astrologers] are seeking to make meaning out of patterns to see in the world," says Dr. Brown. "Isn't that what I do? What is not to love?"[4]

Good News: Pluto Is Now a Dwarf Planet!

In astronomy, B5 and B6 aren't vitamins. They are International Astronomical Union (IAU) resolutions stating the definition of a planet in the solar system (B5), and specifically addressing the reclassification of Pluto as a dwarf planet (B6). So Pluto isn't a "real" planet anymore. Really. But you can still use it in all of your horoscopes, because Pluto's orbital period, mythology, astrological keywords and symbolism remain the same, whether it's known as a dwarf planet or not. Pluto still plows its devastating way through natal and horary charts, symbolically showing complications and power struggles, regardless of its classification. It's still as valid and useful astrologically as it was when it was a "real" planet.

Pluto's reclassification as a dwarf planet was as earth-shattering to the astronomical world as it was to the astrological world. In astronomy, it forced scientists to re-think and re-evaluate the entire origin, structure and foundation of the solar system. Unfortunately, the astrological world, and particularly horary, is not so progressive. Uranus' discovery in 1781 showed that the traditional Ptolemaic system of astrology was completely inaccurate; the outer planets could not be contained within the outmoded paradigm of ancient astrological thought. Since they didn't fit within the Ptolemaic model, instead of correcting the model to accommodate them, or discarding it entirely to create a new one, traditional astrologers relegated the outer planets to a second-class status, and dismissed them as transpersonal, generational, and therefore not as relevant as the seven classical planets. This error is exceptionally glaring in horary. Uranus, Neptune and Pluto have a tremendous personal impact in horary charts. And since Pluto, like all Kuiper belt objects (KBOs), is a trans-Neptunian object (TNO) and has been all along, after 81 years of astrological use and counting, it proves TNOs can be used effectively, whether in horary or another branch. Pluto has also shown that Kuiper belt objects (KBOs) aren't particularly generational from an astrological perspective after all—they are immutably personal and representative of an entirely different astrological perspective that we are only now beginning to understand.

The reclassification of Pluto underscored the necessity of astrological knowledge of the different types of astronomical objects in the solar system, how they integrate, and how they are then symbolically interpreted in horoscopes. No more sweeping scientific fact under the rug, or pretending various astronomical objects don't exist or aren't relevant because the ancients didn't know about them. Pluto's reclassification also exposed the fraudulent system of planetary hierarchy that has existed throughout astrological history. (To paraphrase George Orwell, some planets are considered more equal than others.) The idea of planetary rulerships is a symbolic relic of ancient cultural mores; from an era of kings, queens, and their courts, customs, and deference to hierarchy. The 21st-century alignment is horizontal and democratic, equalized by science. With astronomy-based astrology, science strips away the cultural subjectivity, demonstrating that the myths and symbolism can stand in their own right, without hierarchy, within a whole and open system, and not a closed circuit of "planets only."

Reintegrating the standardized objectivity of science, specifically astronomy, is imperative for astrology's continued growth and evolution, increased accuracy, and ease of learning. But because science had fallen by the wayside, and the full and complete solar system wasn't being utilized, astrology became stuck in its Ptolemaic rut, unable to grow, change and evolve. In order to progress, astrologers have to change what they believe to be true that isn't, and finally make a long-overdue split from Ptolemaic astrology, of trying to fit every new discovery that comes along into its outmoded form, or ignoring them entirely. Needless to say, it's a tall order. Why? Because far too much of astrological practice is based on subjective beliefs, spirituality, philosophy, personal experience, and antiquated dogmas, rather than astronomical science, reasonably standardized interpretive methods, empirical research, verification, and symbolic correlations applied and attributed to reality instead of heavenly influence.

The solar system consists of numerous parts that form a whole and balanced system, just like the human body. In the medical world, no one would declare that the cardiac system is superior to the neurological system, so it would be equally ridiculous to favor specific pieces of the solar system over the whole merely because of ancient astrologers' lack of knowledge of what they couldn't see, and the subsequent lore that was built upon their inaccuracy. The traditional or classical planets are pieces of the astrological puzzle, but they are not the entire picture. Pluto's reclassification opens the doorway to explore the region of the solar system beyond Neptune that the vast majority of astrologers ignore. The entire solar system, and our understanding of it, is changing rapidly. Astrology will change with it. The outer planets, asteroids, TNOs, and beyond, aren't going away. Instead, they're coming closer into focus.

Solar System 2.0 for Astrologers

In the 1940's and 50's, astronomers Kenneth Edgeworth and Gerard Kuiper independently predicted that a reservoir of icy rocks lay beyond the orbit of Neptune. In the summer of 1992, astronomers David Jewitt and Jane Luu officially discovered the 2-billion-mile-wide region, now formally called the Edgeworth-Kuiper belt (but commonly truncated to Kuiper belt).[5] Within it are geologic fossils consisting of material from which the solar system formed 4.5 billion years ago—long before the planets came into being. The entire solar system is enveloped by the Oort cloud, an enormous sphere of nascent comets extending more than 9 trillion miles into space, far beyond the Kuiper Belt.[6] (Fig. 2.1)

Fig. 2.1: The solar system surrounded by the Kuiper belt; all enveloped within the Oort cloud.

So Pluto wasn't the end of the solar system at all—it was merely the beginning of the next segment of it. Pluto's reclassification ultimately showed that there's something more, in fact, a whole lot more, beyond what we thought we knew both astronomically and astrologically. It's not about preconceived notions of what the new objects represent and how we think they should fit. It's not about trying to force newly discovered objects to conform to a long-outmoded Ptolemaic system. The ancients, via classical astrology, tried to organize the heavens on their terms; to make the heavens conform to fit their limited understanding and spiritual beliefs. Modern astrology in the 21st century seeks the exact opposite—to see and understand the solar system as it is scientifically, and to adjust and change the astrological symbolism, knowledge and practices accordingly as the astronomical knowledge expands and changes.

Second century astronomer and mathematician Claudius Ptolemy's geocentric theory of the universe prevailed until the 17th century. It was as factually inaccurate then as it is now. (His historically important work, *Geography*, which charted the then-known world, was also factually inaccurate, suffering from a lack of reliable information, the same as his astrological work, *Tetrabiblos*.) Due to the technical and scientific limitations of his time, he didn't know that planets revolve around the Sun rather than the Earth (heliocentric theory, which Copernicus and Galileo would pioneer). So there was no way he could possibly have been aware of asteroids, Uranus and Neptune, and trans-Neptunian objects. There is also no historical evidence to give any indication that had the astronomical reality of the solar system been available to Ptolemy (or any other astronomer before or after him), he would not have utilized it and incorporated it into his astronomical, and subsequent astrological models and theories.

The Ptolemaic system involves hierarchy and splitting up 12 zodiac signs among five planets and the Sun and Moon, because that was all ancient astrologers could see with the naked eye. Since that was all they had to work with, the five planets were given dual-sign rulerships, and the Sun and Moon singular rulerships. Ptolemy (and others before him) based his astrology on his inaccurate astronomy, and future astrologers not only never corrected the error, but instead endorsed and defended its use. When the reasons for believing astrological principles are based on the authority of ancient astrologers and astronomers, future astronomical discoveries will completely undermine and destroy the rationale for those beliefs.

In order to understand a science-based astrology, one must first grasp the simple astronomy of what's being symbolized and interpreted astrologically. The solar system consists of four zones (Fig. 2.2):

- The inner solar system, consisting of the terrestrial planets (☿ ♀ ⊕ ♂).

- The asteroid belt, containing the "leftovers" from terrestrial planet formation (⚴ ⚥ ⚶ ⚳, etc.).

- The outer solar system, consisting of the gas giant planets (♃ ♄ ♅ ♆). (The Centaurs, such as Chiron ⚷, also dwell in this region.)

- The Kuiper belt, as the beginning of the trans-Neptunian solar system (♇ — Scattered Disc region). All Kuiper belt objects are trans-Neptunian objects, but not all trans-Neptunian objects are Kuiper belt objects. (See Chapter 12)

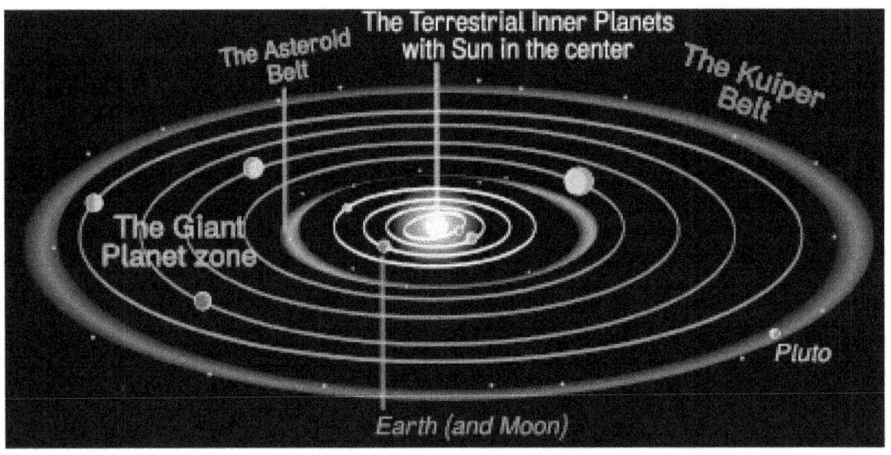

Fig. 2.2: The four zones of the solar system:
1) Inner solar system/terrestrial planets, 2) Asteroid Belt,
3) Outer solar system/gas giant planets, 4) The Kuiper Belt.
Sizes and orbits not to scale; view is tilted.
Image: websters-online-dictionary.org

Astrological consideration by zone, rather than by considerations of visibility to the naked eye, distance from the Sun, or discovery date, is an enormous break from the ancient models of astrological thought. But it puts the astrological symbolism more in line with astronomical reality. By eliminating the astrological hierarchy and dichotomy of "inner" and "outer" planets, in favor of utilizing the full solar system, it removes the focus from planets to allow the inclusion of other, equally important objects.

Inner & Outer Solar System			The Kuiper Belt
☉ – ♆ (including Asteroids & Centaurs)			♇ – Scattered Disc
Inner Solar System Zone 1	Inner Solar System Zone 2	Outer Solar System Zone 3	The Kuiper Belt Zone 4
Luminaries & Terrestrial Planets	Asteroid Belt	Gas Giants (including Centaurs)	TNOs, specifically Kuiper belt objects (KBOs)
☉, ☽, ☿ – ♂	⚴ ♀ ⚶ ⚵	♃ ♄ (⚷) ♅ ♆	♇, Quaoar, Haumea, etc.

So a one-dimensional, rulership-based hierarchy that utilized only one-third of the solar system (five planets and two luminaries) suddenly becomes a multi-dimensional democracy (seven planets, two luminaries, and numerous asteroids, Centaurs, and KBOs/TNOs) working within a whole system. This reality-based model is easily integrated astrologically, horary or otherwise. It makes a huge difference in chart interpretation, allowing for easier access to vaster, deeper, primary detail that is readily apparent, and it also provides a standardized, science-based approach, because the solar system is the same for everyone, regardless of culture, awareness or beliefs.

So the basic idea is to get the astronomy right first, *then* apply the astrological symbolism. Then apply whatever specific technique is preferred to interpret. Astrology from an astronomical perspective is the ultimate democracy; the hierarchy is an entirely erroneous, man-made creation. Modern astrology is about understanding astronomical reality and the heavens as they are, rather than trying to order and conform them to our perceptions and demands, or those of ancient astrologers. Science, the great equalizer, allows this to happen.

Clarity & Confirmation, Not Clutter

Astrology and horary worked successfully throughout antiquity with just the classical planets alone. It still worked when Uranus, the asteroids, Neptune and Pluto were discovered and utilized. It continued to work when the TNOs were discovered and integrated into interpretations. Astrology does not stop working when new objects are discovered. The new objects don't negate the old—they refine and improve upon them.

Planets aren't the only named objects in the solar system, nor are they the only objects of importance in an astrological chart. The other objects have an equal, not supporting, role. The symbolism represented by the TNOs and asteroids provides information and details the planets alone cannot describe precisely or consistently (e.g., Venus in Capricorn is not going to come close to describing the relationship problems Juno in Leo can show). The symbolism of these nonclassical bodies is long known, as their core mythologies are well established and relatively standardized, making them easy for anyone to learn and use.

In the 21st century, there is no justifiable reason not to use the astronomically accurate model of the solar system. Since a whole works better than its parts, using only 1/3 of the known solar system in chart interpretations is to give only 1/3 of the picture (and answer) to querents. That may be all a querent needs or can handle, or that the astrologer is capable of. But having the full picture of primary information, and great depth of detail at the ready, all leading to accurate predictive outcomes, is the pinnacle of horary interpretation.

While an antiquated black and white television will still produce a viable image, a full-color, high definition, high-resolution television image is infinitely clearer, sharper and crisper. More pixels make the picture sharper and clearer, not cluttered. Figure 2.3 is an example of a traditional horary chart (left), with only the classical planets, and a modern one (right) utilizing as much of the full solar system as the software allows. Notice where your eyes are drawn to. Then ask the same of a non-astrologer, since they have not been biased by other astrologers into believing that using anything more than classical planets clutters up a chart.

Additional astronomical objects don't clutter up a chart—they help with analysis and confirmation to render a detailed and correct answer. Where there's smoke, there's fire, so you'll know where and what to look for. It allows the chart to lead you because it's easy to see where to focus, instead of blindly following and trusting antiquated rules that may not even be applicable. In horary interpretation, you are looking for specifics, and allowing what's not directly relevant to remain in the background.

Besides astronomical objects other than planets, any non-physical astrological body that can be placed in a natal chart (e.g., Vertex, Aries Point, etc.) can be used in a horary chart. After awhile, charts with only planets in them start looking a bit thin *without* the details the other objects provide. Once you know how to think about a horary chart, and the mechanics of what to look for, you can utilize as few or as many objects and techniques as you prefer in your interpretations.

Horary astrology is not fixed and unchangeable—like the solar system it reflects, astrology is inherently a living, changing, dynamic organism that can't be constrained by ancient beliefs or contemporary edicts. Science has been missing from horary astrology all these centuries, not more horary rules. But most importantly, at the end of the day, horary querents live in reality, here and now, and not a world of philosophies or make-believe, or as viewed by astrologers in antiquity.

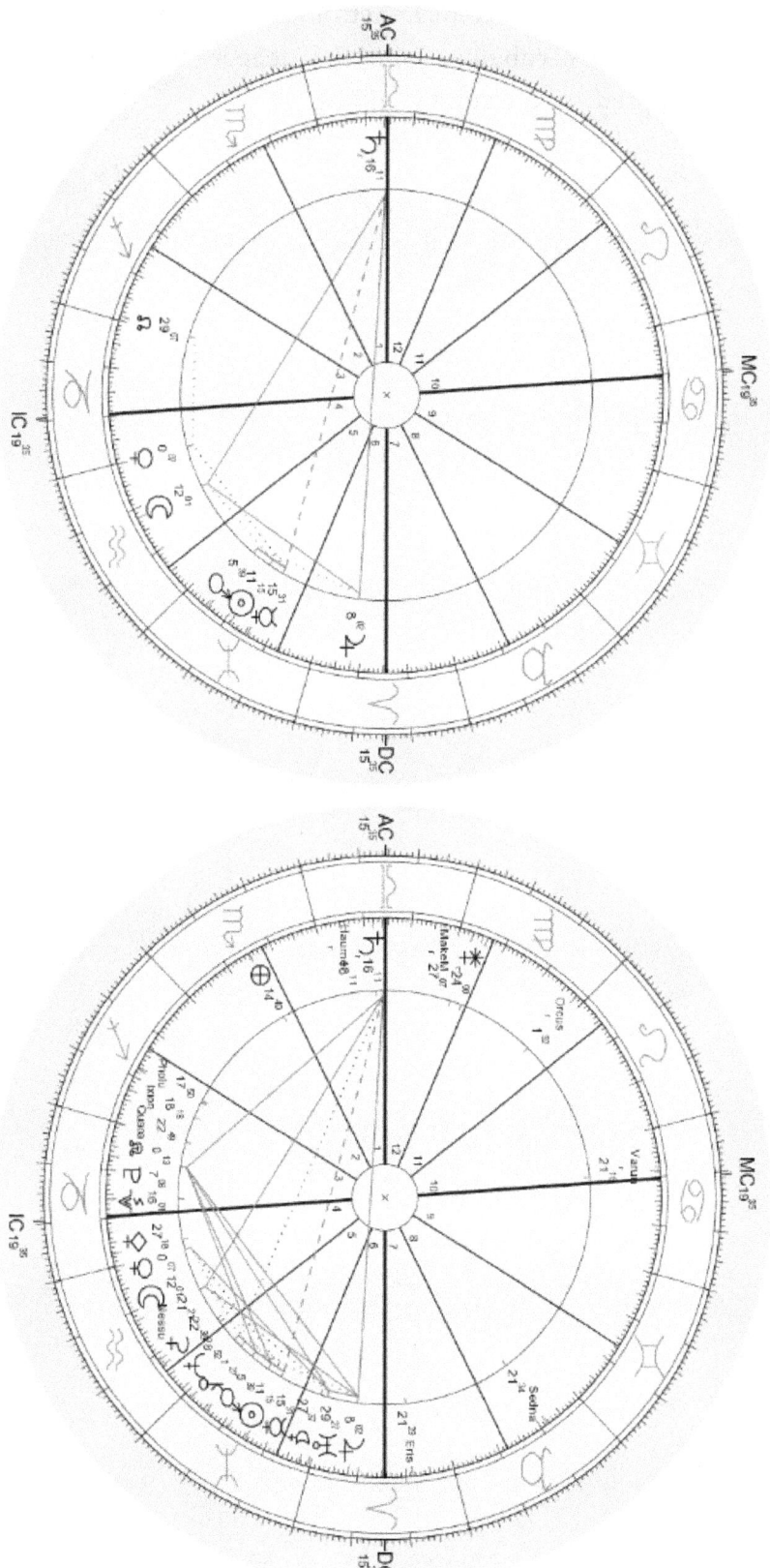

Figure 2.3: Traditional Planets Only (l.) and Whole Solar System (r.)

Life is much deeper, richer and infinitely more complex than what the classical system of only five planets and two luminaries can possibly depict. Astrology is a symbolic language, and the more you understand, the larger your vocabulary, and the deeper, more specific, and precise your interpretive descriptions and predictive accuracy will be.

3 PHILOSOPHICAL DIFFERENCES BETWEEN MODERN & TRADITIONAL HORARY

> *"When are you going to use your own consciousness? When? How long are you going to remain tethered to the dead past? The Gita was born five thousand years back; life has changed so much. If you want to read the Gita, read it as beautiful literature—but just like that, no more than that. It is beautiful literature, it is beautiful poetry, but it has no dictums to be followed and no commandments to be followed. Enjoy it as a gift from the past, as the gift of a great poet, Vyasa. But don't make it a discipline for your life; it is utterly irrelevant.*
>
> *And everything becomes irrelevant, because life never remains confined. It goes on and on..."* [1]
>
> — *Osho*

> *"It's not a great idea to let cultural attachments dictate scientific categories."* [2]
> — *Mike Brown, Caltech astronomer*

Modern and traditional horary astrology are both viable methods that yield correct answers. Neither is superior to the other. They are simply two different perspectives and methods of looking at and interpreting the same data. Just as three different doctors can examine the same x-ray and come up with the same (or different) diagnoses and treatment plans, the different horary techniques can have the same variation. The horary techniques aren't at issue—they all work. But problems and hostilities arise when the teachers' and practitioners' beliefs and dogmas *about* the techniques prevail, and one branch attempts to negate the validity and undermine the credibility of another.

"It becomes increasingly questionable for any of us to attempt to find the 'One True Astrology' which will provide us with absolute spiritual and ideological security while identifying heretical astrologies as 'incorrect,' 'bad,' or 'false.'" says astrologer Liz Greene.[3]

"There is not one astrology with a capital 'A.'" astrologer Alexander Ruperti wrote in an article shortly before his death. "In each epoch, the astrology of the time was a reflection of the kind of order each culture saw in celestial motions, or the kind of relationship the culture formulated between heaven and earth."[4]

"Astrology reflects the historical period in which it is practiced," writes Anthony Louis in his text *Horary Astrology*. "A rule that was sound centuries ago in a desert climate may not be viable today. The same Sun that brings life to the Eskimo may parch the Arab to death."[5]

Disagreement over horary methodologies is nothing new. In *Horary Astrology*, Louis, who studied astrological history, writes, "Although thousands of years old, horary astrology is still in its infancy.[6] Traditional astrology is a hodgepodge of many diverse traditions from various cultures, and some of these traditions contradict one another at certain points. There is no logical and mathematically precise astrology. It's more of an art than a science."[7]

Traditional horary practitioners generally consider modern horary to be anything that doesn't pre-date William Lilly, the 17th-century British author of the traditional horary bible *Christian Astrology*. Many traditional horary rules were formulated based on ancient and pre-17th century societies, morals, superstitions, belief systems and cultures that are long obsolete. From a modern standpoint, one would no more think like a denizen of the 1600's (or prior) than they would dress like one. Contemporary issues and problems are approached and resolved using the logic, methodologies, and realities of today, not the 17th century and prior.

Modern horary practitioners tend to be familiar with the traditional technique, often getting their start in horary that way, but prefer to use the faster, easier, more progressive, streamlined, updated methodology. As the late Joan McEvers explained, "The rules and strictures against judgment seemed to be much too complicated, and to me, too time-consuming. I am not saying that the old systems do not work. They do. But I am a very busy astrologer and use whatever tools are at hand to speed up the process. I would never go back to calculating charts by hand, now that I have a computer; consequently, since I have developed a modern way of dealing with horary astrology, I cannot go back to the ancient methods that take so much longer to use."[8]

Factions and Dogmas

In general, American astrologers tend toward the modern horary approach, while Europeans favor the traditional methods.[9] Unfortunately, there is a small but vociferous, dogmatic faction of British traditional horary practitioners who are dismissive of anything that does not fit their extremely limited and narrow view of what they believe horary astrology is.[10] And in their orthodoxy, they vituperatively dismiss or negate what doesn't fit their myopic vision of the art. They then pass that myopia on to their students and the cycle perpetuates. It's woefully apparent from the ill-informed criticism and unsubstantiated assertions by the traditionalists who deem modern horary unreliable, inferior or unproven, that these detractors know nothing about modern technique—they mistakenly assume it's little more than misunderstood traditional technique that includes the outer planets. What they fail to understand—or more precisely, choose not to understand—is that it's an entirely different method and approach to interpreting a horary chart. And so instead of honest research, scholarship and critique, they seek to denigrate and subsequently dismiss it.

"Some people love the Greek classics, for example, and devote the time to mastering ancient Greek so they can read them in the original," offers Anthony Louis. "This is admirable, but does not mean that modern literature is worthless."[11]

"It's a cancer on astrology, arguing about who's right and whose research is credible," says astrologer Diana Stone. "Modern and traditional can merge and forget about the cult following and fanaticism...It's a disservice that this has turned into a fight and labeling. Too bad it has devolved into such a hostile situation. The arguments have caused a loss to so many people who could have used it [horary]."[12]

Trying to address astronomical reality with the British traditional horary sect is reminiscent of Galileo and Copernicus's attempts at explaining it to the ruling religious orthodoxy: belief supersedes fact, and defending antiquated and scientifically inaccurate dogmas is more important than acknowledging and adjusting to reality. In the southern United States, there are popular bumper stickers that read, "God said it, I believe it, and that's the end of it!" as justification for a Biblical worldview. In this typical example, the dogmatic British traditional horary practitioners' mindset toward modern horary technique is essentially the same:

> "Little is known about the trans-Saturnians, at least, little that can be shown to be consistent. Therefore, they are to be used with caution and, in most instances, secondary to the seven traditional planets. At the beginning of this century, some tried to include them into the traditional scheme, it is our opinion that they have not done this with any success and these planets should be treated separately. It might be worth thinking again about what astrology is: a geocentrically based system, it is about how the heavens appear to us on Earth, not how they are in astronomical reality. Therefore, since these planets can't be seen with the naked eye, thus have no 'rays', would they have been accepted into the scheme had the ancients known about them? However, it would be wrong to discount them entirely, although in most cases they seem to have little relevance.

> Most modern books on horary astrology carry their supposed signification. I recommend caution when using these planets and in any case, as I have already mentioned, you will find that there are very few charts where the new planets do more than add information or description to the main significators." [13]

Unsurprisingly, there is no evidence provided to support assertions such as these, and each statement withers under closer examination:

The knowledge, consistency and "supposed signification" of the outer planets are well established, simply because their symbolic meanings come from the same Greco-Roman mythology as the classical planets. There is no more doubt about the symbolic or archetypical meanings of Venus or Mercury than there is about Uranus or Pluto because they all originate from the same mythology source.

Astrological books about the trans-Saturnian planets abound (See Appendix A - Part I), particularly on the natal side, and those meanings carry over seamlessly to horary for the reason mentioned above: the symbolism comes from the same source and remains the same regardless of astrological branch. The modern horary texts re-affirm use of the natal meanings via the empirical evidence of case studies. If astrological knowledge is built on consensus from empirical evidence, then there is plenty of consensus and consistency as to the effectiveness and accuracy of the outer planets' symbolic interpretation in horary. One only has to seek out the local or online bookseller, websites, astrology conference workshop CD and DVD lectures, or the public library to find the information and case studies. Ironically, the same traditionalists who swoon over the discovery and translation of ancient astrological texts, horary or otherwise, will turn around and assert that modern information based on either empirical evidence or astronomical science is either questionable, unreliable, secondary or irrelevant. They will readily embrace limited and inaccurate ancient knowledge, but completely turn a blind eye to modern research, verifiable case studies, and scientific fact.

A planet is simply a planet from an astronomical classification standpoint, and astrologically, each planet symbolizes a different archetype or function, with no subjective "superior" or "inferior" relationship to each other. Mercury is not better than, superior to, or more important than Neptune. Further, there is no evidence of a lack of successful integration of the outer planets in horary, or of the use of outer planet rulerships, since the modern horary texts and case studies clearly show otherwise. (See Appendix A - Part III)

The ancients worked with the extremely limited astronomical knowledge they had at the time, and as stated previously, there is absolutely no evidence to suggest that they would have negated and ignored any further scientific discoveries had they been available to them. Since the basis of astrology and horary is the use of astronomical objects translated into symbolism and applied to specific questions about human affairs, it makes sense to use the most astronomically correct model available.

Scientifically, planets and other objects in the solar system reflect the Sun's light off their surfaces (albedo)—there is no basis in reality for the medieval fiction of planets "casting rays," which originated from a lack of understanding of how optic vision works. Additionally, it makes no difference if a telescope is needed to see an object, because to do so has no effect on the symbolic meaning of the object. Simply because something can't be seen with the naked eye doesn't mean it doesn't exist astronomically, or shouldn't be utilized astrologically.

"Just because Pluto was not sighted before 1930 does not mean it was not there. If we cover our eyes, does the environment disappear?" asks astrologer Erin Sullivan. "Just as Uranus and Neptune were there before they were sighted, so was Pluto, but what was it doing? Same old thing, but without any human consciousness of its orbit, influence and so on. As with Uranus, it was there, just one orbit beyond Saturn, but it took an invention, a telescope, to allow us to see it. The rest is industrial, technical, and consciousness history."[14]

Finally, if the outer planets are used as significators, the horary interpretation is going to be considerably different than using only what the ancients designated. For example, an Aquarius ascendant, utilizing disruptive Uranus as ruler and significator, is going to tell a *very* different story than using stodgy Saturn as the traditional ruler and significator, since Uranus and Saturn represent diametrically opposite archetypes and symbolism.[15] And major outer planet configurations—such as the T-square of Uranus, Saturn, Jupiter and Pluto in the summer of 2010—resonate within every horary question asked during the duration of the configuration. To overlook such important, core pieces of information sitting right on the surface and directly impacting the outcome is senseless and self-defeating. Also, additional information or description above and beyond traditional significators is a benefit, because a querent should be given as much specific information as possible to make an informed decision.

"I just do not agree that the new [modern planetary] rulers are not primary rulers and tell nothing of a personal nature," says Diana Stone. "I have dozens of charts to disprove that notion. Times change. People evolve. The new planets simply represent these influences."[16]

Astronomer Mike Brown says, "We will always be learning new things about the universe. Sometimes, those new things will cause us to revise what we had thought before...So, we change our understanding to reflect what we now know about reality. Wherever we are confronted with the limits of our knowledge—as we are in the distant parts of the solar system—new discoveries are always going to update how we think."[17]

If modern horary technique is as inconsistent, irrelevant, secondary, unproven, unreliable or fallible as the British traditional sect purports, it would not be possible to consistently provide accurate answers to horary questions at a level greater than chance. The voluminous research, case studies and texts clearly show the consistency and validity of the technique. Trying to have it both ways, traditional horary practitioners will often claim that the same correct answers modern practitioners arrive at could have been concluded using only traditional rules and methodology. That claim only further proves that the faster and easier modern horary technique is just as accurate and viable as traditional methods, since both arrive at correct answers.

The dogmatic traditional British horary practitioners have to insist on heavy denial of astronomical reality, as well as the modern horary body of evidence, because if they don't, their entire platform of proprietary superiority collapses under its own falsity and hubris. Until the traditional British dogmatists can *prove* that modern horary interpretations are ineffective or inaccurate due to technique, use of outer planet rulerships, or whatever other excuse they can come up with—they can't and they know it, because the querents' affirmative feedback of the modern interpretive details and predicted outcomes provides the vindication—the ill-informed criticism and baseless superiority complex (not to mention the practitioners' credibility) should be completely debunked and thoroughly dismissed. (As Christopher Hitchens stated, "What can be asserted without proof can be dismissed without proof."[18])

It's intellectually dishonest to willfully ignore research, case studies and other evidence that doesn't fit preconceived notions of what can be effectively utilized in horary astrology. However, the confirmation bias is not altogether surprising. A University of Michigan study from 2005-6 showed that presenting facts that counter incorrect beliefs actually strengthens the person's hold on the misinformed beliefs. The study also showed that beliefs are the basis for facts, not vice versa.[19] Even worse, an earlier University of Illinois study showed that those who hold the most factually inaccurate beliefs tend to express the most confidence in them.[20]

"Being wrong is not shameful," says astronomer Mike Brown. "But being wrong and refusing to look at and seriously consider the contrary evidence gets you nowhere in your quest to understand reality."[21] Or interpret a horary chart.

The Advantages of Modern Horary

Ancient horary practitioners and William Lilly (and the contemporary, self-appointed apostles of their work) do not have any kind of monopoly on horary thought or technique. "There is a disturbing fundamentalist trend among some practitioners to take Lilly's word as almost divine revelation about matters horary and to avoid modern and creative approaches to the art," Anthony Louis points out in his text *Horary Astrology*.²² What traditionalists tend to conveniently overlook is that "Lilly did not consider his textbook [*Christian Astrology*] the final word on the subject. Unfortunately, Lilly died before he was able to revise it." writes Louis.²³ So there's a high probability that some of the technique so staunchly defended and in use today by traditional horary practitioners would not be used by Lilly himself—and no one will ever know what he would have discarded or replaced with new information.

So why is there such a huge gap in time and knowledge between traditional and modern horary methods? It wasn't because its historical practitioners felt there was nothing to be improved upon. Instead, the prominence of the Church and its repressive views of anything not officially sanctioned, as well as the perception of astrology as the devil's work and witchcraft from roughly 1450-1750, played a large role (Lilly being a notable exception). The Inquisitions and religious persecution were a formidable deterrent to the practice and advancement of the body of astrology in general, including traditional horary. The real threat of being drowned or burned at the stake would be a strong deterrent for anyone.²⁴ But more importantly, "During the time that William Lilly enjoyed great success as a horary astrologer, astrology itself was falling on hard times," writes Louis in *Horary Astrology*. "Advances in astronomy and the physical sciences increasingly strained astrology's credibility. Sensing a demise of their art, astrologers set about making their subject more scientific. The divinatory arts apparently raised the scientists' hackles the most."²⁵

"The pseudo-scientists had a mythology that did not adequately describe the physical universe," says astronomer Mike Brown. "Physical reality is not terribly amenable to the intuitive arts.²⁶ Science and the scientific method developed not because they are obviously the correct thing to do, but because they worked.²⁷ As a scientist, I have a particularly hard time with people who reject the use and conclusion of science for the things that science is particularly well-suited for."²⁸

With the dawn of the Age of Reason in the late 1700's, a logic- and science-based reality supplanted a mythical, religious and superstitious one. Discovering information through observation, rather than the study of authoritative sources such as Aristotle or the Bible, became the standard. Astrology almost died as a result.

There was more "pirating and parroting" of existing traditional horary knowledge, particularly in the last half-millennium, rather than advancement through new information or original thought. Many traditional astrologers have mistaken this to mean the knowledge is "tried and true," when, more realistically, and especially since Lilly's time, it's just been repeated and rehashed, inaccuracies, limitations and all. In that regard, modern horary astrology has several distinct advantages over traditional horary astrology:

1) Modern horary practitioners have more advanced scientific knowledge, education and critical thinking skills than ancient or medieval authors and practitioners, who operated from a base of incomplete models, spiritual beliefs, and superstition.

2) Contemporary, primary sources of information—both astronomical and astrological—can be easily contacted to discuss their methodologies, new discoveries or theories. From an ancient standpoint, dead men tell no tales.

3) Horary interpretation outcomes are able to be validated much faster in modern times because information travels more quickly, thereby establishing and compounding the empirical body of evidence far more rapidly than in ancient times.

4) Modern horary practitioners have current astronomical science as a base to work from, rather than superstition and lore that could vary between cultures and centuries.

5) Literacy is common and information is much more widely available and disseminated, as well as more intact, than was possible in ancient eras. Literacy and information are no longer limited to the wealthy, educated classes of antiquity.

6) Empirical research, replication of results, corroborating documentation, case studies, empirical evidence, and third-party verification and critique are more extensive in modern times, and virtually non-existent in traditional eras.

7) Modern horary astrology can grow, change and adapt as fast as the astronomical discoveries that fountainhead it are made. Traditional horary is a closed, finite body.

Scientific knowledge didn't stop with Newton any more than medical knowledge did with with Hippocrates. If those bodies can evolve beyond antiquity as new scientific information becomes available, horary astrology can as well. Horary faltered not because there was nothing new to be learned or discovered, but because science and the Age of Reason rightfully took over. Notably, not long after the asteroids and outer planets were discovered, astrology revived and started evolving again.

The Proof Is In the Accuracy

Horary skill lies in interpreting symbolism and synthesizing the information into a cohesive, accurate answer. No school of thought has a monopoly on the information or ways to do this.

Horary astrology is not now, has never been, nor will ever be proprietary to any technique, method, person, or school of thought. There is no "one and only way" to do almost anything in this world, and horary astrology is no different. No astrologer, no matter how experienced or authoritative, can credibly say that a method or technique is inferior, unproven or doesn't work because it's different from what they do, or doesn't follow what William Lilly or any ancient did or knew. Consistent, accurate answers are the only proof of technique or methodology required, regardless of what is used to interpret a chart. If you are consistently accurate most of the time (no astrologer is infallible), your technique is sound, whatever the method you use.

Astrology is about the work itself and the people who benefit from it, not the personalities who practice or teach it. Personal beliefs, dogmas or opinions about horary technique will never supplant empirical evidence of successful application. An intelligent horary teacher would *want* a student to explore other methods in order to gain a broader perspective—and appreciation—of the different approaches, and possibly incorporate some of those methods into their own. "If you, as a typical eager student, accept our perspectives as the absolute truth, then your understanding of astrology is based on preconceived notions that are limited to the experience of the astrologers whose ideas you read or study," says astrologer Donna Cunningham.[29]

Ultimately, querents don't know or care about which technique is being applied to their charts, or who William Lilly was. They only care about an accurate answer to their question. They want to know if they will get the job, not which terms and face Venus is in. "Astrology is about the relationship between the astrologer and the client," says Diana Stone. "If the astrologer lacks the ability to understand and meet the needs of the client, they should get out of the business."[30]

"We astrologers make choices based on our observations and differing points of view, all open to challenge, question and interpretation," says astrologer Michael Lutin.[31] "We have to focus on being able to pass on what we know, versus technique fascism."[32]

4 TECHNICAL DIFFERENCES BETWEEN MODERN & TRADITIONAL HORARY

"The wise investigator of horary art will ultimately set up his own rules and standards." [1]

— *astrologer Marc Edmund Jones*

One of the biggest technical differences between modern and traditional horary technique is that traditional horary tends toward perpetuating the observations and methods of ancient authors and texts virtually intact, while modern horary takes a critical thinking and analysis approach of testing and observing astrological correlations to build empirical evidence.

"This branch of astrology [horary] is rooted in antiquity and many astrologers still apply an antiquated approach, even in this modern day and age," wrote astrologer Joan McEvers in her 1994 horary text, *The Only Way To Learn About Horary & Electional Astrology, Vol. 6*. "I have updated these ancient rules and my new method, which was evolved through trial and error and thousands of charts...I have found over the years that my greatest learning did not come from the wisdom of the ancients, but through understanding and applying planetary rulerships, and the intricate structures of the houses and their derivative meanings."[2]

Ignoring traditional horary rules will not impinge upon the accuracy of modern horary interpretations. As stated earlier, it is a trading of perceptions. There are many traditional considerations not used in modern interpretive technique because they are all overpowered by other more primary factors inherent in the chart. One of the core themes of horary astrology is that there is always more than one way to find the same information in a chart utilizing different methods, which is another reason why all the different techniques work.

"If students could but master the fundamentals, they wouldn't need to memorize trivial facts," writes Anthony Louis in *Horary Astrology*. "By understanding the basics, they could avoid slavishly following rules they don't understand. Horary is like that. Either you understand the basics or you blindly follow a thousand rules on the authority of the ancients."[3]

"Ivy [Goldstein-Jacobson] said, 'Things always change.'" says Diana Stone. "The traditionalists only fill in what's been missing in horary, they don't supplant it. Traditionalists and moderns don't contradict each other's rules, they add to them. It's just an extra set of rules because through the years, astrology has lost a lot [of its rules and information. Who knows what was burned?]. You can keep learning all along."[4]

The ultimate goal of modern horary is to evolve beyond rules, not look for more of them. Symbolic interpretation is primary, and technique is secondary, as technique is the application of the interpreted symbolism. Despite traditional practitioners' claims to the contrary, technique does not determine horary interpretive abilities, because all of the different methods yield accurate answers.[5] New techniques advance the body of knowledge to incorporate new information and paradigms as they unfold. The body of knowledge will continue to change and adjust as more astronomical discoveries are made. This is perfectly natural.

If a method employed by traditional horary is scientifically impossible (e.g., casting rays, collection and translation of light), it can be ignored for methods that are science-based and realistic (e.g., midpoints). Some would argue that *all* of astrology and its symbolism is subjective and inventive fiction, and therefore not accountable to reality-based standards. At that rate, anything goes, and it may be a key reason for some of the stranger, fringe approaches to the art. However, the problem is that symbolism, too, has its limits, and crossing that boundary can subjectively distort things beyond recognition from their reality-based purpose and function. For example, it crosses a line when the outer planets are symbolically twisted into consideration and usage as something they aren't and never will be, such as fixed stars, because acknowledging them for what they truly are would undermine and destroy the prevailing traditional dogma regarding outer planets. Astrology does not supersede natural laws or science, because people on the receiving end of the interpretations must live in and deal with reality as it is. So dogma must conform to reality, not the other way around.

Some traditionalist practitioners claim they've "tried" modern technique and couldn't get it to work as well as traditional technique. If there were any merit to the claim, *no one* would be able to get modern technique to work as well, not even once, let alone repeatedly. And yet the reality is that modern horary astrologers, working independently with separate data, over time, have consistently attained successful results—as the books, other publications and case studies show. So the failure by traditional horary practitioners to utilize the technique correctly to attain similar successful results is far more likely due to "user error" rather than a problem with the method.

This book will often refer to traditional methods in order to compare and contrast application and interpretation with modern methods. Below are just a few of the major technical differences between modern and traditional horary technique.

In a most generalized sense, traditional horary is a hierarchy-based, dignity- and debility-driven system, while modern horary is aspect-driven, inclusive and democratic. Traditional horary practitioners use Lilly's point system of planetary strengths and debilities as well as Ptolemy's table of essential dignities and debilities as the foundation for their technique. Since both exclude the outer planets, asteroids, and TNOs because they were unknown in Ptolemy and Lilly's time, these tools are not useful to the modern horary practitioner.

Borrowing instead from natal astrology, modern horary primarily uses all aspects (not just the Ptolemaic ones), dispositors, current transit configurations, primary rulerships, reception, midpoints, Nodal axis position, asteroids and TNOs, and other various chart considerations as needed to arrive at an accurate conclusion. The methods applied may vary from chart to chart depending on the question. Modern horary also utilizes transits and progressions in horary charts, particularly for timing. For example, if there is an outer planet T-square in the horary chart that will reconfigure itself transit-wise over the course of a few months, it will reactivate the issue or matter inquired about for the querent when the reconfiguration occurs. Progressed aspects between significators are also very reliable for timing. (See Figure 5.4 in Chapter 5 for an example.)

Non-Ptolemaic aspects are not overlooked in modern horary as they are in traditional. All aspects are equal, with no distinction between major and minor, because the research and case studies show that they all work successfully.[6] A circle is 360 degrees of mathematical objectivity for everybody, and there is no "better" or "superior" way of splitting it up. In a horary chart, a biquintile or semi-sextile can bring an event to culmination just as easily as a trine or sextile. And most of the non-Ptolemaic aspects are natural midpoints of the Ptolemaic aspects, with midpoint usage being a major component of modern horary.

A few decades ago, modern horary practitioner Gilbert Navarro convinced staunch British traditionalist Olivia Barclay to test, and subsequently admit, that a chart cast for the date, time and place of the querent was just as accurate as one cast the traditional way, for the date, time and location of the astrologer when he or she hears the question.[7] Both methods work equally well. After all, it's not the querent's fault he or she was on the other side of the world when the question was birthed, and the astrologer was asleep and couldn't be reached immediately.

In modern horary practice, the traditional strictures against judgment are considered red flags, but do not prevent a horary chart from being interpreted. Particularly disregarded is the traditional horary myth about Saturn in the 7th house impeding the judgment of the astrologer. Saturn is exalted in the 7th house, and there's a 1-in-12 chance it will be found there. Its placement there speaks volumes about the situation under consideration, and is key to interpreting the chart and answering the question. It has nothing to do with the astrologer.

Traditional terms, faces, decans, triplicities, almutens, solstice points (antiscia and contrascia), most fixed stars, moiety, cazimi, under the sunbeams, occidental/oriental, increasing/decreasing in light, nocturnal/diurnal, masculine/feminine, hayz, planetary hours, houses of joy, rays, collection and translation of light, natures of the planets and signs, and out-of-sign aspect culmination are also not used in modern horary interpretations. Some modern astrologers use Arabic parts, of which the Part of Fortune is frequently considered. However, as derivative calculations rather than astronomical objects, they are descriptors and cannot act.

Traditional rules regarding the peregrine status of planets aren't considered in modern horary, because modern case studies have proven that planets or significators don't need essential or accidental dignity to act or bring an event to culmination. The term peregrine, indicating "out of bounds" or moving through unfamiliar territory, originates from the ancient sport of falconry, which virtually no one practices today. And planets simply do not "wander aimlessly" as William Lilly poetically stated. Basically, a planet doesn't need essential dignity to act or bring a matter to culmination any more than a person needs fame and fortune to live. It's helpful, but not required.

In modern horary, the mother is designated by the 4th house and the father is ruled by the 10th house. Traditional horary reverses this for reasons based on outmoded, patriarchal cultural mores. In the modern designation, the 4th house is the natural house of the Moon and the sign of Cancer, which rules motherhood. The 10th house is the natural house of Saturn and the sign of Capricorn, symbolic of the father. Traditional horary thought generally considers house meanings completely separate from planetary symbolism.

Traditional Myths About Outer Planets Debunked

By far, the biggest technical difference between modern and traditional horary astrology is in the use of the outer planets, meaning the trans-Saturnians: Uranus, Neptune, and until its reclassification, Pluto. Many traditional horary practitioners do not consider the outer planets, asteroids or TNOs because they utilize an antiquated model of the solar system. As Uranus, Neptune and Pluto were discovered, traditional horary practitioners erroneously dismissed their relevance by considering them transcendental, social, generational and political, with no possibility of being personal, primary or capable of sign rulership in horary. They then ignored the extensive evidence that proved otherwise.

In a horary chart, when Uranus, Neptune, and the TNOs meet the inner solar system planets, it shows the point where a circumstance beyond the querent's personal control is going to have a direct and personal symbolic effect on the situation or person inquired about. While the classical planets are a large part of the foundation of a chart, they are by no means the walls, windows, roof and entire house. Astrologers have had over 200 years to observe and analyze the asteroids and Uranus, and more than 150 years for Neptune. This is plenty of time to make accurate observations, especially since information has been exchanged at a far more rapid rate over the last two centuries than the whole of antiquity combined. More than three-quarters of a century to integrate Pluto is plenty of time as well, and its reclassification has no effect on its use or symbolism. "I think that the modern planets make the picture clearer, whereas traditional astrologers tend to think the modern planets make the picture less sharp," says Anthony Louis. "And that may well be their experience based on the types of questions and charts that come their way. It may be that as astrologers we attract charts that fit our point of view—a type of synchronicity."[8]

Utilized as primary rulers, the outer planets reflect the big picture of the world affecting an individual at the personal and immediate level of the matter inquired about. The outer solar system planets represent huge, irrevocable changes in a person's life caused by the world around them, rather than self-generated life changes, which are symbolized by the inner planets. Both types of change are visible in a horary chart. Inner planets are one-to-one relationships, while outer planets represent a one-to-many relationship, both in horary and natal astrology. And if the querent is that "one," it's *very* personal.

Traditional horary practitioners' specific claims against the use of outer planet rulerships are opinion- and philosophy-based, and as such contain no supporting evidence. The traditionalists claim that outer planets aren't personal in nature and therefore can't rule signs. They also assert they've never seen effective use of modern rulerships, or that there's a clear disadvantage to using them in horary, and that traditional rulerships "undoubtedly" work best.[9] Opting for actual research over opinion, philosophy, and adherence to dogma, the late Marion March concluded the following:

> "In the late 1970's, I spent two years using Saturn as well as Uranus as ruler of Aquarius in all my chart interpretations, in comparison/ composites and especially in electional work where some old-time astrologers claim that the 'old' rules work much better than the new ones. Since that little experiment, I am totally convinced that in today's world, Uranus rules Aquarius and Neptune rules Pisces, and that we don't need Saturn or Jupiter as co- or sub-rulers."[10]

March and her co-author, Joan McEvers, present 100 case studies in their horary text demonstrating that the outer planet rulerships are just as effective (and personal) in horary and electional astrology, and work as well as the classical rulerships in providing accurate and detailed answers. Other modern horary practitioners' case studies demonstrate this as well. (See Appendix A-Part III).

The traditional philosophy of sign rulership is exactly that: a philosophy. And the opinion-based, standard traditional horary philosophies negating the outer planets as sign rulers or primary significators generally fall along the lines of the following:

1. The original sign assignments were based on a symbolic structure that is inherently complete, and to break apart the structure destroys the strength and logic of the whole.[11]
2. The outer planets show conditions or events that have an impersonal or universal quality.[12]
3. The closer a planet is to the Sun, the more it affects the individual.[13]
4. Slow movement of the outer planets doesn't convey personal "influence" or show details of events or actions of the querent.[14]
5. Outer planets symbolize political or social events, rather than personal or individual ones.[15]
6. Because horary astrology deals with personal questions over which the querent has some control, it makes sense to limit rulerships to the most personal of planets.[16]

The flaws and fallacies of these philosophies are apparent upon closer examination:

1. The original sign assignments were based on a symbolic structure that is inherently complete, and to break apart the structure destroys the strength and logic of the whole.

The traditional rulerships came about because the ancients had more zodiac signs than known planets at the time, and somehow had to make it all fit. It's still a problem, which is why Mercury and Venus still have dual rulerships. What would planetary rulerships look like today had there been 15 planets known to the ancients, and only 12 zodiac signs?

In 1781, William Herschel discovered Uranus. "So it was that very discovery of Uranus that shattered the foundations of the celestial art," writes Anthony Louis in *Horary Astrology*. "The neat, ancient scheme of seven divinely appointed planets ruling an earth-centered universe fell apart. The theoretical structure which held up Ptolemaic astrology crumbled."[17]

If you have five planets and two luminaries (Sun and Moon) to work with due to incomplete scientific information, you can contort the 12 zodiac signs to fit and make it look like a balanced system. However, what happens when it turns out there are actually *seven* planets (not including Earth, of course), plus the two luminaries, for a total of *nine* to work with? Then it turns out the original structure isn't "inherently complete" after all. You don't get to just ignore the two planets that don't conveniently fit the theory and still call it a strong and logical system. You have to change it to come up with something that fits the actual parameters. As such, the sign rulerships must be adjusted to accommodate the new parameters.

2. The outer planets show conditions or events that have an impersonal or universal quality.

All of the planets can represent impersonal or universal qualities, not just the outer ones. Qualities such as falling in love (Venus), communicating (Mercury) and optimism (Jupiter) can be shown by the classical planets, just as much as denial and self-delusion (Neptune), illegal activities (Pluto) and divorce (Uranus) can be shown by the outer planets.

3. The closer a planet is to the Sun, the more it affects the individual.

By that logic, Mercury would be the most important and influential planet. It isn't; it's only one piece of the symbolic picture. If a planet has a slow orbit of the Sun and is generational, or even millennial, in natal, transit and progressed astrology, that doesn't mitigate its symbolism, relevance and immediacy in a horary chart. Object distance and orbits are important when looking at astrological cycles, which are clearly beyond the scope of horary.

4. Slow movement of the outer planets doesn't convey personal "influence" or show details of events or actions of the querent.

Orbital speed is not the only way to describe the events and actions of the querent. As significators, Pluto in the 8th can show illegal activity by the querent; Uranus applying or separating from the ascendant can show a separation in process (applying) or past (separating) due to extreme desire for independence in the matter; and Neptune in the 11th house in aspect to or on a midpoint of Saturn or Uranus or other relevant house ruler can depict the querent's recent formation of a philanthropic foundation.

The outer planets are indeed slow, yet they are still capable of having a direct, immediate impact on the matter inquired about. Uranus can make an applying square to Pluto in a horary question with Aquarius and Scorpio as significators, and all the outer planets can apply to faster ones while retrograde via mutual application. These slow-moving and distant objects can be significators and aspect other bodies, angles, midpoints and the Moon just like the faster and closer objects. Transits of the Moon and other faster bodies to the midpoints of the slower planets can catalyze events in lieu of the slow-moving bodies themselves. This is important because querents don't always drive or generate the action, events or outcome in the matter inquired about; often, circumstances take the querent for a ride, and not the other way around.

The houses of a horary chart are also an enormous equalizer, because they are the fastest and most changeable component in astrology. All of the planets and other astronomical objects move through the 12 houses of a horoscope almost equally over the course of the Earth's 24-hour rotational period. The relevance of those objects' placement within the houses are then applied to the specifics of the horary question.

In a horary chart, the sloth of Pluto can show clearly and pointedly how long an estate takes to settle before an inheritance is distributed. Neptune can show long-standing denial of a substance abuse problem, and the refusal to treat it. And just because a horary question is asked—urgent or not—doesn't mean that the answer is going to unfold overnight. For example, if a querent is trying to buy or sell a home, and Pluto retrograde shows up as his Scorpio significator, he can count on financial complications and delays that can take months or years to clear up, such as dealing with a lien on the property due to back taxes.

Also, the sloth of the outer planets' movements gives them the power to hold things up and put the kibosh on the querent's plans and timelines. As Michael Lutin observes, "The slowest planet always wins."[18] Part of the reason for this is precisely because there is no personal control over them—it's the other way around. If you doubt this, think about it next time you're at the grocery store and the elderly person at the front of the line takes forever to unload their cart. And then waits until it's all rung up before they even think of taking out their checkbook. And then tells the cashier all about their seventeen grandchildren while writing the check. Planetarily, it's no different.

The relationship chart in Chapter 5 (Figure 5.4) is an example of how Pluto can effectively rule Scorpio, depict events and actions of the querent, and be used for timing as effectively as any other planet.

5. Outer planets symbolize political or social events, rather than personal or individual ones.

The outer planets are social, political and generational only when discussing the speed of its orbit around the Sun in relation to an individual's life span (cycles), which is the domain of natal astrology and outside the parameters of horary questions. Almost all horary questions are individual and personal, so the outer planets and their mundane keywords don't just vanish. Instead, they are applied to the horary question via aspects, house placement, etc., just like any other planet. And political or social experiences symbolized by the outer planets directly affect people individually. People are not islands unto themselves, unaffected by the events of the world at large. The outer planets represent the world that is beyond personal control, *and the individual effects of such*, whether it's a hurricane or tsunami (Neptune) that destroys a home or an entire city, or a financial crash (Pluto) that vaporizes a 401(k), both putting a person's living in jeopardy and instantly and permanently changing their way of life.

For example, Pluto, as ruler of Scorpio and not Mars, has dominion over financial corruption, abusive power and domination. (It's called "plutocracy" and not "marsocracy" for a reason.) One only has to look at the worldwide financial crash in September 2008, beginning one week after Pluto turned direct en route to leaving Sagittarius' dead degrees (party's over) to ingress long-term into Capricorn (fiscal austerity) to see that fleeting Mars couldn't possibly have been responsible (in detriment and squaring Jupiter at the time) for the mess we still find ourselves mucking through today and for the foreseeable future. This global collapse, in turn, affected individual ability to obtain credit, employment and mortgages, not to mention the personal retirement funds that were destroyed. And the fallout of it all was reflected in horary charts cast in response, as querents asked panicked questions such as "Should I sell what's left of my stock portfolio?" or "Should I put my house on the market?" That is Pluto at work, not Mars.

When Pluto in Capricorn demolishes an economic system, and a person loses his job or a home as a result, it's *very* personal. Pluto is going to tell the backstory of how the querent got into the predicament, not Mars. See the relocation chart (Fig. 8.2) in Chapter 8 for precisely such an example.

6. **Because horary astrology deals with personal questions over which the querent has some control, it makes sense to limit rulerships to the most personal of planets.**

Since horary questions are inherently personal, all objects within the chart are going to specifically relate to the question in some way. From a horary standpoint, Venus under personal control is when the querent has the choice and ability to leave an unhappy relationship they are inquiring about. But Venus beyond personal control is when cultural acceptance of economic strictures of control by the querent's spouse (Pluto in the 7th squaring Venus in the 4th) prevents the querent from obtaining economic security to escape the abusive relationship, or file for a divorce.

The reality is that people simply do not control their day-to-day lives and circumstances to the level they think, wish or hope.[19] If they did, they wouldn't be asking horary questions. Instead, they'd be busy controlling the jobs or relationships, etc., that they are asking about. Choices and personal responsibility are imperative in life, but they are only half of the story. The other half is where people are stuck with what life gives them in spite of their wishes and choices. This is the tremendous value of the outer planets and TNOs—they amplify the parts of a person's life they *don't* have control over, including matters inquired about in horary questions.

Modern Horary Rulerships

If Scorpio is on the ascendant, use Pluto, not Mars, unless there's a compelling reason to use Mars. (Remember, there are no absolutes in astrology.) The red planet rules overt and constructive Aries. Scorpio is covert and destructive, with Pluto fitting that description on a far bigger and more powerful scale than Mars can. Mars is a skirmish in your life; Pluto is a complete annihilation of a way of life you'd been living that will never be again. Mars is a gun or sword; Pluto is a nuclear bomb. All of which is relevant at a personal level in a horary chart, if not moreso than in a natal chart, because of the immediate effect on the question posited. For example, if it's a relationship horary question, and Venus is conjunct Pluto, issues of power and control (who wears the pants in the relationship), or sexual intensity between two people either inappropriate for each other or with little in common, or relationship triangles are going to be indicated based on their placement within the chart.

With Aquarius, use Uranus and not Saturn, because they are diametric opposites symbolically. Uranus will not be confined or restricted by anything, period; Saturn is about containment and limitation. Uranus conjunct the Moon in an employment horary chart with Aquarius rising shows someone who likes to work freely and independently. To use Saturn as the traditional significator in the same example would indicate a corporate drone, rendering an incorrect interpretation. As a significator, restless Uranus in a horary chart can make a person antsy and agitated to act. Saturn prefers to wait patiently. Uranus can indicate the breakup of a relationship, where Saturn embodies the entrenchment of one (for better or for worse). Squares to Uranus can indicate separations or divorces, and conjunctions can mean disruptions or interruptions in relationships or other activities. If a harshly aspected Uranus transits a natal chart's 7th house, and symbolically indicates a divorce after 40 years of marriage, that's personal, not transcendental or generational. And if the subsequent horary question of "Will I receive a fair financial settlement in the divorce?" has Aquarius rising, Uranus in Aries in either the 1st or 2nd house will tell the story and reflect the reality of a battle with twists, turns and reversals throughout the process—not steady, stay-the-course Saturn.

If Pisces rises, use Neptune as significator. Neptune and Jupiter, and therefore Pisces and Sagittarius, also rule over two entirely different types of symbolism. Jupiter is active and expansive, while Neptune is passive and retreating. The exuberant and direct fire sign, Sagittarius, is a tremendously different quality than elusive and vague Pisces. Neptune rules over non-reality and all that's illusory. Not in any airy-fairy sense, but as an antithesis to Saturn's cold hard reality.

Movies (simulated versions of reality on celluloid) and romantic fantasies don't exist materially; hence they fall under Neptune's domain. Neptune signifies delusions and self-deception, especially when rising, by not seeing the matter clearly or realistically. Venus may rule relationships, but if Neptune is involved, it plays a bigger role—there's a reason the divorce rate is close to 50%, because what was obtained wasn't what was imagined or dreamed. And the heartbreaking disappointment and disillusionment that inevitably follows belongs to Neptune, not Jupiter.

Neptune as a significator conjunct Chiron in the 7th house with Pisces on the cusp in a horary chart, showing a drug-addicted husband who won't get help, is enormously personal to the querent asking "Should I demand that Tom get treatment or divorce him if he won't?" There's nothing impersonal, transcendental or universal about that—it's a bad situation, compounded front-and-center in the querent's life.

Finding Your Own Way

Modern horary highly encourages exploration. If something exists astronomically—*and you understand its meaning*—you can use it in a horary chart. Objects other than the classical planets can easily be integrated into a horary chart if you are willing to learn their symbolism. Techniques adapted from other astrological branches, such Uranian astrology or Cosmobiology, can also be utilized to interpret a horary chart. Consistent accuracy should be the barometer of whatever interpretive methods you choose to employ.

There's a huge difference between choosing not to use something out of personal preference, and stating something is ineffective, inferior, irrelevant or doesn't work, in spite of the contrary evidence, for no other reason than it doesn't fit someone's narrow horary paradigm or ancient dogmas. The equanimous Anthony Louis states, "My view is that we should respect each other's work and always try to learn new things."[20] To the open-minded, modern and traditional horary are an and/also proposition, not an either/or one. Thankfully, most people in the astrological world tend to keep an open mind, and practice a live-and-let-live-there's-room-for-everyone approach. Also, there are many "hybrid" horary practitioners who borrow from both (or more) techniques, with excellent results, as their case studies show. The true power and mystery of the art is how it all works out anyway, correctly and accurately, to give the querent the information they need, *in spite of* all the contradictions and differences of philosophy and technique between the various methods.

5 THE MODERN HORARY TOOLBOX

*"Astrologers are agreed that the squiggles called a horoscope
contain some sort of message to be decoded."* [1]
— *astrologer Dennis Elwell*

The core of horary astrology lies in the matter inquired about. In Bill Cain's masterful play *Equivocation,* Father Garnet instructs William Shakespeare to consider of his hostile inquisitors, "What is the question they are *really* asking?" Such is the approach of the horary astrologer. It's best if the querent can discuss the question with the astrologer first, and then have the astrologer cast the chart so that both understand the intent of the question. It doesn't always work that way however, and that is perfectly fine.

The two most common types of horary questions are either forensic or predictive. Forensic horary questions are where the outcome is known, but the querent is seeking details on the whys and hows of what happened. "Did my friend commit suicide or was it a natural death?" or "Did so-and-so steal the data?" are examples of forensic horary questions. It asks for details surrounding past events. Predictive horary questions are questions speculating on the future. The outcome is unknown, and consists of "Will I...?" or "Should I...?" types of questions. "Will my daughter get into Harvard?" or "Should I take the trip to Rio?" are examples of predictive horary questions.

In 1940s detective movies, a suspect was hauled into a police station, shoved into a chair, a bright light was shone in his face, and he was roughed up to force him to talk. Today, military interrogators and scientists state that "enhanced interrogation" returns the least reliable information, while rapport-building with suspects yields better results.[2] The same holds true for horary charts. Instead of manhandling and strangling a chart to death with rules, modern horary technique employs an active listening style to allow the chart to openly and readily reveal and unfold its message. It's a dialogue rather than an interrogation, which yields deeper and more accurate information faster. It's about *letting* the chart tell the facts in the story, versus *forcing* it to say what some arbitrary and ancient rules think it should.

Carefully consider the variables within the chart, and don't think in terms of absolutes. Sometimes a chart will have nothing to do with the question asked, involving an entirely different matter instead. Address the discrepancy with the querent to see what the real issue is. Sometimes a chart will have a simple storyline, sometimes there will be multiple, complex storylines happening simultaneously. Sometimes more than one house (e.g., the 5th and 7th for relationships, or the 6th and 10th for work or career issues) will yield the same answer, and point you in the proper direction as you gather evidence for your analysis. Sometimes what you use will vary from chart to chart, depending on the question. Let the chart lead you; don't force it. Report what you see, even if it doesn't make sense at first.

Here's an alphabetical guide to the modern tools used to interpret a horary chart:

Aspects

Aspects are the engine of the modern horary chart. In modern horary, there is no designation of "major" and "minor" aspects—research and case studies show that all aspects work equally well and in their own right, not just the so-called major or Ptolemaic aspects.[3] As mentioned previously, a circle is 360 degrees of mathematical objectivity for everybody, and there is no "better" or "superior" way of splitting it up. Looking objectively at function, a 45-degree aspect (semisquare) is no more or less valid or worthy than a 90-degree aspect (square). Both have a different, but equally important message to convey. (See Appendix B for a table of the aspects and their meanings.)

In general, the non-Ptolemaic aspects are more subtle and indirect in their action, while Ptolemaic aspects are more dynamic and active. For example, a Ptolemaic sextile aspect is similar to picking up the phone and calling someone, and talking directly to them to give them information. A non-Ptolemaic semi-sextile aspect is the equivalent of sending the same information to them via text message: same outcome, different dynamic. Therefore, quincunxes, semi-sextiles, semisquares, sesquiquadrates, etc., are all considered, especially when determining whether the Moon is void-of-course or not.

In horary, generally (but not always), if there's no aspect between significators, there's no action. "A bad aspect is still a connection between the two parties," says Diana Stone. "It may be a bad idea, but it can be accomplished."[4] An aspect involving mutual application (i.e., a planet moving forward to aspect one retrograding back to meet it), underscores and emphasizes the event signified by the planets and aspect involved.

An abundance of harsh aspects between significators, and significators to the Moon, generally indicates a "no" answer. A preponderance of positive aspects indicates a "yes" answer. However, just like life, charts usually aren't that black and white, and there are other factors to consider in addition to aspects.

Asteroids & Lilith

The main asteroid belt is located between Mars and Jupiter and forms a "buffer zone" between the inner solar system terrestrial planets and the outer solar system gas giant planets. In the 19th century, the asteroids Ceres, Pallas, Juno and Vesta were considered full-fledged planets, and were taught as such in schoolchildren's texts. But when it became obvious to astronomers that there were too many of them in the same location, and that their orbits crossed and overlapped, they were all quietly reclassified to asteroids (meaning "starlike") by the early 20th century.[5] (See Appendix F - Part II)

The myths and legends constituting the astrological symbolism of the asteroids are just as important and influential as the archetypal symbolism of the planets. Also, the symbolic meanings of the asteroids, dwarf planets, comets, etc., are the same in horary as in natal astrology. In horary, the asteroids' symbolism provides sharper detail to amplify a specific meaning that can't be shown by just the signified planet alone.

Asteroids do not rule signs, nor do they need to; they are strong or weak by sign according to their founding myth. For example, Ceres does not do well in Scorpio, ruled by Pluto, who kidnapped her daughter Persephone to the underworld. Pallas is strong in Sagittarius, as she sprang from the head of Jupiter in her founding myth.

Like any other planet or object, they act as co-significators by house placement, and synthesize either strongly or weakly with other objects and the planets, particularly significators, through aspects, dispositors and midpoints. If an asteroid connects to a significator, midpoint or an angle, it has an important message to tell about the situation inquired about. Relevant asteroids can also supersede planets and be used as primary significators in a matter. Below are just a few of the most commonly used asteroids in horary; there are many others, such as Eros, Psyche, etc., that can be targeted to specific types of horary questions once you learn their meanings.

CHIRON (Half asteroid, half comet)

Chiron is a hybrid in both the mythical and physical sense: It is half asteroid and half comet according to NASA (Comet 95P/Chiron and Minor Planet 2060).[6] It is an object known as a Centaur that orbits mainly between Saturn and Uranus, and its key symbolism is the Wounded Healer archetype. Chiron reveals tremendous weaknesses or flaws that bring a person to his knees rather painfully in order to reveal a hidden strength and generate an authentic healing. Astrologer Michael Lutin calls it "Your greatest ironic twist. You become a teacher in the area in which you feel the weakest. It represents the pain that precedes a great transformation."[7] Sign and house placement will show in what area, and aspects will show the ease or difficulty. Look to Chiron for horary questions about health issues and healing, either physically or mentally. Chiron is also used to address any situation where a painful double life or duality exists. Use it particularly in questions relating to mentoring or teaching.

⚳
CERES (Dwarf planet, but previously classified as an asteroid)

Ceres is a non-Kuiper belt dwarf planet that resides in the asteroid belt between Mars and Jupiter. She represents nurturing capacity and the ability to care and empathize, as well as how well one treats and takes care of themselves or others. Ceres is strong when the Moon and Venus are involved, and neutralized with Saturn and Pluto. For example, Ceres paired with the Moon or Venus will show a deep connection within a relationship chart, while emotional coldness and distance is indicated if she's aspected to Saturn or Pluto. Ceres in Capricorn conjunct Pluto is one of the weakest possible places for her, indicating a person who is alienated from closeness and nurturing from others; they must provide it themselves. Look to Ceres for questions about family matters, motherhood and children, and nutrition in health horary questions.

⚸
LILITH (Lunar Apogee)

There are four types of Lilith that can be calculated for a chart: The traditional Black Moon Lilith is the position of the mean lunar apogee as measured from the geocenter; variants of the Black Moon include replacing the mean orbit with a "true" osculating orbit or with an interpolated orbit; charting the empty focus of the Moon's orbit instead of the apogee; and measuring the desired point's barycentric or topocentric position instead of its geocentric position.[8]

Regardless of which calculation you choose to utilize, the archetype of Lilith is a form of personal protest or outrage as a result of being outcast, misunderstood or dismissed. Lilith is like a miniature, more personalized Uranus, steeped in Mars outrage and anger, with Plutonian revenge thrown in for good measure. This is not necessarily a bad thing, especially in cases of personal injustice. Lilith is very deep and intense, but not always at the conscious level, which can cause acting out. Her placement will reveal much in a relationship horary chart, especially near an angle or conjunct a significator.

Lilith is the ultimate rebel. Her revolt is against personal injustice, versus Uranus' mass societal change via revolution. Lilith pairs well with Uranus and Jupiter and is restrained or inhibited when paired with Saturn or Venus.

PALLAS (Asteroid)

Pallas represents strategic planning and wisdom. In horary, Pallas shows the wisest course of action; if afflicted, it shows what's preventing such a course. Pallas is very powerful when combined with Jupiter, and genius-like with a flair for creative intelligence with Mercury or Uranus. Pallas is debilitated with Venus, because Pallas is about commanding rather than relating. Pallas is very difficultly paired in aspect with Neptune, indicating a lack of planning and vagueness. Look to Pallas in all business, employment, government and political charts, and charts of a decision making nature, such as "Should I do X?"

JUNO (Asteroid)

Juno represents struggles in committed personal relationships and marriages, especially due to inequality or injustice. Her symbolism provides more accurate insight into relationship horary questions than Venus alone. Juno is strong with Jupiter and Saturn, but poorly paired with controlling Pluto and disruptive and freedom-loving Uranus. Juno should be used in all spousal or intimate relationship horary questions, in addition to the 7th house. For example, Juno in Pisces quincunx Saturn in Libra shows an ambivalence about the commitment a relationship, but the problem can be worked out in time and with effort. Juno conjunct Pluto indicates tremendous jealously and mistrust in the relationship, including infidelity. Juno opposing Uranus means breaking free of the relationship is the best possible option.

VESTA (Asteroid)

Vesta, as Goddess of the Hearth, represents supreme dedication and a place of tremendous focus and devotion in the house it occupies. Vesta works well with the Moon and Saturn, but not with Neptune and Uranus. Vesta provides specific details about home and family matters, relationship questions, and shows where focus and dedication is either shown or needed. For example, Vesta with Neptune is a lack of focus or a commitment that falls through; with Uranus, a lack of commitment to begin with, or someone unreliable; and with Pluto, an outright obsession. Vesta in the 9th house can show a successful university career, or in the 7th, a lifelong marriage commitment.

Astromaps

If a picture is worth a thousand words, then using astromaps (also called local space maps) generated from a horary question's data can be of immense value and validation for geographic questions. Astromaps are very useful for horary questions such as "Should I attend school in Rome?" or "Should I Move to Toronto or New York City?" or "Should we vacation in Brazil?"

In the astromap in Figure 5.1, generated with data from the horary question, "Should I accept the job in Northern California?" (in which the querent has Capricorn rising), the querent should definitely accept the position. The Pluto, Mars, Mercury and North Node lines are incredibly strong ascending, with Saturn at home on the MC, literally providing an opportunity for complete control to rebuild a business empire. The querent accepted the position.

Figure 5.1: Astromap for the question: "Should the querent accept the job in No. Calif.?"

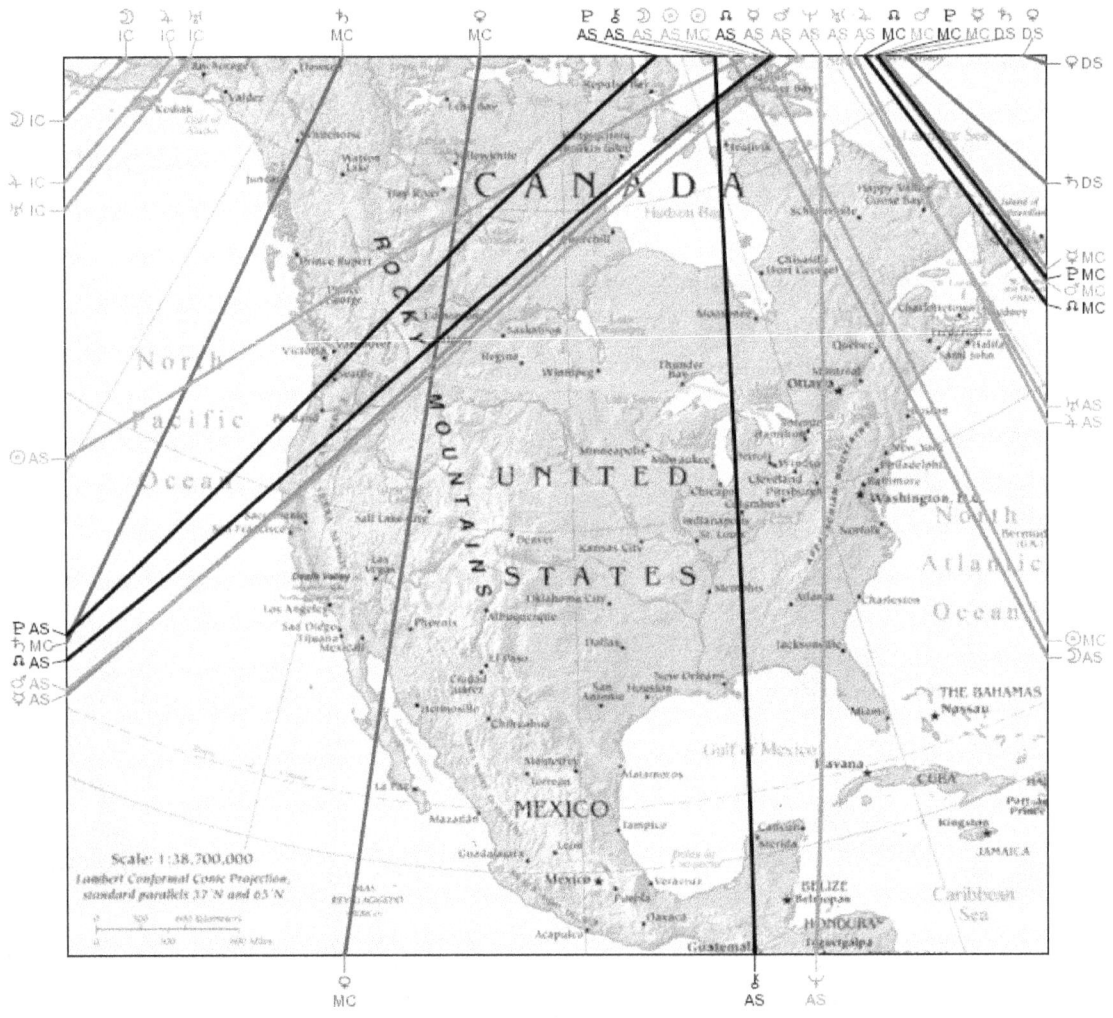

Astromap courtesy of Astro.com

Co-significators

Any planets in the first house are co-significators of the querent, and show additional sides of the story and circumstances surrounding the querent in the matter. For example, the Sun or Jupiter in the 1st house may mean the querent is optimistic about the matter, while Neptune in the 1st house can show confusion or denial. Also, planets in the house of the quesited become co-rulers of the quesited.

Combust the Sun

Combustion occurs when the unaided visibility of a planet is obscured by sunlight. A planet that is within 8 degrees of the Sun is considered combust (i.e., Venus at 19 degrees Leo conjunct the Sun at 25 degrees Leo). Symbolically, the effectiveness of the combust planet is weakened, "burned up" and overwhelmed by stronger forces, as is the person or thing ruled by the combust planet. It's a high anxiety situation for the person involved. Like looking directly into the Sun, the person is somewhat blinded by the overwhelming brightness, and as such, can't see the matter clearly.

In general, a significator combust the Sun is not good, but it does not necessarily preclude a positive outcome as the example in Chapter 8 (Fig. 8.3) shows. However, if a significator is combust the Sun and retrograde, that's worse, and if it's combust, retrograde, intercepted and in detriment or fall, forget it.

TNOs are immune to the symbolism of Sun combustion due to their distance and orbital eccentricities, as well as the fact that they were forged from the birth of the solar system.[9]

Critical Degrees

Critical degrees represent high anxiety or a desperate situation for the planet or house cusp (particularly angular cusps) at the critical degree. Zero degrees and 29 degrees of all signs are critical because they signify beginnings and endings.

Traditional horary utilizes additional critical degrees (below) based on the ancient concept of lunar mansions. Modern horary practitioners generally don't utilize these additional degrees to no ill avail.

Cardinal signs	0, 13, 26 degrees
Fixed signs	9, 21 degrees
Mutable signs	4, 17 degrees

Derived or Derivative Houses

Deriving houses means turning the wheel of the original chart (called the radix or "root" chart) to place the quesited house on the ascendant so it becomes the first house. This is done to signify someone other than the querent, in order to assess the details of their involvement in the matter inquired about. For example, if the querent is asking about a friend, the chart is turned to put the 11th house of friends as the first house cusp, and interpreting around the chart from there to see the friend's point of view. If a lover is the quesited, the wheel is turned so the 5th house becomes the first house.

Derivative houses are also utilized to show a sibling-like or third house relationship between similar items or circumstances. For example, if someone owns two homes, the primary residence would be the 4th house. The second residence, bearing a sibling relationship to the first home, would be located in the 6th house, which is the derived third house from the radix (root) 4th house. This three-house spacing is used only if both items are owned by or related to the querent. Each subsequent instance would be located in a derivative third house. For example, in questions about children, the 5th house designates the first child, the 7th house the second child, and the 9th house the third child, etc.

If there is a similar item, and it *doesn't* belong to the querent, such as looking to purchase a second home, *don't* use a sibling relationship. Use the derived natural house from the original natural house. In this example, the current home would be the radix 4th house, and a *potential* second home would be located four houses away in the 7th house. In a relocation chart, the 4th house is the current residence, and four houses over is the 7th house, signifying the residence that would be moved into.

For questions about money, use derived 2nd houses. For example, the 1st house is the querent and the 2nd house shows the income of the querent. In real estate sales, the 4th house is the property and the 5th house is the 2nd house of income from the 4th house of the property. For a 7th house partnership, the 8th house shows the income and finances from the 7th house couple. The 10th house rules a business or enterprise, and the 11th house shows the income of the business, since it's the 2nd house from the 10th house.

Each house also has a derivative fourth house of outcome or endings. For example, if the question is 11th-house related, such as a question about a friend, colleague, or business income, then as the derived 4th house from the 11th, the radix 2nd house (in addition to the other factors in the chart, of course) will show the outcome of the question.

Dispositors

A dispositor is the ruler of a sign that another planet is in. For example, Mars in Virgo would disposit to Mercury, because Mercury is the natural ruler of Virgo. Venus in Sagittarius would disposit to Jupiter, the ruler of Sagittarius. The trail is followed until its natural end or "final" dispositor, or until it reaches the end of its trail before repeating. Dispositors are utilized heavily in modern horary to help follow the trail of the significators to unfold the story and outcome. Dispositors connect significators and relevant houses to the question for better or for worse. If there is a strong connection, coupled with positive aspects, the greater the likelihood of achieving the desired outcome. (See Appendix G - Part III for an example of how dispositors are used.)

Early or Late Degrees

If the ascendant or a significator, angle or quesited house cusp is between 0 and 3 degrees, it indicates that the matter too early or premature. In particular, it can take up to 5 degrees for planets and other objects to establish themselves in a sign.

If the ascendant or a significator, angle or quesited house cusp is between 27 and 29 degrees, it indicates that the matter is too late to do anything about, as the outcome is out of the querent's hands, or that the situation is about to change. Planets or other objects at 28 or 29 degrees of every sign are in "dead degrees," where they act like they are "at the end of their rope" as astrologer Ivy Goldstein-Jacobson described it.[10] The dead degrees show the situation is ripe for change, and the impatience that ensues from the desire to get on with something new. It can also indicate the situation has met a dead end.

If a chart has late degrees rising, and the Moon or other significators are in early degrees, it can indicate the matter was over before it ever had a chance to get started. This is common in employment charts, for example, where an internal candidate may have had the inside track. Conversely, if the ascendant or significators are in early degrees and the quesited in late degrees, it can indicate a need to start over or begin anew.

Fixed Stars

Traditional horary reference material on the meanings of fixed stars are vague and often contradictory. Ptolemy blended two classical planetary influences via statements such as "Antares is of the nature of Mars and Jupiter," while other authors tend to provide a description of vague or contradictory keywords shrouded in superstition: "Antares: Destructiveness, broad-minded, liberality, evil presages, danger, violence, etc."[11] Or: "Natives with this particular configuration have to be prepared at all times for sudden incidents, unforeseen events and potential accidents."[12]

Astrologer Joseph Crane posits, "The brighter fixed stars can have an outer planet feel to them—they were what our forebearers used millennia before the outer planets were discovered to relate to experiences of extremes or fate."[13] Traditional horary practitioners utilize fixed stars moreso than modern horary practitioners. Fixed stars won't override planetary action—they merely act as additional descriptors. Benefic fixed stars tend to be mitigated if afflicted.

Due to precession in the tropical zodiac, fixed stars advance approximately one degree every 72 years. For example, the benefic fixed star Regulus, known as the "Heart of the Lion" because of its earlier location in the constellation of Leo, is now located at 0 degrees Virgo. By no means exhaustive, below is a list of a few of the most commonly used fixed stars, their current degrees, and traditional meanings:

Caput Algol (26° Taurus)	More of a message than a malefic. Losing one's head in a matter to the extent that things aren't being seen clearly or rationally. Over-attached or over-invested to where a person can't think straight, to their own detriment.
Pleiades/Alcyone (0° Gemini)	The Weeping Sisters constellation; a significator here will give you something to cry about.
Aldebaran (10° Gemini)	Related to Mars with its energy and drive, but considered volatile.
Sirius (14° Cancer)	Success through your own efforts. Benign action and results. A flourishing.
22° Leo	Not a fixed star but a malefic fixed degree. One's own worst enemy in a more overt way than the 12th house meaning. A no-win degree. Not free to act on your own behalf.
Regulus (0° Virgo)	The most benefic fixed star. Enhances or glorifies a significator, but can also exaggerate or create grandiose hopes.
Spica/Arcturus (Spica 24° Libra, Arcturus 25° Libra)	Benefic oasis in the otherwise fiery and turbulent Via Combust zone. Helps matters.
Serpentis (19° Scorpio)	Also not a fixed star, but a malefic fixed degree. Considered the worst place in the zodiac.
Antares (10° Sagittarius)	The need to defend or fight back in a given situation. Valorous at best, vengeful at worst. Conflict.
Fomalhaut (3° Pisces)	Considered to bestow great and lasting honors. A benefic influence if conjunct a significator.

House Systems

The choice of house system to generate horary charts is a matter of the astrologer's personal preference. There is no "official" or "correct" house system in horary. The most commonly used house systems for horary are Placidus and Koch (modern) and Regiomontanus (traditional). Some people prefer an Equal House system. Vedic horary practitioners use something entirely different. Many Uranian and Cosmobiology horary practitioners don't even use houses; they use a 90-degree dial instead. Having interpreted querent-generated charts that used all of the various house systems at one time or another, accuracy was never impeded due to house system choice. Any one of them will work just fine.

Houses

The symbolic meanings of the twelve houses in natal astrology are the same in horary. For example, the 8th house rules death, legacy and taxes in horary, just as it does in natal astrology.

There are three types of houses: angular (1st, 4th, 7th, 10th), succeedent (2nd, 5th, 8th, 11th) and cadent (3rd, 6th, 9th, 12th), which correspond to the cardinal, fixed and mutable modes or qualities. Planets and objects in angular houses show things or circumstances that are overt and out in the open, as well as quick activity. Succeedent houses sustain momentum in matters, and cadent houses indicate things that are hidden, slow, or delayed, hindered and covert.

Traditional astrology considers cadent houses malefic. Modern horary drops the superstition, as cadent houses aren't any worse than any other houses. Instead, they aptly describe situations and circumstances. For example, the cadent 9th house rules immigration and foreign travel, so a significator there for a question such as "Should I immigrate to Canada?" is entirely appropriate, and not malefic. See Appendix B for brief synopses of the meanings of all twelve houses.

Interceptions

When a sign doesn't rule a house cusp, it is intercepted. Interception is a result of trying to turn 3-D spatial reality into a flat, 2-D chart wheel. Many traditional horary practitioners ignore interceptions, but modern practitioners find they provide valuable pieces of information.

Interceptions inhibit or restrict the action or expression of whatever planet(s) may be "trapped" within them. According to Diana Stone, "If you want to know what the interference or inhibition is with the intercepted planets, look for the ruler of the sign they are trapped in."[14] For example, if Venus is intercepted in Cancer in the 5th house, look to the house and sign of the Moon, since it rules Cancer. In this example, if the Moon is in the 8th house in Scorpio (thereby in fall by house and sign), there may be a secret sexual affair that doesn't end well if it's a relationship question.

Stone also mentions that interceptions can indicate a yielding, or one situation giving way to another—an interception in the 7th house can mean replacing one person with another, such as changing doctors in a health horary question.[15]

Interference/Prohibition, Frustration, and Hinderance/Impedition

These circumstances are considered primarily by traditional astrologers and are included for the sake of comprehensiveness and because they are so poorly understood; they are usually ignored by modern horary astrologers.

Interference (called prohibition in traditional astrology by William Lilly) occurs when one of the significators applies to aspect another planet before it can aspect the other significator. For example, Mars is applying to conjoin Venus, but Mars trines Saturn first. This is interference, indicating a limitation, distraction or delay on the part of the Mars person.

Frustration occurs when a third planet steps in to thwart an applying aspect to two significators. For example, Mars is going to conjoin Venus, but Mercury squares Mars first. So a third party (in this case, Mercury) steps in to interrupt with the two people represented by Mars and Venus, thus hampering the outcome, but not necessarily foiling it completely.

The key difference between interference and frustration is that interference is internal (one of the two significators causes the snafu) while frustration is external (a non-significator, third-party or outsider planet causes the problem). Both signify a hampering or delay or even an interlude, but not necessarily a defeat in the matter, depending on the aspects involved and other factors in the chart.

Hinderance and impedition (the term used by Lilly) are anything that weakens a significator. Both are general terms for things such as combustion, retrogradation, besiegement, etc., that obstruct significators from acting fully and freely in a horary chart.[16]

Malefics and Benefics

There are planetary good guys and bad guys in horary. The general rule of thumb is that malefics afflict or harm a situation, while benefics are fortunate and assist a situation. Traditionally, the malefics are Mars (lesser malefic) and Saturn (greater malefic), and the benefics are Jupiter (greater benefic) and Venus (lesser benefic).

From a modern standpoint, each planetary archetype has both fine and dark qualities. It's the rulerships and aspects that determine whether for better or for worse in all planets, not just the alleged malefics. For example, an afflicted Mercury can lie and deceive, while a well-aspected Saturn can solidify or culminate a goal.

Traditional astrology only recognizes Mars and Saturn as malefics; modern horary adds Pluto. Depending on the matter inquired about, Saturn, Mars and Pluto aren't always malevolent, and rational minds today can handle the doom and gloom that spooked the ancients. Some modern horary practitioners also consider Neptune and Uranus malefic, but it's a pretty big stretch to consider everything in the solar system beyond Jupiter to be a place where evil lurks. For the most part, consider Uranus and Neptune as malefic only if they are afflicted, debilitated, or harshly aspecting a significator. Otherwise, a Moon-Uranus sextile can bring a pleasant surprise, Venus trine Neptune can make a dream come true if other influences in the chart support it, and a Mercury conjunction to Pluto can unearth a long-withheld, key piece of information from a witness in a courtroom.

Additionally, the term "besieged" describes a significator or the Moon between two malefic planets, no matter how far apart. "Duress" is besiegement within a tight orb (7 degrees or less) between two malefics.

Midpoints

Midpoints are the mathematical halfway point between two planets (or other astronomical objects or points) in a horary chart.[17] They are important interactions between planets that are often overlooked in favor of more obvious connections such as aspects, reception or disposition. Midpoints can depict alternate routes, particularly if the main inroads (aspects, etc.) between significators are missing.

Just as in natal astrology, midpoints are amplified sensitive points, specific descriptors, as well as event triggers in horary charts. They are also easy to utilize as an extra support of confirmation of judgment. The use of midpoints in modern horary has been adapted and integrated from Uranian astrology.

Midpoints amplify the connection between two planets or objects, specifically the more challenging ones (squares, sesquiquadrates, etc.). As event catalysts, midpoints can be used to analyze past, present and future events, particularly if the Moon (or other planet or object) has either recently transited or will transit the significators' midpoint. When a third planet transits the midpoint of two significators, it triggers an occurrence in the situation based on the symbolic qualities of the planet, sign and house placement of the triggering planet. For example, if Pluto is at the midpoint of a Venus-Jupiter square (at which point Pluto is semi-squaring both), the ability to otherwise work out differences harmoniously and benevolently takes a sudden turn toward jealousy, suspicion and paranoia.

If your astrology software is capable of generating a list of midpoints and midpoint trees, they are very easy to work with. As with horary charts, focus only on the midpoint trees of the significators and Moon, and ignore the other trees. The shorter the list of midpoints involving significators, the fewer the difficulties, and the better the chances of the matter culminating easily. Figure 5.2 is an example of a 90-degree midpoint tree for a 10th house career question, where Uranus rules the Midheaven. The Moon and Venus are the querent's significators in the horary chart wheel (not shown). In the midpoint trees, the Moon is on the Jupiter-MC midpoint while afflicted by Saturn; Venus is afflicted by (but not directly on) the Jupiter-Uranus midpoint, while afflicted by the Sun and Mars; and the Midheaven itself is directly on the Moon-Venus midpoint. So with those three strikes, unsurprisingly, the querent did not get the job.

[As a quick primer, note that the "D" following the midpoint pair means that the focal point planet in the colored box is sitting directly on that pair's midpoint (D=direct). Planets at the very bottom of a box are in some sort of challenging aspect to the focal point planet. Use the chart wheel's aspectarian grid to see what aspect they make.]

If your astrology software *doesn't* have the capability to generate a midpoints list or tree, the easiest way to work with midpoints is to note how the aspects relate to each other through mathematical division:
- Conjunctions (0 degrees) don't have a midpoint.
- Semi-sextiles (30 degrees) are the midpoint of sextiles (60 degrees).
- Semi-squares (45 degrees) are the midpoint of squares (90 degrees).
- Sextiles (60 degrees) are the midpoint of trines (120 degrees).
- Quintiles (72 degrees) are the midpoint of biquintiles (144 degrees).
- Squares (90 degrees) are the midpoint of oppositions (180 degrees).
- Sesquiquadrate (135 degrees) midpoints are sesquioctiles (67.5 degrees, or a semi-square and a half). Quincunx (150 degrees) midpoints are called squiles (75 degrees; a hybrid of a square and a sextile). Both sesquioctiles and squiles are primarily used in Uranian astrology, rather than modern horary.[18]
- Quindeciles (165 degrees) are the midpoint of a quincunx (150 degrees) and opposition (180 degrees).

Figure 5.2: Midpoint Tree for the Horary Question "Will the Querent Get the Job?"

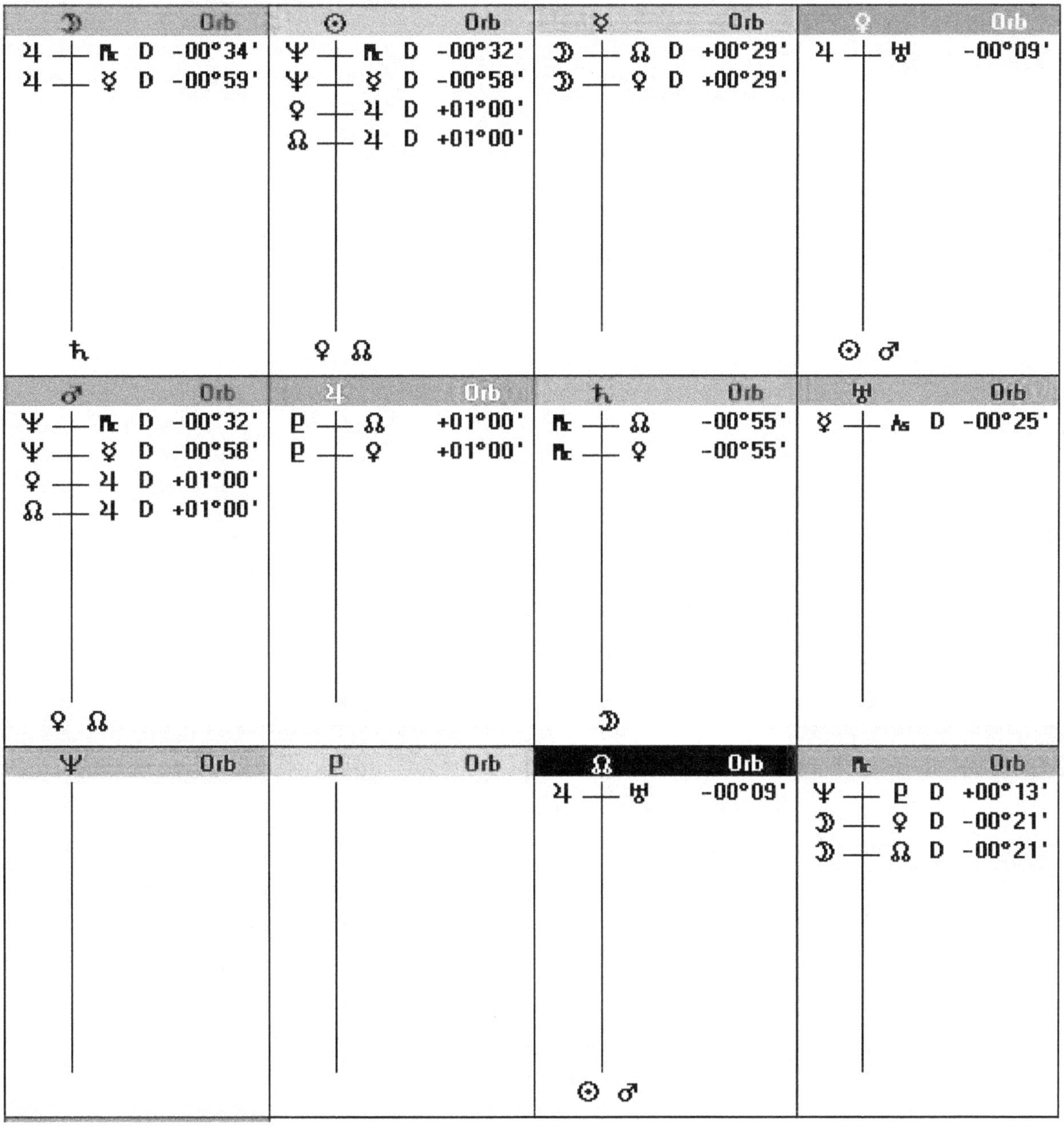

☽	Orb	☉	Orb	☿	Orb	♀	Orb
♃ — ☊ D -00°34'		♆ — ☊ D -00°32'		☽ — ☋ D +00°29'		♃ — ♅ -00°09'	
♃ — ☿ D -00°59'		♆ — ☿ D -00°58'		☽ — ♀ D +00°29'			
		♀ — ♃ D +01°00'					
		☋ — ♃ D +01°00'					
♄		♀ ☋				☉ ♂	

♂	Orb	♃	Orb	♄	Orb	♅	Orb
♆ — ☊ D -00°32'		♇ — ☋ +01°00'		☊ — ☋ -00°55'		☿ — As D -00°25'	
♆ — ☿ D -00°58'		♇ — ♀ +01°00'		☊ — ♀ -00°55'			
♀ — ♃ D +01°00'							
☋ — ♃ D +01°00'							
♀ ☋				☽			

♆	Orb	♇	Orb	☋	Orb	☊	Orb
				♃ — ♅ -00°09'		♆ — ♇ D +00°13'	
						☽ — ♀ D -00°21'	
						☽ — ☋ D -00°21'	
				☉ ♂			

Midpoint Tree Copyright © 2006 Matrix Software, Inc.

Use the chart wheel's aspectarian grid to spot the aspects, rather than trying to count in your head. Also note whether they are applying or separating, using orbs of two degrees or less, which is the standard for midpoints.

There is a wealth of detailed information contained within a horary chart that can be easily mined with the use of midpoints. Master the horary fundamentals first, and then learn to look for and integrate midpoints.

The Moon

The Moon in horary astrology is particularly important for several reasons: It is the co-significator of the querent, it is the fastest body in a chart, and it is used to determine the tone of how events unfold and ultimately end.

The key difference between natal and horary in using the Moon is that in horary, all the past, present and future aspects the Moon makes while in a single sign at the time of the chart are utilized, rather than the natal approach of considering only what's within a specific, and often compact, orb. Past events are designated by the Moon's most recent aspects, while present and future circumstances are shown by current and future aspects. For example, if the Moon is at 5 degrees Leo, and most of the rest of the planets are at 20 degrees or later, there will be a time of idling where it seems like nothing is happening in the matter, until the Moon comes to the later degrees and forms aspects with the other planets or objects.

Aspects of the Moon are secondary to aspects between significators. Marc Edmund Jones described the Moon as "Pertinent, but trivial."[19] Diana Stone states, "The Moon's aspects in the order that they occur shows the sequence of events before the matter is resolved. The Moon's last aspect generally indicates how the matter ends. It's not the whole story, but it's a big piece of the answer. The Moon's last aspect to a retrograde planet means that there is always something that you don't like about the way the matter ends." If the Moon sextiles or trines a malefic as the last aspect, it eases the consequences, but doesn't alter the negative outcome if one is otherwise indicated in the chart.[20] "Sometimes when the Moon's last aspect is positive in an otherwise negative chart, it just means that things turn out okay in the long run, even if the matter at hand is disappointing," adds Stone.[21]

In modern horary, *all* aspects to the Moon are considered, not just Ptolemaic aspects. For example, if the Moon's last *true* aspect is a quintile to Venus, it can soften the blow of a Ptolemaic square to Mars, which would traditionally be considered the last aspect.

Since life isn't one-dimensional, it is normal for the Moon to tell one story while the significators tell quite a different one. The astrologer must reconcile the duality while rendering an accurate judgment.

New moons and full moons are not considered malefic in modern horary. Traditionally, the new Moon is considered combust the Sun, and therefore malefic. Instead, in modern horary, it describes a situation as either a beginning (new Moon) or culmination (full Moon). The new Moon describes the beginning of a new cycle, having been symbolically "re-energized" by its conjunction with the Sun. Its house placement and aspects determine in what area the focus, energy and nurturing will be applied. The full Moon, as an opposition aspect to the Sun, represents closure and separations, or finality in a matter.

Eclipses and Occultations

Eclipses symbolize endings and beginnings. Lunar eclipses are essentially high-powered oppositions on steroids. They bring up long-standing issues and core tensions that unresolved, lead to separations. A lunar eclipse will create emotional upheaval that causes the end of a matter, such as a relationship. Diana Stone states that eclipses upset the matter of the house where they occur.[22]

Solar eclipses are high-powered conjunctions that reveal something obscured or that had not been previously considered. It can also "reboot" or renew the matter inquired about. It represents a momentary loss of power and then a change in direction or circumstance based on the house axis it falls in. Strength and will in that area disappear momentarily due to the deep, unresolved issues invoked by the preceeding lunar eclipse, and then a reboot occurs once the missing piece is addressed. A solar eclipse can also show activity that has come to overshadow the event.[23]

When the Moon conjoins and eclipses a planet by declination, it's called an occultation. This relatively uncommon phenomenon can repress, disempower or literally overshadow what the afflicted planet is trying to represent. If the occulted planet is a significator, it indicates the person may not succeed. One thing an occultation *can* do is somewhat mitigate a malefic. According to Diana Stone, "Occultations are usually unfortunate. However, when the Moon makes an occultation to a malefic, the aspect is bad, but not as bad as it could have been. It works well for the querent because the Moon is always the co-ruler of the querent."[24]

Mutual Reception

Mutual receptions are a great way out of a jam and a querent's best friend. "A mutual reception is when two planets occupy the ruling sign of the other and can trade places," says Diana Stone. "Mutual receptions allow you to move a planet—with its original degree—back to its own sign that it rules. One of the meanings is that it shows a way out of the matter."[25] For example, Uranus in Pisces is in mutual reception with Neptune in Aquarius because both planets are in the sign each other rules. As medieval horary astrologer Guido Bonatus noted, "Reception abates all malice."

Retrograde status can (but not always) negate a mutual reception. Stone observes that the querent will be disinclined to take the way out offered by the mutual reception when one or both planets are retrograde.[26]

North and South Nodes

The Moon's Nodes are points where the orbit of the Moon around the Earth intersects with the ecliptic, which is the orbit of the Earth around the Sun. The Nodes are calculated in one of two ways: Mean and True. Traditional horary practitioners use the Mean Node, which is the Node's rate of motion averaged out over the course of its backward revolution through the zodiac. The Mean Node is always retrograde. Modern horary practitioners tend to use the True Node, which is closest to the *actual* position of the Nodes, because it takes into account the wobble in the Moon's orbit. The True Node is direct at times. Both the True and Mean Nodes differ by a little more than a degree and a half.

Regardless of Nodal preference, the Nodes of the Moon are one of the most widely misunderstood influences across all branches of astrology, not just horary. In a natal chart, the Nodes are literally the chart's DNA. All relationships, jobs, health issues, etc., will spring out of the Nodal placement and aspects. It's just as important in horary, especially in relationship charts. In a horary chart, the Nodes by house, sign and dispositor will depict the DNA of the question: why it was asked, hidden agendas, and what the true goal is.

Michael Lutin's masterpiece, *Sunshines: The Astrology of Being Happy*, is a landmark realistic and pragmatic work on the meaning of the Nodes and how to synthesize them in natal astrology. *Sunshines'* power and depth carries over seamlessly from natal to horary, with phenomenal results. The "boring" North Node, as Lutin describes it, "never fails you." It is where a person always finds success, but essentially takes it for granted, and goes looking for something more exciting and glamorous to pursue in the South Node. The South Node according to Lutin, "never fails to fail you." It is where a person tries to get in the present what they didn't get in the past, in an attempt at "this time it's going to be different."[27] It is an over-attachment due to deprivation. The outcome is always the same: disastrous.

According to horary astrologer Ivy Goldstein-Jacobson, "Any planet or angle in the same degree as the Nodes points to a catastrophe, casualty, fatality or tragedy in a horary or natal chart, the more far-reaching when a malefic is involved."[28] Traditional horary considers the Nodal catastrophe scenario only if a *significator* is in the Nodal degree. Regardless of which method you use, it's an extra red flag to consider in light of the rest of the chart.

When there is a square to the Nodes involving a significator, it indicates the person faces a "damned if you do, damned if you don't" situation. [29]

Part of Fortune

The Part of Fortune, consisting of a derivative calculation of the Sun, Moon and Ascendant, is one of the many Arabic parts primarily used by traditional horary astrologers. Some think the Part of Fortune strengthens a significator and acts as a small benefic. It is thought to be unfortunate if conjunct the malefic fixed star Caput Algol, or located in the 8th or 12th houses. Since it's a derivative calculation and not a moving body, it can't create action; it's basically a static descriptor. Like fixed stars, it won't override the basic tone of the chart or action of the planets, but it can be helpful in providing additional information if needed.

Planetary Rulership (Dignity & Debility)

Dignity and debility show the strength and weakness of planets. Planets in rulership or exaltation show power and strength to act, while planets in detriment and fall show distress or weakness or inability to act effectively. For a list of planetary dignities and debilities by sign and house, see Appendix B.

Rulerships apply only to planets. An object, such as a TNO or asteroid, does not have or need any form of dignity in order to function effectively in a horary chart, as their strengths and weaknesses are conceptually different from planets. (See Chapter 12)

Contrary to traditional horary rules, a planet does not need essential dignity (strength by zodiac sign) or accidental dignity (strength by house position, etc.) to be able to function or act. It's helpful, but not required. A beat up Volvo will get you from point A to point B just as a brand new Ferrari will; the same as a person flying alone in coach will arrive in Paris at the exact same time as the person sitting in first-class with an adoring entourage. Symbolically, it's no different with the planets.

Querent & Quesited

The querent is the person asking the horary question. The querent is always ruled by the first house, unless using a derivative chart to inquire about another person. (See: Derived or Derivative Houses) The quesited is the object, person or matter inquired about.

Having a single planet ruling both the querent and quesited (e.g., a Gemini ascendant with Virgo on the 4th house cusp for a family-oriented question; both ruled by Mercury) is common, indicating emphasis on or a common bond in the matter inquired about. Only Venus and Mercury are affected, since they are the only planets that rule two signs, as the outer planets supplant the rest of the traditional dual-sign rulerships. (See Appendix G - Part III for an example of a single planet ruling both querent and quesited.)

Traditionally, when the same planet rules both querent and quesited, the Moon is used as the primary significator of the querent. From a modern standpoint, there are several other ways in addition to using the Moon to glean deeper detail. In the above-mentioned Gemini ascendant-Virgo 4th cusp quesited example:

- Look to the house placement of and aspects to Mercury.
- Look to Mercury's dispositor, aspects to it, and its house placement. Does the ruler of the house cusp Mercury is in make any aspects to Mercury or its dispositor?
- Look for other planets as co-significators in the houses of querent and quesited, and what aspects they make to Mercury. Also see what and where they disposit to.
- Look at any midpoints and aspects to midpoints of a) Mercury and its dispositors, b) Mercury and the ruler of the house cusp Mercury is in, and c) to any co-significators.
- Look at the Moon's aspects to Mercury, its dispositors, and pertinent midpoints.

The more direct connections, the more primary the focus and action, and the greater the chance the matter has of culminating. The fewer connections, the more indirect and secondary the focus and the action, and the lesser the chances of culmination. Whether for better or for worse depends on the types of connections, either harsh or favorable.

Reception

How planets relate to each other by sign—via rulership, exaltation, detriment and fall—is known as reception. It is the astrological concept of "I am attracted to what is familiar and favorable to me, and repulsed by what is unfamiliar and harmful." For example, in a relationship horary question, if the querent's significator is Mercury in Capricorn, and the quesited's significator is Jupiter in Pisces,

Mercury is in the sign of Jupiter's fall, and Jupiter is in the sign of Mercury's detriment, indicating the two people are not compatible.

How the Moon receives significators is another important factor to look for in interpretations. For example, if the Moon, as co-ruler of the querent, is in rulership in Cancer, and Saturn as quesited is exalted in Libra, both people are strong in their own right but in completely different ways. However, the Saturn person is at a disadvantage in the situation with little to gain from collaborating with the querent, because Saturn is in detriment in Cancer, the sign the Moon (and co-ruler of the querent) is in.

For a list of planetary rulerships, exaltations, etc., see Appendix B.

Refranation

Refranation is where an applying aspect between two significators "refrains" from occurring, indicating the matter inquired about will not come to pass. It is the failure of an event to happen—literally, the matter or event falls through or comes to naught—because one of the two significators leaves its sign before the aspect with the second significator can perfect.

Think of a horse race, where the tired horse in the lead staggers beneath the wire as the horse on the inside rail comes charging along at full speed and misses by a neck. The charging horse on the inside rail "runs out of real estate," while the planet "runs out of sign." This usually happens with planets in late degrees. For example, if Mercury is at 28 degrees Libra and the Moon is at 1 degree Aquarius, Mercury will ingress into Scorpio before the Moon can transit to the late degrees fast enough to form the trine at 28 Aquarius.

Retrogrades (Rx)

Retrogrades invariably cause delays or snafus in horary matters. Diana Stone states that retrograde planets "lie" or provide misinformation, and to look to the house cusp the retrograde planet rules to see what it's lying about.[30]

Astrologer Beverley Rostant describes the different retrograde scenarios clearly and concisely:

> Retrograde motion is the apparent backward motion of a planet. In horary, this motion indicates returning or going back to a previous condition. The area ruled by the retrograde planet could change its mind, or a key person involved in the situation may cause the person to return.

> With the issue of retrograde motion, an item may be in a damaged state, may return to something, or to someone. If the answer to the question asked is positive and the ruler of the question is retrograde, then if the objective is gained it may well fall short of your expectations and you should reconsider moving forward with the matter.
>
> Retrograde Saturn in the 1st house of the question may signify a negative outcome or less favorable outcome than expected. A retrograde 7th house ruler may mean...in a relationship question, that the person can't commit at this time. Mercury retrograde will affect the outcome of the question asked. Usually the person asking the question will change their mind, or what looked good during the retrograde period will have a serious flaw once Mercury goes direct. In a lot of cases, Mercury retrograde can often give a negative outcome to the question asked. [31]

When a planet is stationing, the matter is stalled and about to change. When stationing retrograde, reversals and delays can be expected. When stationing direct, activity resumes or is revitalized. "Clearing its shadow" is when a planet (or other object), by direct motion, finally transits beyond the degree and sign where it originally turned retrograde. Matters untangle and progress can then be made.

If afflicted, Mercury retrograde can indicate someone may be lying or withholding facts or information. Venus retrograde creates doubts about and discomfort in relationships. Mars retrograde slows down activity considerably, causing enormous frustration and impatience in the process—kind of like driving with one foot on the brake and one on the gas simultaneously. Jupiter retrograde can indicate unwarranted optimism or flat-out denial.

If Saturn is retrograde, especially near the ascendant, it generally means matters won't work out, unless the rest of the chart can overcome it with extraordinarily positive aspects.[32] It's like beating your head against a brick wall and generally indicates a bigtime "no" of an answer. It also can bring endless delays and frustration. Matters rarely come to a satisfying fruition with Saturn retrograde in the 1st house.

Uranus retrograde will bring unexpected rude awakenings from out of the blue, severely throwing the matter askew. If you try to count your chickens with a retrograde Uranus, they're sure not to hatch. It is the wildest of wild cards. Neptune retrograde indicates something hidden, mistaken or erroneous, or a misunderstanding or lack of facts or details. Pluto retrograde indicates difficulty in managing power in a given situation, as well as "compounded complications."[33]

Significators

A significator is the planet which rules the querent, and the planet ruling the house of the quesited. The planet ruling the sign on the Ascendant is the significator of the querent. If you can't quite figure out a quesited significator, and rulership books and online sources don't help, the chart will often point you in the right direction. Let the significators guide you by seeing if they occupy the house(s) most relevant to the question. For example, if a querent asked "Should I open a Roth IRA?", retirement and investments are ruled by the 8th house, but personal finance is ruled by the 2nd house. If the reason for wanting to open the Roth IRA is for tax purposes, use the 8th house. If the Moon or a significator of the querent or quesited, or both, were in the 8th, use the 8th house. If the ruler of the 8th is in the first house, use the 8th house. If a stellium appears in the 2nd house, however, look there first and foremost.

Strictures Against Judgment

Traditionally, if one or more specific factors known as "strictures" appeared in a horary chart, the astrologer deemed the chart unfit to be judged and wouldn't read the chart. Modern horary doesn't take an avoidance approach to the traditional strictures. Anthony Louis states, "They simply caution the astrologer to be aware that the question is complex and the chart may be difficult to interpret."[34] According to Marc Edmund Jones, "The chart will contain a reliable answer if the stricture describes some fundamental aspect of the situation."[35] Modern horary case studies support this. Therefore, err on the side that the chart is always right in its existence, and it's up to you to figure out why it is throwing out red flags. The situation may be complex, complicated, and even muddied, but the chart can still be interpreted.

The traditional strictures against judgment are:

- Less than 3 degrees rising indicates a premature question.
- Greater than 27 degrees rising indicates a post-mature question; the matter is already decided, the querent already knows the answer, or it's too late to affect the outcome.
- Moon Via Combust —Not safe to judge unless conjoined benefic fixed star Spica (24° Libra).
- Moon Void of Course in Gemini, Capricorn or Scorpio. May function in Taurus, Sagittarius, Pisces or Cancer.
- Saturn retrograde in the first house indicates matters generally don't work out well.
- Saturn in the seventh house means the astrologer's judgment may be impaired.
- Seventh house ruler afflicted means the astrologer will have difficulty answering the question.
- If the ascendant ruler is combust the Sun, it means the querent is worried, or the astrologer may have too little information.[36]

The strictures can be easily integrated within the chart. Via Combust shows that the situation or the querent is unstable, and a trial by fire is at hand. Saturn is exalted in the 7th house, and has nothing to do with the astrologer's ability to interpret the chart as much as it provides a key piece of information, especially if the matter is 7th-house related. A significator that is combust the Sun does not preclude a successful outcome, albeit a high-anxiety and stressful one. And a void-of-course Moon can be overcome by significator aspects, midpoints or other primary factors in the chart.

Timing

Ironically, this is a part of horary that can be very hit-or-miss for both traditional and modern practitioners. There are four types of timing: modal degree timing, lunar timing, ephemeris timing, and significator progression timing. Try to use more than one timing method to confirm.

Modal degree timing, as depicted in the table below, is a traditional horary method where the number of degrees until the exact or partile aspect between the significators is converted into days, weeks, months or years depending on whether the faster of the two significators is in a cardinal, fixed, or mutable sign, and in an angular, succeedent or cadent house.

Modal Timing	**ANGULAR**	**SUCCEEDENT**	**CADENT**
CARDINAL	Days	Weeks	Months
FIXED	Weeks	Months	Years
MUTABLE	Months	Years	Unknown

So, for example, if the querent's significator is Mercury at 3 degrees Libra in the 1st house, and the quesited's significator is Venus at 5 degrees Capricorn in the 4th house, the matter will culminate in two days because the difference between the degrees of the planets is two, and both are angular and cardinal, signifying days. Modal degree timing is the least reliable; consider it but don't rely on it exclusively. Modal degree timing's limits become apparent when it's impossible for an event to occur during the chart timing indicated. For example, if a querent's surgery is definitively scheduled for six weeks, but the modal degree timing method indicates 15 years (succeedent/mutable), obviously you'll have to have a back-up plan to reconcile and rectify the timing.

Open Source Modern Horary Astrology 65

Figure 5.3: Lease Signing Depicting Lunar Timing

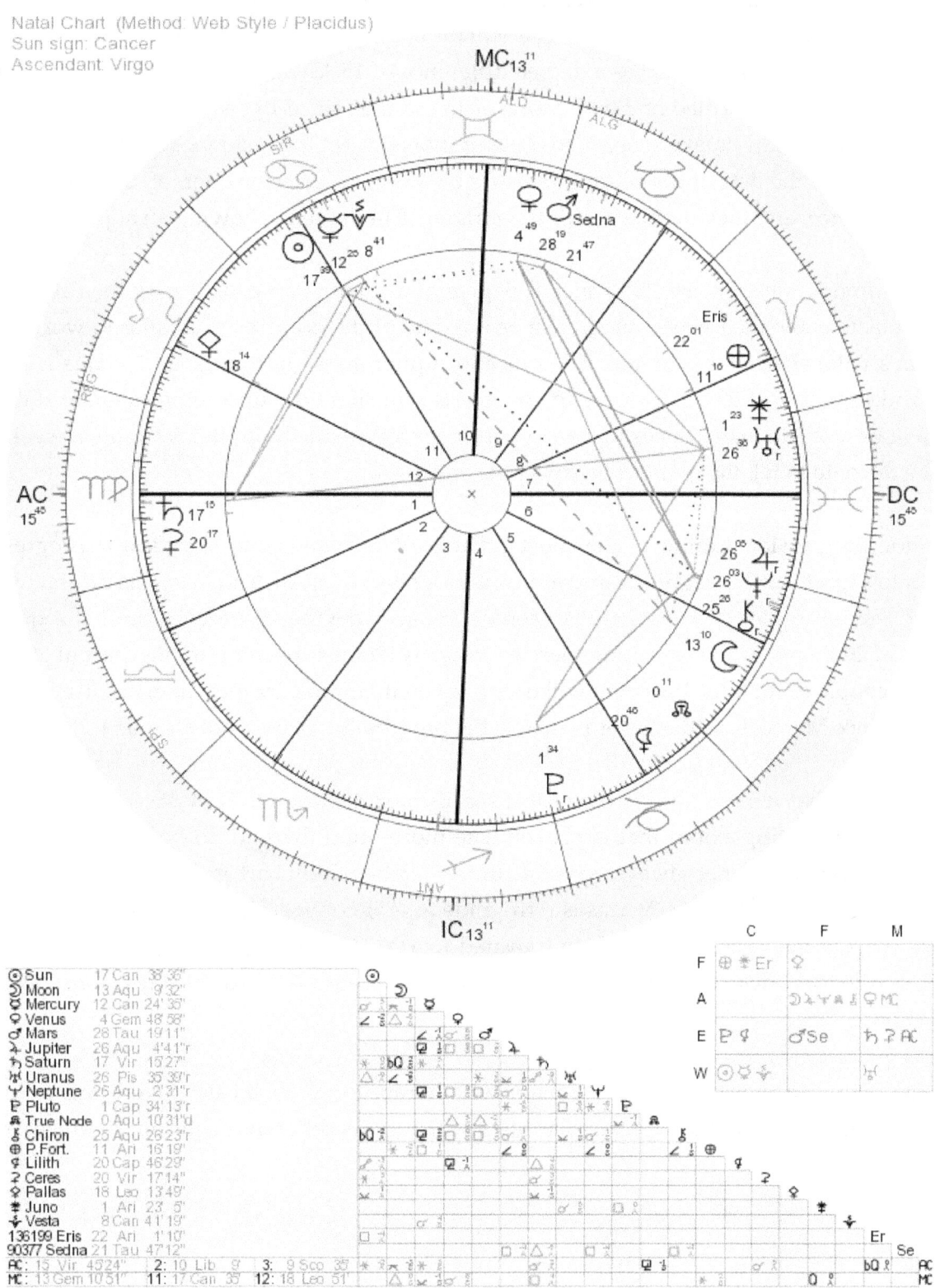

Lunar timing is when the Moon is used with the modal degree method, rather than a significator, to determine when an event will occur. In the event chart in Figure 5.3 for a lease signing, the querent wanted to know how long he would reside at the location, as it was a transitional situation. The Moon's last aspect before void-of-course is a square to Mars, ruling severance. Mars' 28 degrees, minus the Moon's 13 degrees, leaves a degree difference of 15. Given Mars' cadent house and fixed sign, the querent was informed of a time frame of 15 months, since 15 years according to the modal degree table above didn't make sense. The querent moved from the residence exactly one week shy of 15 months from the date of the chart. Interestingly, Mercury rules the querent, and Jupiter the 4th house of residence, and they quincunx in a time frame of 14 degrees, showing an adjustment.

Ephemeris timing is better than both modal degree and lunar timing, as it uses the calendar date the two planets make their aspect via transit as the date of the occurrence, similar to working with transits in a natal chart. For example, if Venus and Jupiter are significators, and Venus is at 17°32' Taurus and Jupiter is at 22°52' Cancer, an ephemeris will show the upcoming calendar date when Venus will be at 23 degrees Taurus to form a partile (exact) sextile to Jupiter (roughly a week). That would be the date to tell the querent to expect the occurrence.

Significator progression timing is the most reliable. It is where one significator progresses or advances to aspect another significator that is not progressed, but instead keeps its original place in the chart. For example, if the querent's Mercury is at 5 degrees Capricorn, and the quesited's Uranus is at 29 Pisces, when transiting Mercury reaches Uranus' position in the chart at 29 degrees Pisces in a couple of months, the event will occur. (Even if Uranus, by that time, has itself ingressed into Aries, since Mercury, as the faster planet, is the progressing planet, not Uranus.)

Note, however, that it's not always the fastest significator making the contact. Astrologer Michael Lutin has an interesting axiom that is proven true more often than not in both natal and horary: "The slowest moving planet always wins."[37] In the relationship chart in Figure 5.4, using the 1st and 7th houses for significators, Venus is retrograde at 4°55' of Scorpio, and Pluto is direct at 3°20' of Capricorn. On the calendar date Pluto transited to 4°53' Capricorn, within 24 hours of an exact (partile) sextile to Venus' 4°55' position in the chart, the event occurred, 51 days from the time of the question.

Also, just as you can convert coins into dollars, with horary timing you can convert time units, such as twenty weeks (i.e., mutable sign, angular house, 20 degrees difference between significators) into five months.

Figure 5.4: Relationship Chart for Significator Progression Timing

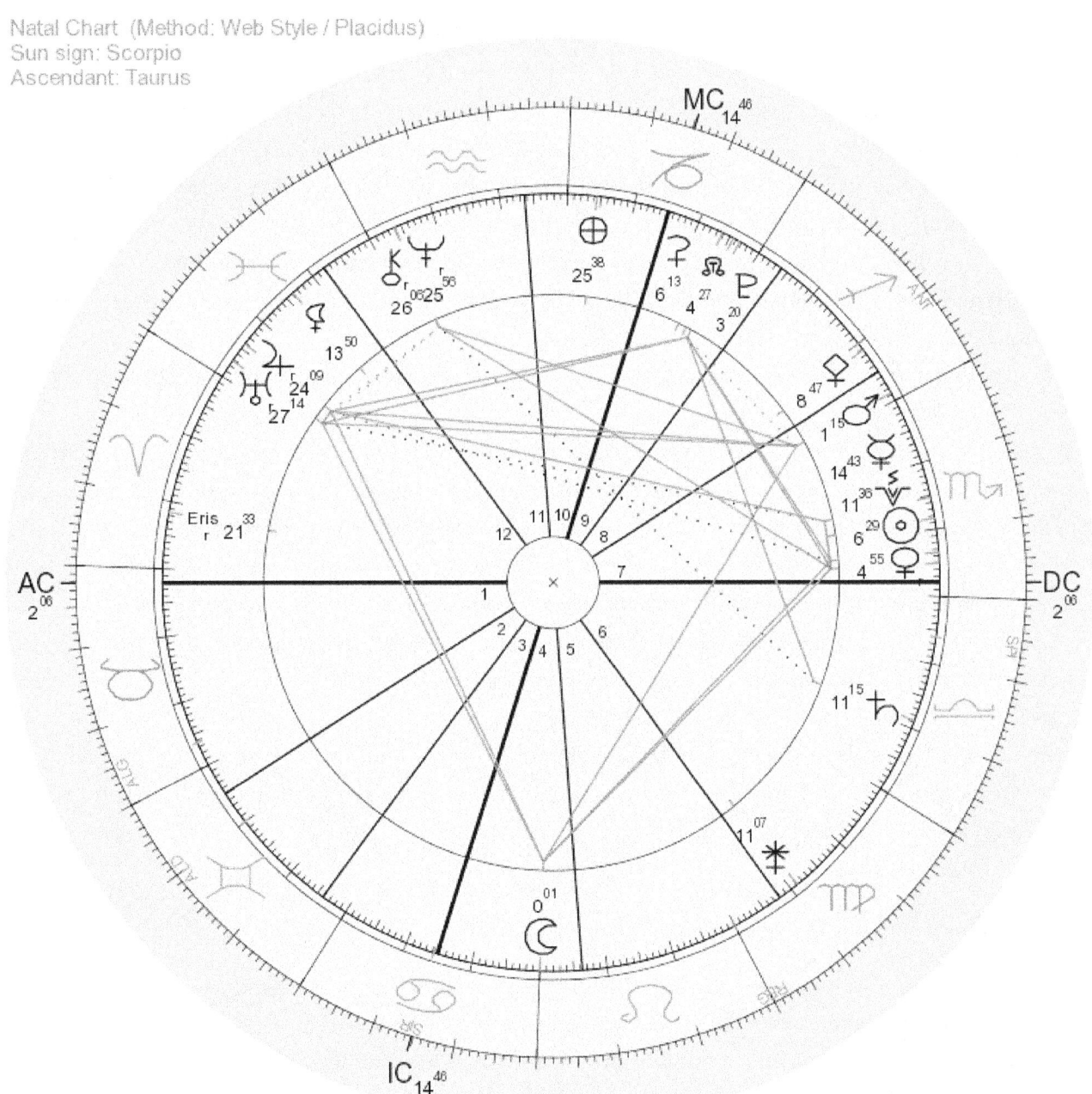

Trans-Neptunian Objects (TNOs)

In the past decade, astronomers have realized that Pluto is not the true edge of the solar system.[38] All of the objects on the frozen, outer edge of the solar system are called trans-Neptunian objects (TNOs) because they orbit further from the Sun than Neptune. Other odd misfits that are in between the Kuiper belt and the Oort Cloud, including Sedna and Eris, are also trans-Neptunian objects.[39]

Trans-Neptunian objects add a whole new layer of depth, meaning and understanding to a horary chart. TNOs provide primary information and details that the planets alone can't describe or act out, rather than just additional or secondary description. Though they operate very differently from traditional astrological paradigms, TNOs are every bit as powerful and meaningful as the inner solar system planets. The vagaries and vicissitudes, subtleties and nuances of contemporary human consciousness and experience are not confined to only two luminaries and seven planets within an astrological chart, horary or otherwise. Life and the world are more complex in the 21st century.

So why not welcome dwarf planets, and their Kuiper belt neighbors such as cubewanos, scattered disc objects (SDOs) and other trans-Neptunian objects? It's time to tell their stories.[40] Besides, fixed stars (which aren't even part of the solar system) and asteroids have been used successfully for years in natal and horary charts. Adding TNOs isn't going to suddenly confuse matters or harm accuracy. And integrating the new objects' symbolism into horary interpretations, aside from providing richer, deeper answers for querents, can build the empirical evidence of correct meaning and use more rapidly for the other astrological branches to integrate.

Chapter 12 provides an in-depth description of these objects and their appropriate use in horary charts. Appendix G - Part I gives instructions on how to recover TNOs in horary charts in order to study their symbolism and use.

Via Combust: The Burning or Fiery Way

"The region from 15 degrees Libra to 15 degrees Scorpio is considered an ancient malefic tumultuous zone of the nature of Mars, Saturn, and now also Uranus," writes Anthony Louis in his text *Horary Astrology*. "The Moon here is a stricture against judgment and traditionally may render the chart unreadable...In traditional horary the chart was considered safe to read only if the Moon was conjunct the benefic fixed star Spica.[41] This is a controversial stricture and many astrologers ignore it."[42]

Contrary to traditional horary doctrine, Via Combust doesn't just apply to the Moon; it applies to anything relevant to the question falling in the Via Combust way, including other planets and house cusps. It's a difficulty or trial by fire for the querent, experienced as a high-anxiety, tumultuous, unsettling and unpredictable situation.

Modern horary practitioners consider the chart valid or radical, and therefore readable, completely ignoring both the stricture and Spica rules. Instead, note and apply the characteristics of the Via Combust zone in relation to the question, as having a significator Via Combust in a chart is usually relevant to what's being asked. It could indicate a love affair or relationship in turmoil, trouble at work as layoffs loom, or other types of difficulties depending on the question.

Void-of-Course (VOC)

A planet, luminary, or other object is void-of-course when it makes no further aspects before leaving the sign it occupies. The Moon has special significance when void-of-course in a horary chart.

"Some astrologers believe that when the Moon is void-of-course that nothing ever comes of the matter," says Diana Stone. "That is often true, but I have charts to prove that it is not always true. The horary astrologer is well-advised to study the entire chart...If there is powerful, positive testimony and everything lines up just right, the void Moon can act. However, always be very aware when you are dealing with the void-of-course Moon...Even when it does bring things together, there is usually something wrong with the picture when all is said and done."[43]

"If two significators will complete an aspect during the void-of-course Moon, before the Moon leaves its sign, the matter may still perfect," says Anthony Louis.[44]

A planet or object, usually in a late degree, is void-of-course when it neither makes or receives any applying aspects before leaving the sign it occupies. Planets and other objects void-of-course mean that the energy represented by the planet or object is spent; it is out of gas, drifting and passive. Retrograde planets or objects can be void-of-course in early degrees (e.g., Mercury retrograde at 1 degree Gemini) if all of the other planets are in middle degrees and therefore out of orb.

In particular, if Saturn (symbolically known as "Father Time") is void-of-course in a horary chart, it generally that means matters should wait.

6 MODERN HORARY INTERPRETATION, STEP-BY-STEP

Horary begins by clearly forming the question and casting the chart. For the most part, you'll probably discuss and "co-create" the horary question with people who have no horary or astrological experience at all. If the querent has any astrological skill, they can ask the question, cast the chart themselves, and hand it over to you to interpret. There will also be those in the middle, who will ask the question and write down the date, time and place, and then give you the data to cast the chart. All are viable. If the querent texts or emails the horary question to you, or if the question is asked over the phone, use the date, time and place for the querent's location, rather than when and where you actually received, read or heard the message. This is because the querent is the one birthing the question; the astrologer is just the midwife.

Once you have a well-thought-out question, you shouldn't have to ask the querent for any additional details or background—everything will be contained within the chart. Once the chart is cast, the question is placed into the correct houses. "Always identify all the houses that pertain to the querent [and quesited] and limit your interest to those houses," instructs Diana Stone.[1] This is the most crucial part of horary, regardless of technique, as it is the primary "point of entry" into a horary chart. Use rulership books for ideas, and foster your own thinking. Also, let the chart lead you. "The sharp-eyed and focused horary astrologer always pays close attention to 'the grain of the chart' as Marc Edmund Jones described it," notes Diana Stone. "The chart needs to speak to you in a way that you know is really seriously communicating about the question asked."[2] So if the question is related to a spousal matter, use the 7th house, or if a friend, the 11th, and check the planet that naturally rules the issue, such as Venus for relationships, Uranus for friends, etc. Look for related planets or significators in those houses.

Don't be fooled by the wording of the question—focus on the core of the question for house placement, rather than the descriptors about what's being asked. For example, the question "Is he lying about the house sale?" is a third house question, because it pertains to facts and veracity of the matter. The fact that it's regarding a house sale isn't primary, though those houses (derivative 4th and 5th) will likely play a role in the answer. Similarly, a question such as "Will my father die from his illness soon?" is not inherently a 6th house question about health or an 8th house question about death. The subject is about the father, so it starts as a 10th house matter. Then, the derivative 8th (death) and derivative 6th (health) houses would be used in connection with the 10th house.

At its core, a horary chart is a snapshot of current transits applied to a specific situation. It's another point of entry into a chart, as the transit configurations almost always supersede horary "rules." Consider what is the most significant transit in the sky at the time the question is posited. Is there a configuration such as a Saturn-Uranus opposition, or a Uranus-Pluto square, that will be active (and activated by future transits) for months, or even a couple of years? This is important because the recurrences and transit activations will often generate more horary questions by the querent about the same matter, particularly if it's a long-term situation that remains unresolved. Is there a singleton or a stellium? Or are the planets mostly retrograde and off doing their own thing in different parts of the zodiac? Any such indicators will impact the horary chart as well, even if the lineups don't involve significators, but even moreso if they do. Also, in acute situations, current transits tend to provoke horary questions, either in their own right or because they are triggering the querent's natal placements.

Horary charts will reflect other things going on in the querent's life, even if not germane to the question. The key is to focus on what's relevant to the question first, and then if the "background noise" needs amplification because it's tied to the significators, do so. If something isn't applicable, don't try to force it to be. In horary, there's no need to use every last object in the chart—instead, start by looking at what's happening with the significators and the story that tells. Avoid taking the broad, natal approach of "touch-every-planet-and-explain-it." You can explore outward from the significators to gather information, but start with them first, and see what direction they point you in. Then look at aspect sequences to see how the events will unfold.

Bonds and connections between significators are a major, core component of horary interpretation. Just as in chemistry, some bonds in horary are stronger than others. Connections are primarily made via aspects, reception, disposition, and midpoints. The more frequent and benefic the connections between significators, the greater the ease and likelihood of accomplishment of the matter inquired about. The fewer and more malefic the bonds, the less easily and likely. But don't be fooled into a yes/no or good/bad mindset about connections. A chart with a few heavily malefic bonds can still bring a matter to culmination, though with great struggle, effort, and frustration, with the outcome falling short of what was desired or not worth the effort, rather than not culminating at all. This is where the astrologer's ability to pick up on subtlety and nuance in a chart greatly assists in rendering a correct judgment.

Traditional horary interpretation along the lines of William Lilly is a linear pattern of thought. It's almost checklist-like as you apply his point system and other rules. The details are pieced together first, and the practitioner works from the inside-out to obtain the big picture. Modern horary interpretation is more like cloud computing, and takes an outside-in approach. The big picture view of the chart is studied first, in order to see what's predominant relative to the question, and then deeper investigation ensues, while weighing specific factors to see what the chart says as a blended and interconnected whole.

Think of the components of a horary chart theatrically: Planets, asteroids and TNOs are the actors and actresses; signs are their costumes; houses are the stage and scenery, or set dressing; and aspects are the script acted out. Of secondary importance is the Moon, which is the lighting and the tone of the play (ominous, happy, etc.). Retrogrades, interceptions, fixed stars, etc., are the special effects. If an object orbits the Sun, it can act. If it doesn't, it's a static descriptor or scenery.

The basic formula for horary analysis at its simplest is this: What's strong (dignified), what's weak (debilitated), how does it relate (reception) and act (aspects), and in what arena (house)? What is the tone of the chain of events (Moon)? Can other planets assist or hinder and in what way (disposition)? What is the ease or difficulty of the events in the situation (midpoints)? What does it all indicate? How does it apply to the specific situation? Look at the symbolism and connect it to the question. The way to do this is to apply it via this sequence: S.A.M.E. = Significators + Aspects + Moon + Extras. These core pieces will combine to help you form your conclusion. (See Appendix B).

Aristotle, in *Poetics*, stated that all stories have a beginning, a middle, and an end. A horary chart is no exception. The three phases of interpreting a horary chart are: 1) Getting an overview, or the lay of the land, 2) Action, and 3) Confirmation and synthesis. The significators are the nouns, the aspects are the verbs, and everything else, adjectives and adverbs. It's the synthesis of it all that forms the sentence and the statement—and the answer.

I. HEADLINES – Nouns & Overview

Getting the "lay of the land" involves taking a broad view of the setting and relationships of the situation within the chart. Is the chart in the querent's favor, or is it against them? Begin with these key indicators:

- Assign houses and significators appropriate to the question. Don't be fooled by the wording of the question—get to the essence of what is really being asked.
- Note any co-significators, and the natural planetary ruler of the matter inquired about (e.g., Mercury rules cars if the question is about purchasing one; Venus rules relationships). Check to see if it is tied to a significator in a positive or negative way, or not at all.
- Is there an early or late degree on the ascendant? Are the Moon or significators in early or late degrees, or a mix? Are things on the brink of change, or are they just getting established? Is it too soon to tell, or too late to do anything about?

- Look for dignities and debilitations. Planetary strength is considered by sign, house and aspect. See if the significators are either strong by rulership, exaltation, angularity, dignity by house, or mutual reception. Or note if they are weak by besiegement, retrograde motion, combustion, interception, fall or detriment, malefic influence, or refranation.
- How do the significators relate to each other by sign (reception)? Are they in each other's rulership (mutual reception), exaltation, detriment or fall, or a mix thereof?
- Note interceptions, if any (which inhibit a planet from acting), and investigate what's "trapping" them and why. To do this, look to the ruler of the sign that is intercepted, and see what house it's in and any aspects it makes.
- See if the Moon is void-of-course, which can indicate that nothing will come of the matter, or that the status quo will continue. Check the Moon, ascendant, and significators to see if any are Via Combust, indicating an unstable, unsettling and unpredictable situation.
- See if there are critical degrees among significators or angles, showing chart crisis points, indicating amplified anxiety over the matter.
- Note asteroids and TNOs by sign and house placement. Note their connections to significators and the Moon by reception and disposition.
- Weigh the predominance of significators in angular, succeedent, or cadent houses. Angular objects act overtly, or out in the open. Succeedent objects are sustainers that continue to move matters forward. Cadent objects are passive, hidden, and behind the scenes.
- What is the status of the angles? Are they cardinal, fixed, mutable or a mix? Is the situation actively initiating, stable, or changing? As a result, does it indicate action, entrenchment, or change?

II. DETAILS – Verbs & Action

What is the tone of the action or activity in the chart indicating? Are there a lot of difficult aspects indicating obstacles to be overcome? Or are there trines and sextiles greasing the rails to an easy culmination? Are there multiple or complex storylines? Or is the chart screaming the answer everywhere you look? Start putting the pieces together. This is where to look for specifics, honing in on the developments as they unfold, and noting the tone and sequence of events via aspects. Focus on what's of primary importance and relevance; don't get lost in trivialities.

- Aspects, aspects, aspects. In most cases (but not all), in order for the matter to culminate or occur, there should be aspects between the main significators. It's even better if either or both aspect the Moon as well. Many hard aspects, such as squares, oppositions, or quincunxes are unfavorable, indicating troubles, difficulty, or outright negation. Many good aspects, such as conjunctions, trines, sextiles, and quintiles, are favorable and indicate ease of accomplishment. Note whether the aspects are applying (strengthening) or separating (weakening). Also see how tight or wide the aspect orbs are: 7 degrees is good, 5 degrees is better, and 3 degrees or less is best.

- All aspects count equally; there is no division of "major" or "minor." Any aspect is better than none at all, as it can bring the matter to fruition, even if things don't turn out well.
- Note the Moon's aspects. Past, current and future aspects of significators to each other and the Moon show past, current and future event sequences, and the unfolding of the plot of the situation. Lots of aspects before the Moon goes void-of-course indicates many events are yet to unfold in the situation, therefore requiring alertness and patience. Though rare, note if there are any occultations.
- If there are no aspects, look at the significators' and the Moon's midpoints, and any planets or objects either directly on the midpoints or aspecting them. Midpoints, and aspects to them, will amplify that particular relationship between the planetary pair for better (if well aspected) or worse (if harshly aspected).
- Check out the significators' dispositors, and the dispositor of the planet that naturally rules the matter (e.g., Mars for surgery). What planets and houses do they lead to? What is the status of the dispositor? Is it strong or weak or hindered in any way?
- Retrograde planets show a repeating or trying again, or the subject in a damaged state, particularly in relationship questions. If the Moon's last aspect is to a retrograde planet, there's something dissatisfying about the outcome, or it can be delayed.
- Look for significator, co-significator and lunar aspects to TNOs and asteroids, and their midpoints. If you find there's a lot of activity (e.g., a Ceres-Pallas conjunction opposing Haumea that forms a T-square with a significator conjunct Varuna), focus on the information contained within those details, rather than just the planets.
- Is there any impediment, frustration, hinderance, or interference involving significators? If so, look to the house ruled by the interloper to see who and why.
- Look at the Nodes and see if they are aspecting a significator, or if they are in the same degree as one. What house axis are they amplifying? Do they aspect, or are they in the same degree as any other planets or angles?
- Extras: If you use them, look to the Part of Fortune, the major fixed stars, etc., to see if they are conjunct angles or significators. Check the house the Part of Fortune is in and its dispositor. The Part of Fortune is considered unfortunate in the 8th and 12th houses, as well as in the sign of Scorpio.

III. CONCLUSIONS – Synthesis & Confirmation

Form your sentence, phrase or paragraph based on your findings. Then, critically think through your conclusion. Sometimes it will be glaringly obvious, other times not. Sometimes it may be necessary to think about a chart for awhile. Most charts reveal their secrets quickly, while a very rare few can take much longer depending on the nature of the question asked.

If a chart "jams" you, don't force it. This is the chart's way of saying it wants to be looked at differently than your normal, standard approach. Like a traffic jam, wait until it clears and then proceed. Keep tinkering. Sometimes a chart only wants to yield a simple yes or no answer without a lot of details. Other times the chart won't shut up. If a chart nags you after you've already rendered a judgment and filed it away, it can often mean you've made a mistake, or there's additional information it's trying to tell you.

In general, if the significators and Moon are afflicted and debilitated, the answer is no. If both are harmonious and well-aspected, the answer is generally yes. But don't fall into a yes/no mindset; look for subtleties and nuances that can have an effect on, or even undermine, an otherwise solid conclusion. If the Moon is okay and the significators are afflicted and debilitated, or vice versa, action can still happen and the event can still come to pass, if haphazardly or with complications, or even unfavorably. Charts, like life, are rarely black and white, and even fewer things turn out all rainbows and roses.

Key things to remember when forming your conclusion are:

- The chart can only reflect reality. It cannot make magic or wishful thinking happen.
- Never rely on only one isolated factor to render a conclusion (i.e., one opposition in the whole chart means "no"). Consideration of multiple factors is necessary to arrive at a solid, detailed, comprehensive, and cohesive conclusion. Synthesize all the evidence.
- Don't let the querent's hopes influence your verdict. If you have to be the bearer of bad news, do so factually, but with encouragement and detailed alternatives.
- Note the Moon's last true or actual aspect before it goes void-of-course, not just the Ptolemaic one. Do things end happily, or on a sour note? Will changes or adjustments need to be made?
- Look at the cusp of the 4th house, which signifies the end of the matter, especially if it's ruled by a significator, or if a significator is located in there. See if there are any other planets in the 4th house affecting the outcome.
- Don't repeat what's already known about the situation—the querent is trying to find out what's unknown and what's going to happen. NEVER give advice. Instead, stick to the facts you see in the chart and explain the scenarios and outcomes.

- K.I.S.S. (Keep It Simple, Simon) — "I always admired Marc Edmund Jones' book on horary astrology in which he approaches horary interpretations according to the principle of Occam's Razor, or narrowing down something to its barest essentials." says Diana Stone. "It is not a mark of skill to see how much you can dredge up after the answer is obvious; stay with the primary indicators only as is necessary to arrive at a definite conclusion. If that means adding Arabic parts, solstice points, and other horoscopic indicators, all these are available to help if you need to go that far."[3]

"In some cases the answer jumps right out at you," adds Stone. "It is not always necessary to delve into endless complexities. In fact, many charts can be read in short order. If you do horary charts, don't try to get more information than you need. It isn't really necessary to know if the person has red hair and drives a Buick. I think it is a good habit to work on the lean and mean side. Learn what the most important indicators are, get your answer, and move on to the next one."[4]

Sometimes the answer will seem puzzling in light of the facts you already know. This is okay. "You won't always know why a chart says yes or no. Sometimes you'll only find out in retrospect." says Stone.[5] "This is where the astrologer must accept each piece of the puzzle and report it to the querent. I have found that the answer will always make sense when the situation unfolds."[6]

See Appendix B for horary cheat sheets to help you stay on track as you think through the interpretive process.

7 ELECTIONAL ASTROLOGY & EVENT CHARTS

"Millionaires don't use astrology; billionaires do." [1]
— *American banker and industrialist J.P. Morgan*

Electional astrology involves finding the best possible time to take specific action. It is so named because one elects or chooses the time, as opposed to using the time it happens to be when a question arises with horary. Electional astrology is used for setting wedding dates, job interviews, trips, business meetings, or any other circumstance that the querent has control over.

With electional astrology, the basic idea is to get as many beneficial aspects, house placements, and rulerships in favor of the querent at a specific time. The degree of difficulty can be high, as querents can't run down to the licensing agency and file paperwork, or hold a grand opening at 3:22 A.M. when the planets are exactly where they want them.

Event charts are a sort of hybrid of electional and horary charts. Event charts aren't deliberately engineered like an electional chart, as the querent doesn't always have control over the time of an event like they would with an electional matter. As the birth chart of a circumstance, an event chart also doesn't ask a specific question like a horary chart, yet it's interpreted using horary rules. In electional and event charts, the time that the matter is officially initiated (with no going back) is the "birth time" of the matter.

To begin casting an electional chart, "The first thing you will do is scan through the dates you are interested in and eyeball the Moon's aspects, carefully noting the final one, of course," advises Diana Stone.[2] The Moon's aspects, and rulerships and receptions, are some of the most important components to consider when engineering an electional chart. Be sure to avoid times when the Moon is void-of-course, because matters won't go as planned.

"You will start the process of elimination, ruling out the days where the Moon ends with a hard aspect to a planet, a hard aspect to a malefic for sure, and ending with a retrograde planet is usually avoided, also," says Stone. "I say it is usually avoided, but there are times when a retrograde planet is desirable. A retrograde planet can repeat something or give the opportunity for a second chance. I avoid it in a surgery chart because there is the danger of having to go back and fix something after an operation. Election charts require the astrologer to analyze exactly what he or she wants to happen in any given situation."[3] Once the best date based on the Moon's aspects is determined, zero in on the best time on that particular date. As with horary astrology, placing the election matter in the correct house is crucial.

"Electional astrologers must be skilled at house rulerships," says Stone. "The ruler of the appropriate house is identified. There must be a positive aspect between these significators. If there isn't, the matter cannot be brought together no matter how great the rest of the chart may be. It is this rule that inexperienced astrologers usually founder on the rocks of failure."[4] The goal is to ensure that the ascendant ruler, the planet that naturally rules the matter, and the ruler of the house of the matter are all fortified, meaning as dignified, well-aspected, received, disposited and connected to each other as benevolently as possible. For example, if a couple wants to get married, make sure that the ruler of the 1st house, 7th house, and Venus, the natural ruler of relationships, are fortified in the chart.

If possible, it's helpful to choose a time where the planet that rules the matter is in the house ruling the matter (e.g., Venus in the 7th house for a marriage chart). The sign of the planet is secondary, unless it's in the detriment or fall of one of the other significators. The idea is to strengthen the relevant planets and have positive connections between them.

It is best to avoid having the relevant significators afflicted or debilitated (e.g., by combustion, critical degrees, Via Combust, intercepted houses, occultation, conjunct malefic fixed stars, in aspect to Eris, etc.). Retrogrades are also undesirable, except as Stone notes above. Also avoid malefic planets in the first house and the other angular houses, especially Eris. If she can kill Pluto, she can do the same to your electional chart.

The ruler of the ascendant should also be strong and in good aspect to the Moon. It's even better if the planets ruling the house cusp governing the matter, and the matter itself, are also well-aspected by the Moon, but that's not always possible. The planets are almost never in perfect harmony all at once, but a major goal of election charts is to mitigate what isn't in the querent's favor. "Sometimes we have to live with some nasty planetary combinations." says Stone.[5]

Guidelines for Electional Charts

There is no such thing as a "perfect" election chart; sacrifice of some considerations in favor of others will be inevitable. In light of that, here are some general guidelines and common denominators to aim for with all types of electional charts:

Moon	The Moon shouldn't be debilitated or hindered: Not void-of-course, Via Combust, eclipsed, in hard aspect or in detriment (Capricorn) or fall (Scorpio). It's preferable if the Moon is in a waxing phase, but far enough away from the Sun to avoid combustion. The Moon should be making positive aspects to the ruler of the ascendant *and* the planet ruling the sign on the house cusp that governs the matter.
Ascendant	The ruler of the ascendant should be in harmonious aspect with the planet ruling the matter, and the planet ruling the sign on the house cusp that governs the matter. The sign on the ascendant should have some jurisdiction over the matter being pursued, such as Cancer rising to start a new restaurant business. Avoid interceptions in the 1st house.
Aspects	Try to avoid putting significators in harsh aspect with malefics, even if the significators are in good aspect to the Moon or other significators. Applying aspects with orbs of seven degrees or less are best. Avoid separating aspects between significators, as it signifies opportunity lost. Keep an eye on significator aspects to difficult midpoints as well.
Houses	Put as many benefics in angular houses as possible. Make sure there are no malefics in angular houses or conjunct the ascendant. Instead, stash them in cadent houses. Keep malefic fixed stars off the ascendant and away from the significators, particularly Caput Algol (26° Taurus) and Serpentis (19° Scorpio). The Part of Fortune should be angular.
Retrogrades	Avoid retrograde significators unless you deliberately want something delayed, repeated or returned to a previous state. Don't have the querent buy a car when Mercury is retrograde, or get married when Venus is. If a retrograde planet is unavoidable, it shouldn't rule the houses involved in the matter, or the ascendant.
Nodes	Put the North Node in the house governing the matter if possible. Also try to have it well-aspected to the significators. Avoid planets in the same degree as the Nodes, as well as significators or the Moon conjunct the South Node.

Travel

In travel event and electional charts, use the departure time on the itinerary, regardless of the mode of travel. It can be rectified later if the plane ends up sitting delayed on the tarmac for three hours. If traveling by car, use the time you pull out of your driveway.

Mercury retrograde works very well for returning to a place you've been before, (such as the city you grew up in), rather than a new destination. Avoid harsh aspects to Mercury and Jupiter, or to the 3rd house for short trips, or 9th house for long trips or foreign travel. Avoid retrogrades and harsh aspects to Neptune, Varuna and Sedna for cruises. Avoid Mercury retrograde or harshly aspected for car trips. Same for Uranus for air travel. Strengthen or fortify these areas with the ruler of the Ascendant and the Moon.

Job Interviews

For job interviews, the event chart is cast for the scheduled time and location of the appointment with the potential employer, not when the querent leaves their home to drive to the appointment. If the job interview is a phone interview, the event chart is cast for the appointment time and location of the querent.

Be sure to place the chart in the proper house. The 6th house rules "common" or non-skilled, part-time and wage-slave types of work, while the 10th house rules careers and professional work. For example, retail clerks and fast-food employment would be ruled by the 6th house, while a foreman for a construction company or an IT analyst belongs in the 10th house.

If the job interview chart is an electional chart rather than an event chart, make sure the ruler of the type of work is well-fortified. For example, if the job is with a restaurant, such as a cook or waitress position, make sure the Moon is strong and unafflicted. If the position is a career with a law firm, Jupiter should be strongly placed and aspected. The asteroid Pallas should be used in employment charts and fortified as well.

Business Startups

For a new business such as a sole proprietorship, use the date and time the business license registration is complete for the event or birth chart of the business. That's the moment an entity is legally permitted to engage in business activity, even though the storefront may not even be built yet. In that case, later on an electional chart can be cast for the best time to hold a grand opening. Similarly, if the business is a corporation, use the date and time when the documents are officially registered with the Secretary of State. These filings can be completed in person, and in many places, online, giving a strong latitude of control over the time of the filing and therefore, the birth of the business. If the filing is done by mail, you can call the registrar and ask what date and time their computer shows the paperwork was entered or processed.

If you were already engaged in some sort of business activity informally or unofficially, such as a hobby that grows into something bigger, the birth chart of the business is not when the hobby began, but when it becomes legal and official through government registration.

The 11th house rules income from the business, since it's the derived 2nd house from the 10th house, so make sure the ruler of the 11th house is well-fortified. If you use the Part of Fortune, try to place it in the 11th house or any angular house. The asteroid Pallas should be used and fortified as well.

The Moon or the ruler of the ascendant should be in line with the type of business, such as Pisces for a bar or tavern, Leo for a child care center, etc. Place the North Node in the 10th or 11th houses if possible, and keep the South Node out of both.

Real Estate

The Moon in rulership in Cancer or exalted in Taurus are the best placements for real estate matters. For real estate *sales* transactions by the querent, the seller/querent is the 1st house and the buyer is the 7th house. For real estate *purchases* by the querent, the 1st house is the buyer/querent and the 7th house is the seller. Escrow, mortgages, etc., are all ruled by the 8th house. The 4th house rules the property itself, so be sure to strengthen this house and its ruler. The best course of action is to have the rulers of the 1st, 4th and 7th houses as strong and well-aspected to each other as possible.

Beware of malefics and debilitated or harshly aspected planets in the 4th house, as it can indicate a defective property based on the qualities of the planet(s) involved (e.g., Saturn could indicate cracks in the foundation; Uranus could indicate electrical problems; Neptune, issues with water and flooding, etc.).

Marriage

Some horary practitioners use the time the wedding ceremony begins (as shown on the invitation) as the election time for a marriage. To others, a marriage is birthed the moment the presiding official announces, "I now pronounce you man and wife." Both methods work just fine. However, if using the latter method, the marriage electional chart should be cast with a large enough window to allow for the sometimes lengthy preamble to the actual vows. For marriages where the time of the vows isn't available or wasn't recorded, an event chart based on wedding invitation data can be used instead.

Venus, and the 1st house and 7th house rulers, should all be as harmoniously aspected, received, dignified and disposited as possible. Venus should *never* be retrograde or debilitated in any manner in a marriage chart. The North Node should be placed in either the 7th, 5th or 11th houses. Mars and Venus should be well aspected, as well as the Sun and Moon. Also ensure that Ceres and Juno are angular, well-aspected, and well-fortified (e.g., Ceres harmonious with the Moon; Juno with Jupiter, etc.). Ideally, the Moon and the significators should not make any aspects *at all* to Eris, Sedna or Lilith. Keep those three, especially Eris, out of angular houses, and particularly the 7th house.

Surgery

Avoid surgery when the Moon is in the sign of the organ slated for operation (See Appendix B for a very general list of body region rulerships, and consult medical astrology rulership books for specifics).

Mars and the 8th house rule surgery, so fortify those areas. The 7th house rules the surgeon. Don't elect for surgery when Mars is retrograde, or the procedure may have to be repeated. If the procedure is cosmetic, make sure Venus isn't retrograde or debilitated.

Strong aspects to the Sun, and the Moon making benefic aspects to both Mars and the planet ruling the 8th house cusp, as well as the ruler of the ascendant, are most desirable. Jupiter in the 1st, 4th or 8th houses, or well-aspected to Mars, the Sun or Moon, and the planet ruling the 8th house cusp is also helpful.

Lawsuits

It may be necessary to call the courthouse to acquire event chart data from the court clerk if the lawsuit was initiated, and documents were filed by the opposing party's attorney rather than the querent's attorney if it is the querent who is being sued. If it's a querent-initiated lawsuit, the ascendant rules the person initiating the suit, while the 7th house is the opponent. The ascendant ruler must be stronger and more fortified than the 7th house ruler to increase the chances for victory. The 9th house rules the querent's attorney; the radix 3rd house becomes the derived 9th to show the opponent's attorney. The judge is signified by the ruler of the 10th house. An angular and cardinal Moon is helpful to ensure the case is not tied up in court for years, which is usually indicated by retrograde outer planets, which should be avoided as significators at all costs if possible. Also, avoid Jupiter retrograde. Pallas should be well-placed and well-aspected.

Electing for a Sales Agreement

The querent wanted to approach a local merchant and have him agree to sell her souvenir item in his very busy and successful coffee shop. She was given a 15-minute window to do the deal, in order to keep the desired placements in the election chart intact. (See Figure 7.1)

With Saturn retrograde in the 3rd house of agreements, and as ruler of the 7th house of the buyer, the merchant showed skepticism, and somewhat reluctantly agreed to a deal. But Saturn is disposited by Mercury, who in turn is disposited by and conjunct Venus in rulership in Taurus. Mercury is also conjunct the exalted Moon in Taurus. Money and success always makes a believer out of everyone—the sales deal is still in place and profitable for both parties, in spite of the economy and its harm to tourism.

The basic election chart considerations were achieved in this chart, namely:

- The ascendant ruler, the Moon (ruling souvenirs), is exalted, and disposits to a dignified Venus.
- Mars, the querent's co-ruler, is dignified by house and rules the Midheaven.
- The Sun is exalted in Aries in the 10th house ruling the querent's business. It is mutually recepted with Mars in the 1st house, the querent's co-ruler. Both are angular.
- Venus in rulership is in the derived 2nd house of business income, indicating small (not millions) but steady profits.
- Malefics are in cadent houses, even if just barely.
- The Moon, Venus and Mercury squares to Mars are all separating.

86   Open Source Modern Horary Astrology

Fig. 7.1: Sales Agreement Election Chart

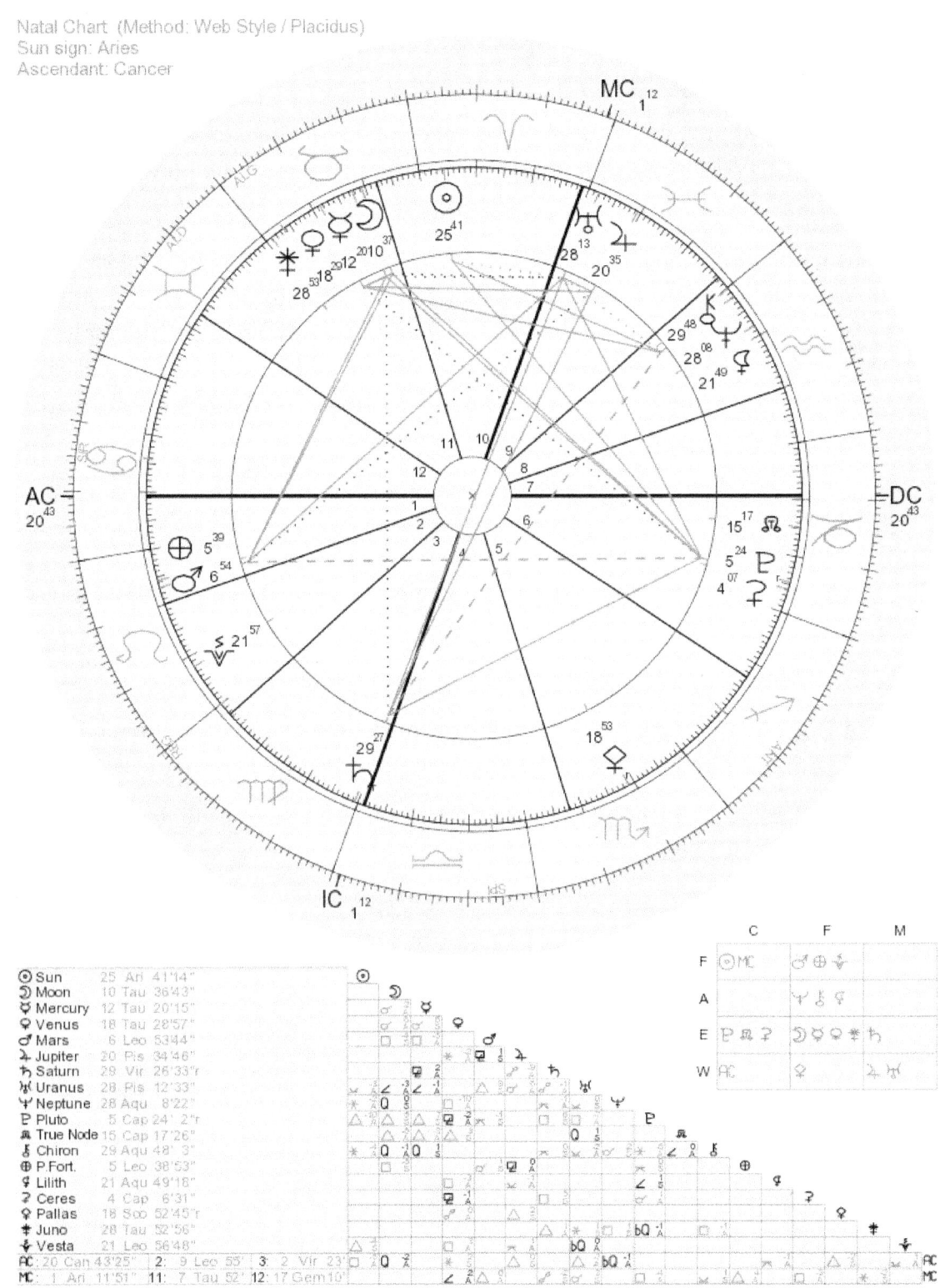

Electing for Divorce

The querent requested the best possible time to file for divorce during a specific month. Like any sane and reasonable person, he wanted as quick, painless and inexpensive an outcome as possible. He also desired a fair settlement; he was not out to stick it to his soon-to-be ex-wife.

In any court case, the party with the most dignified significators, and best aspects to the ruler of the 10th house cusp (signifying the judge) or planets within, is likely to win. Divorce is ruled by the 7th house and Uranus, with the querent's lawyer signified by the 9th house, so these were the areas to fortify as best as possible. The querent was given a 15-minute window to file the papers in order to keep the desired placements in the election chart intact.

In Fig. 7.2, Haumea in Libra is close to the ascendant, depicting the querent-initiated breakup of the marriage. The querent's significators, the Moon-Venus conjunction, show his desire for fairness and lack of ill-will toward his wife, primarily for the sake of their children. The querent's co-significator, the Moon, is strong in rulership and near the benefic fixed star Sirius, thereby overcoming its detriment by house placement. The Moon as 10th house ruler also signifies the judge, and it is conjunct the querent's ruler, Venus, which disposits to the Moon. He is in a very strong position should the case end up in front of the female judge (Venus-Moon in Cancer) assigned to the case.

With Gemini on the 9th house cusp, dignified Mercury rules the querent's lawyer. Mercury is partile conjunct Saturn; the querent's lawyer was an older gentleman with an outstanding reputation for divorce cases, not to mention eons of experience. He continually communicated realistic expectations to the querent based on that expertise.

The soon-to-be ex-wife is represented by Aries on the 7th house cusp, which is ruled by Mars in Gemini in the querent's 9th, showing the two sides letting their lawyers slug it out. Mars disposits to Mercury, the querent's lawyer, who was the one calling the shots in the case. Mars in the derived 3rd house is squaring Uranus in the derived 12th house with Pisces on the cusp, showing the wife did not desire the divorce—it was sprung upon her unexpectedly. Mars is also applying to oppose Pluto, ruler of the derived 8th house of joint assets, so she wished to hit him hard financially in revenge. Juno, describing the wife and to a lesser extent, the marriage, is in hostile Aries opposing the querent's Libra ascendant. Eris is in the 7th house in Aries, the sign where she is strongest. The wife was outraged by the whole situation, and wasn't going to go away without a fight.

Venus, ruler of the querent, is sextiling Mercury, his lawyer's significator, so his lawyer's advice was that a trial would be too expensive for both of them (Venus ruling the 8th house cusp; Venus

Figure 7.2: Divorce Election Chart

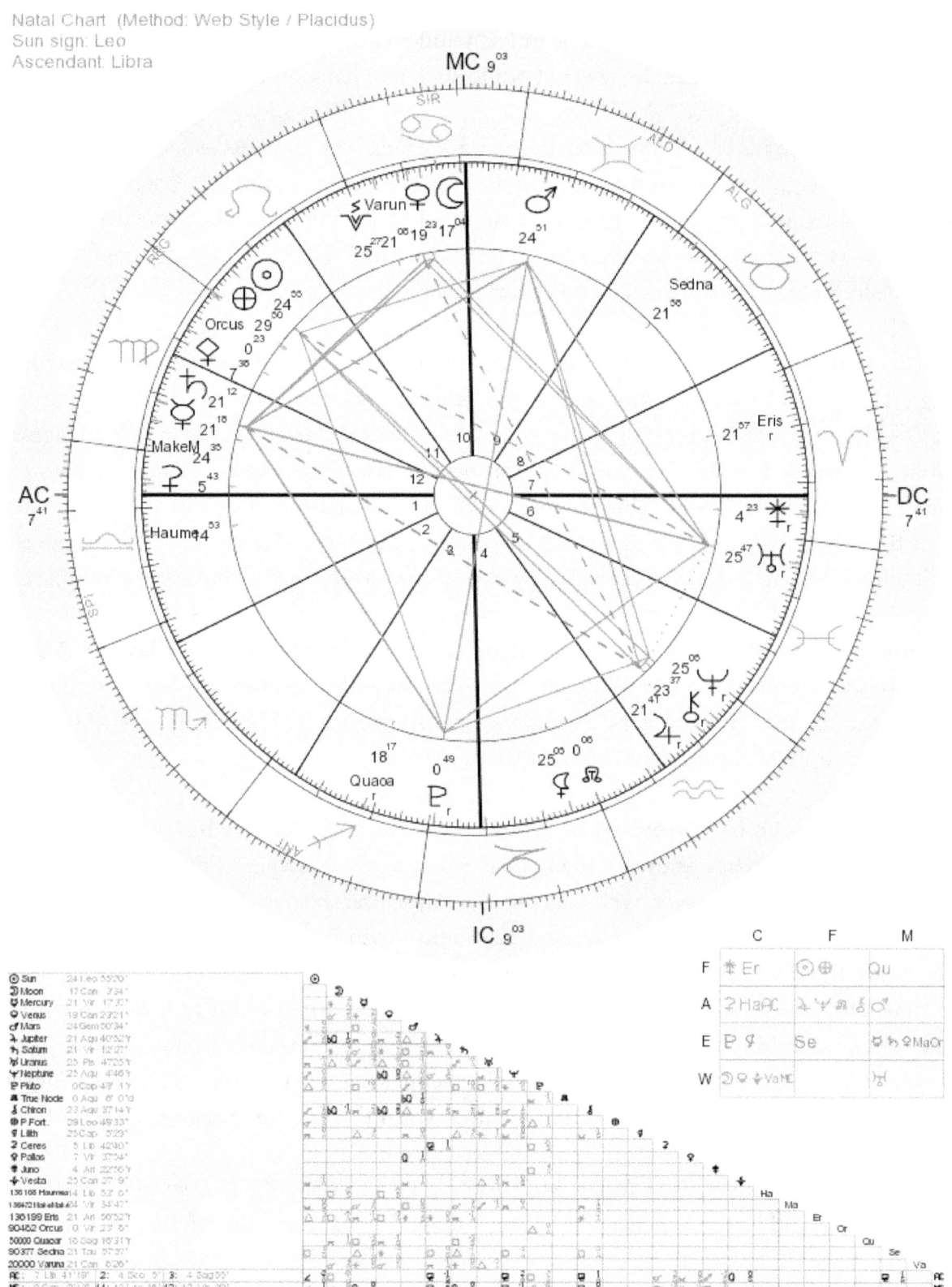

quincunx Jupiter). He pushed them both into and through the mediation process (ruler of the 7th in the 9th) successfully. Both parties settled in less than nine months.

Note that Pluto is at a critical degree (0 Capricorn), and in the same degree as the Node, indicating a catastrophe. Pluto rules the querent's 2nd house and the wife's derived 2nd house, indicating that the financial fallout from the divorce (North Node in Aquarius) would cause the loss of their home (North Node in the 4th house, South Node in the derived 4th house showing the impact to both of them) to foreclosure. (Pluto is in Capricorn, the sign governing foreclosure, and the South Node is in the querent's 10th house of foreclosure.)

As far as timing, the Moon starts off making some nice aspects, such as conjoining the querent's significator, Venus, and then sextiling the Saturn-Mercury conjunction, indicating he had the right lawyer for the job. Things progressed very rapidly at first until the Moon-Jupiter retrograde quincunx and Moon-Neptune retrograde quincunx slowed things down considerably. Jupiter rules the wife's lawyer, and she had some stalling tactics in hand to run up billable hours, as well as a serious health problem that needed tending to (Jupiter conjunct Chiron). The divorce could have been finalized as early as two weeks after settlement if not for these speedbumps.

The Moon's last aspect is a trine to retrograde Uranus, ruler of the divorce. The retrograde underscores the delays involved, as well as some part of the outcome that the querent wouldn't like. The querent was not happy about having to pay spousal support, but the duration of it wasn't anywhere near as long as it could have been. The divorce was finalized 11 months after the filing.

Mars, the wife's significator, is trining the Neptune-Chiron conjunction midpoint, showing she would eventually accept the situation and move on. The election chart goals of the quickest possible resolution in the least expensive way and a fair shake for both of them were met.

Figure 7.3: Job Interview Event Chart

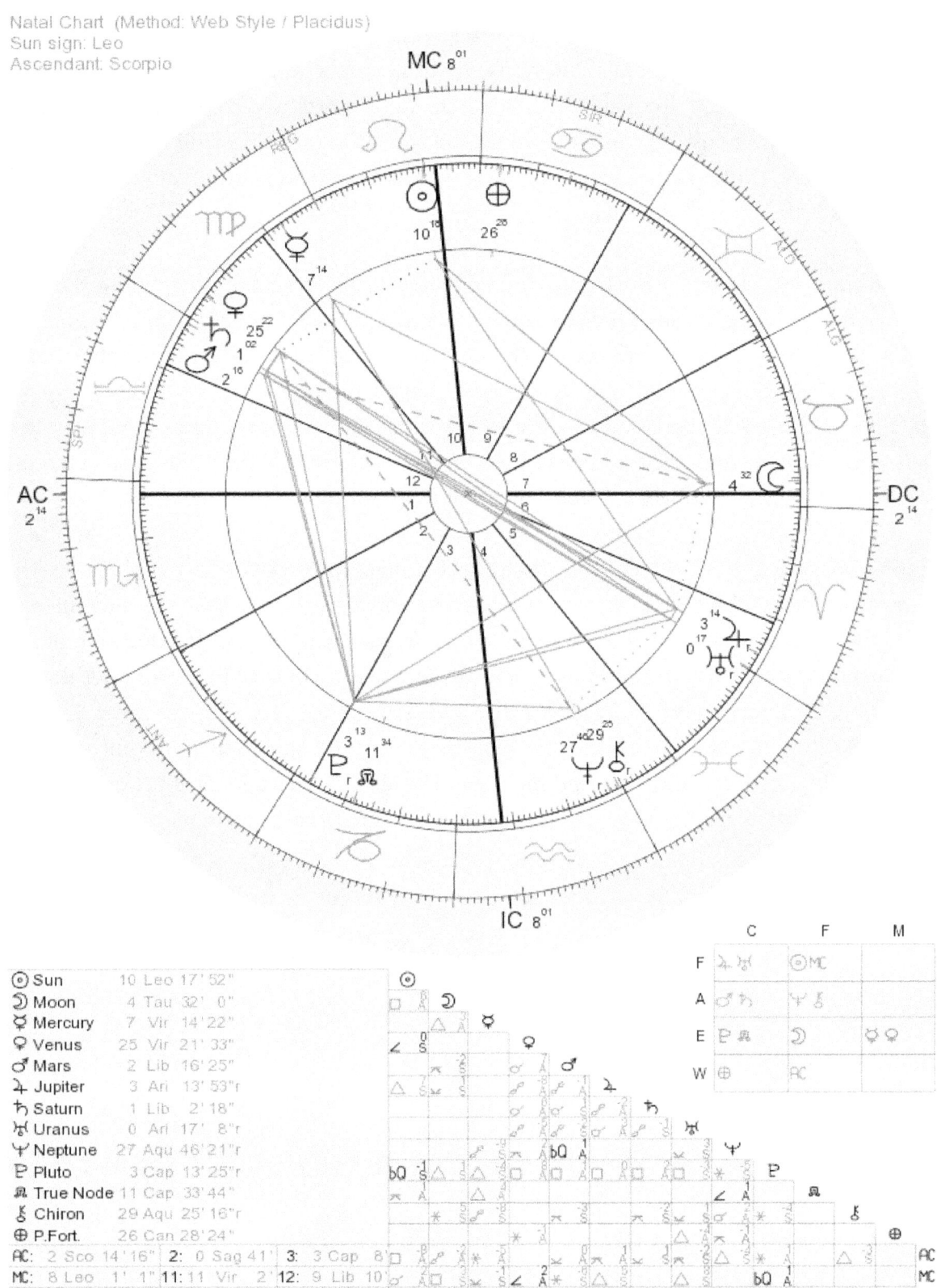

A Job Interview Event Chart

Figure 7.3 is an example of an event chart for a job interview the querent was excited about and felt had a lot of potential.

As part of an ongoing dialogue with the querent (who understands horary astrology, so I spoke using the lingo), I interpreted it as follows: "I'd have to say a 'no go' on this one, too. Early degree Scorpio rising (2 degrees) means it's premature. Also, Moon exalted in the 7th opposes the ascendant and is moving up to square the Sun/Employer in rulership in the 10th house—she may not be able to come up with the funding for your position. The big killer for me is Scorpio's traditional ruler Mars is moving up to square its modern ruler Pluto, and then oppose Jupiter, ruler of your 2nd house of money and finances. That's the most active thing in the chart—the T-square—and it involves both of your rulers. Outcome is Uranus retrograding back to Pisces, but still opposing Saturn and Mars. Moon's last aspect as a square to Neptune retrograde in the 4th house affirms 'no.' The Moon is going to trine Mercury though in the 11th house, meaning more opportunities will be coming your way. So since it's an early degree rising, and the Moon's last aspect is the square to Neptune, let's just see how it develops. I don't like that your Moon is moving up to square the MC/Job. So it may be a case where things start out smooth and then the T-square gets hit and everything goes askew."

The querent described how the interview unfolded. "Yesterday I interviewed...and the first thing that she said was, 'I just felt that you were too good to let get away—now I think I can combine two jobs and get you closer to what you want in salary.' She was very favorably impressed because a mutual colleague sent her a recommendation for me, and she also belongs to the same professional organization that I do. I'm not saying it's a sure thing, because she has to get the approval for the money, but it's by far the best interview I have had. She would also have me back to have another interview with her staff, but she said, 'I decide, but I like the team to buy in.' I could work partially at home, good benefits, etc., etc."

So what was the eventual outcome?

A few days later, the querent said, "[The hiring manager] called today around noon and said they hired someone for their internal job...So it was kind of a disappointment, because the location, benefits and boss were all desirable, it was the salary that wasn't. She didn't have the clout to combine the two jobs, said it was an internal candidate...your reference is all right on. You predicted it correctly."

Worst Travel Event Charts Ever

For a very extreme, but well-documented example of why malefic aspects should be avoided for travel charts, here are two charts for the Uruguayan rugby team plane that crashed in the Andes mountains en route to a match in Chile in 1972, where the survivors had to resort to eating the dead to survive.[6]

In the first chart (Fig. 7.4), the official departure date and time of the beginning of the trip, Pluto, ruler of the ascendant, is in fall and conjunct Mars in detriment, and squaring Jupiter in fall, with the South Node in the 9th house of travel, particularly for a sporting match. And the Moon, ruler of the 9th house and dispositor of the South Node, is in applying opposition to Saturn. Uranus, ruler of air travel, is combust the Sun, and both of them are in the Via Combust zone in the 12th house. Venus, ruler of the 12th and dispositing Pluto and the Sun-Uranus combustion, is in fall in Virgo. Eris and Chiron, both unknown at the time of the incident, are opposing the Mars-Uranus midpoint.

In the second chart (Fig. 7.5), the actual crash chart based on air traffic control data, the Moon in detriment conjunct Jupiter in fall are both squaring Pluto in fall in the house of its fall. Uranus is still combust the Sun and both are still Via Combust, this time in the 8th house, and again dispositing to Venus in fall. But Pisces rising and Neptune most elevated in the 9th house for a plane crash? It turns out the pilots had been drinking prior to takeoff, and were confused as to their actual flight location, believing they were in Chile when they were actually in Argentina. They were completely off course at the time of the crash. The survivors, who depended on teamwork and their friendships to see them through (North Node in the 11th in Capricorn, the sign of endurance), described the ten-week ordeal as having been "a more elevated—almost a mystical—concept of their experience." When they eventually returned home to Uruguay, suffering and privation on the mountain had shown them the frivolity of their lives before the crash. Many of the survivors felt they were the beneficiaries of a miracle.[7]

Figure 7.4: Andes Plane Crash Itinerary Departure

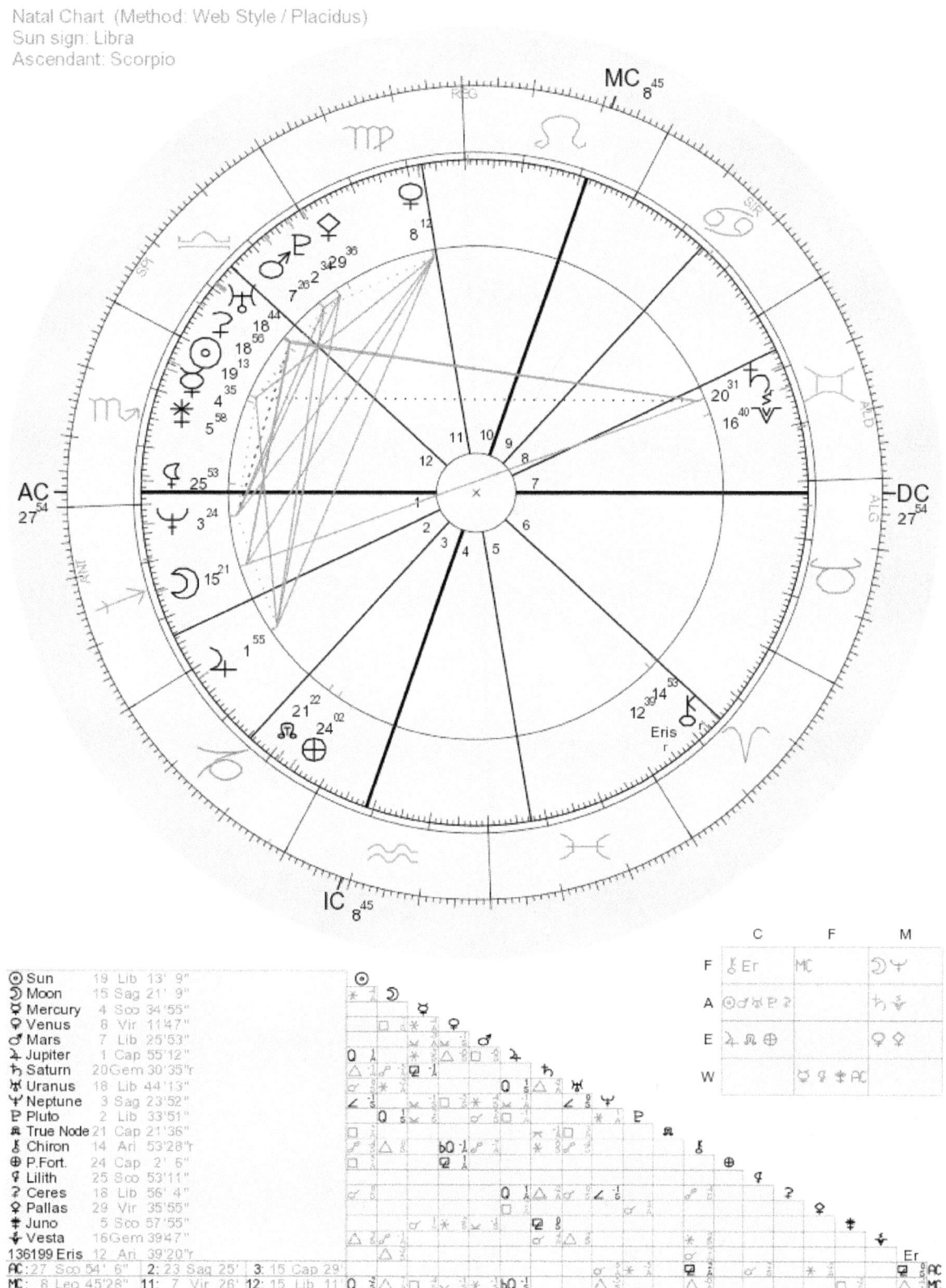

94 Open Source Modern Horary Astrology

Figure 7.5: Andes Plane Crash Air Traffic Control Data

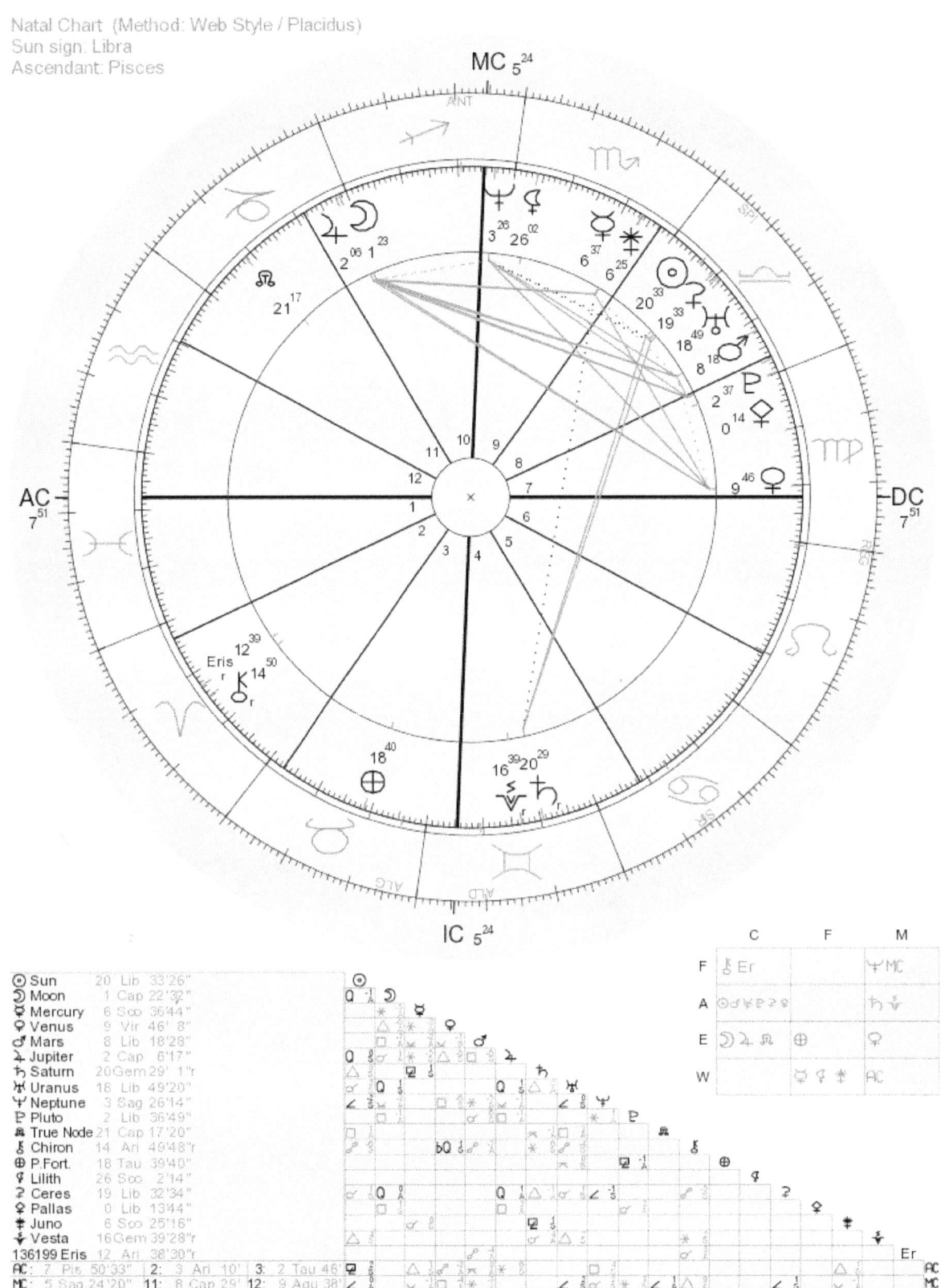

8 MODERN HORARY IN ACTION

An Office Space Question: The Astrologer Sees the Red Flags

The querent had just graduated from massage school and was looking for office space to begin her practice. Starting on a serious shoestring, she was offered to share a space part-time with an established massage practitioner. This prompted her horary question, "Should I rent the massage space from the established massage practitioner?" (Figure 8.1)

The chart has trouble written all over it. The early degree of the ascendant shows the querent is just beginning her practice, and retrograde Neptune conjunct the ascendant rules her 2nd house of money. Venus in rulership by sign is intercepted in the 8th and in detriment by house. Venus rules the third house; the facts in the matter. Something isn't on the level involving money. Uranus, the querent's significator, is also in the first house and retrograde, mitigating its rulership, and opposing Mars in the 7th. Uh-oh, conflict is afoot. Retrograde Neptune quincunx the Sun, ruler of the 7th, shows she shouldn't trust the practitioner offering to lease the space.

The massage space is signified by the 4th house since it's a real estate matter—note the Pleiades on the cusp. She'll have something to weep about or regret. The Moon is intercepted in the 8th, the house of its fall, again indicating something financial is awry in the matter.

I seriously advised her against taking the space, and told her the problems would reveal themselves after a delay due to the retrogrades. The Moon trined retrograde Uranus, a planet that tends to make people antsy and restless, and the querent, feeling desperate (Neptune retrograde conjunct the ascendant) with no other office space leads, chose to share the massage space with the established practitioner.

Figure 8.1: Should the Querent Rent the Massage Space?

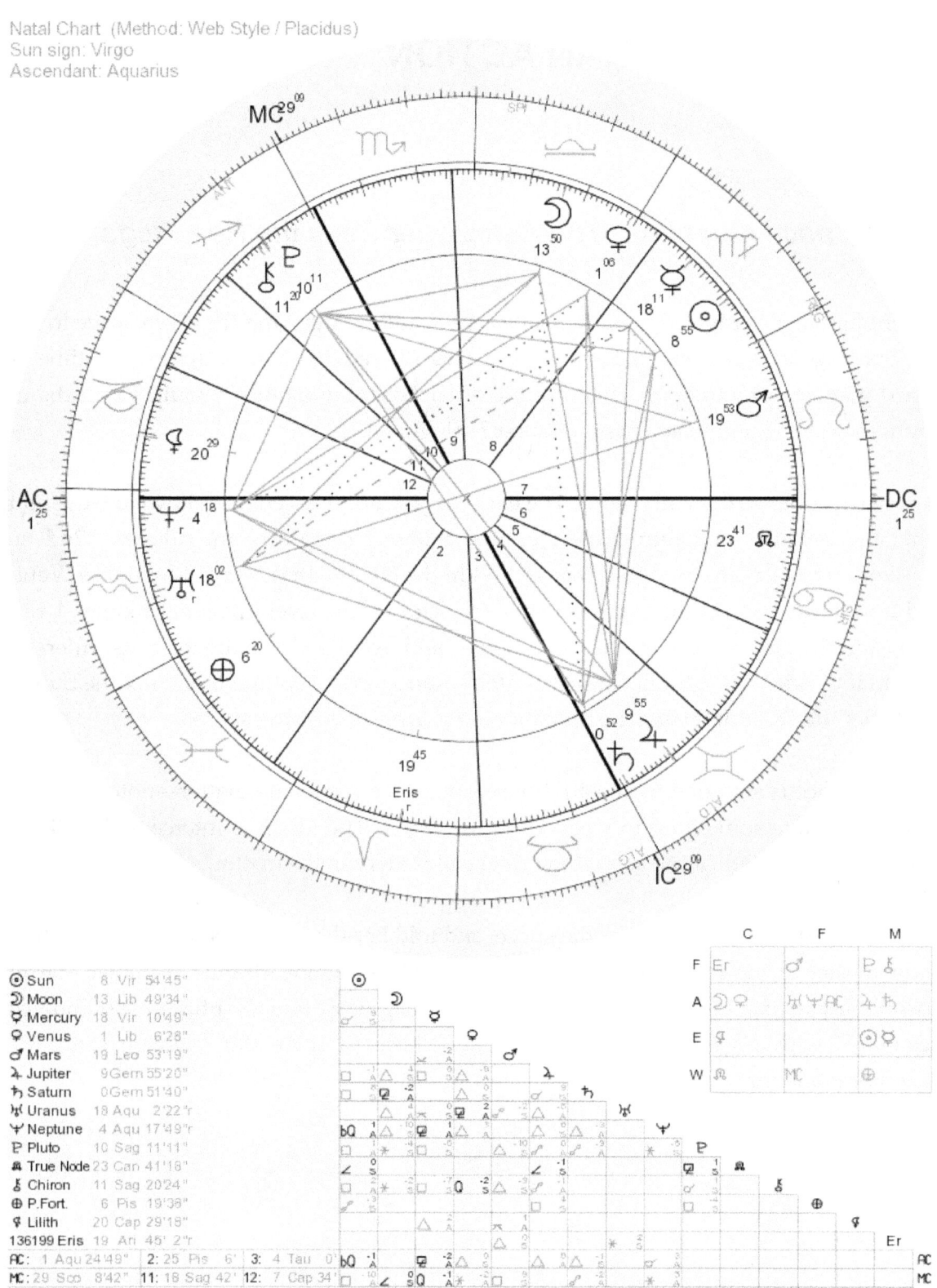

Six weeks later (timed when the intercepted Moon sextiled Mars in the 7th house), the querent found out that the established practitioner was overcharging her for rent. The querent was paying more than 2/3 of the full office rent for less than half the use of the office space. The Uranus-Mars opposition flared, and the querent had words with the establish practitioner, who felt the deal was perfectly reasonable due to depreciation, in spite of the fact that the querent was using almost all of her own equipment and the office space belonged to the building landlord, from whom the established practitioner rented the space full time. The querent immediately moved out and found a much better space a couple weeks later, in a much nicer place less than a quarter of a mile away.

What's interesting is that Eris had only recently been named and was not in astrological use at the time of the question. Lilith also wasn't in prominent horary use like it is today. But in utilizing recovery data in the chart at the time of this writing, the final point is interesting. The Moon's last aspect is a square to Lilith at the South Node in the 12th house of self-undoing, and an opposition to Eris (intercepted in the 2nd house of money). The T-square outlet leg is in the 6th house of massage at the North Node in Cancer, which disposits back to the Moon. Would knowing that back then have changed the querent's mind? Doubtful. But it's interesting how the T-square provides sharper detail, and amplifies and underscores the scenario and event outcome far more specifically than just a Moon sextile to Mars in the 7th (Aries intercepted in the 2nd, a hidden issue about money) before going void-of-course.

A Moving or Relocation Question: Pluto IS Personal and Knows How to Force the Issue

The querent ran into considerable financial difficulty after the global market meltdown, so she inquired if she would have to move from her beloved current residence to a friend's house in another state until she could regroup and get back on her feet. (Figure 8.2)

With Scorpio rising, use Pluto, not Mars, especially for financial matters. Retrograde Pluto embodies complications compounded, and in the second house (its detriment) the financial difficulties are readily apparent. Pluto is squaring retrograde Jupiter, traditional ruler of the 4th house of the querent's current residence. Jupiter, in turn, is conjunct retrograde Uranus, ruler of disruption, at the most dead degree of the entire zodiac (29 Pisces). The querent loves her current home as shown by Jupiter dignified by its traditional ruler, Pisces, and exalted by house. Neptune, modern ruler of the 4th house, is in late degrees, intercepted and retrograde, making it too debilitated to help her. Mars, traditional ruler of Scorpio, at 10 degrees of orb, is too far away from a trine to Neptune to help her. Mars is also in detriment in Libra, affirming that she's out of luck.

Figure 8.2: Querent Stay at Current Residence or Move in with Friend?

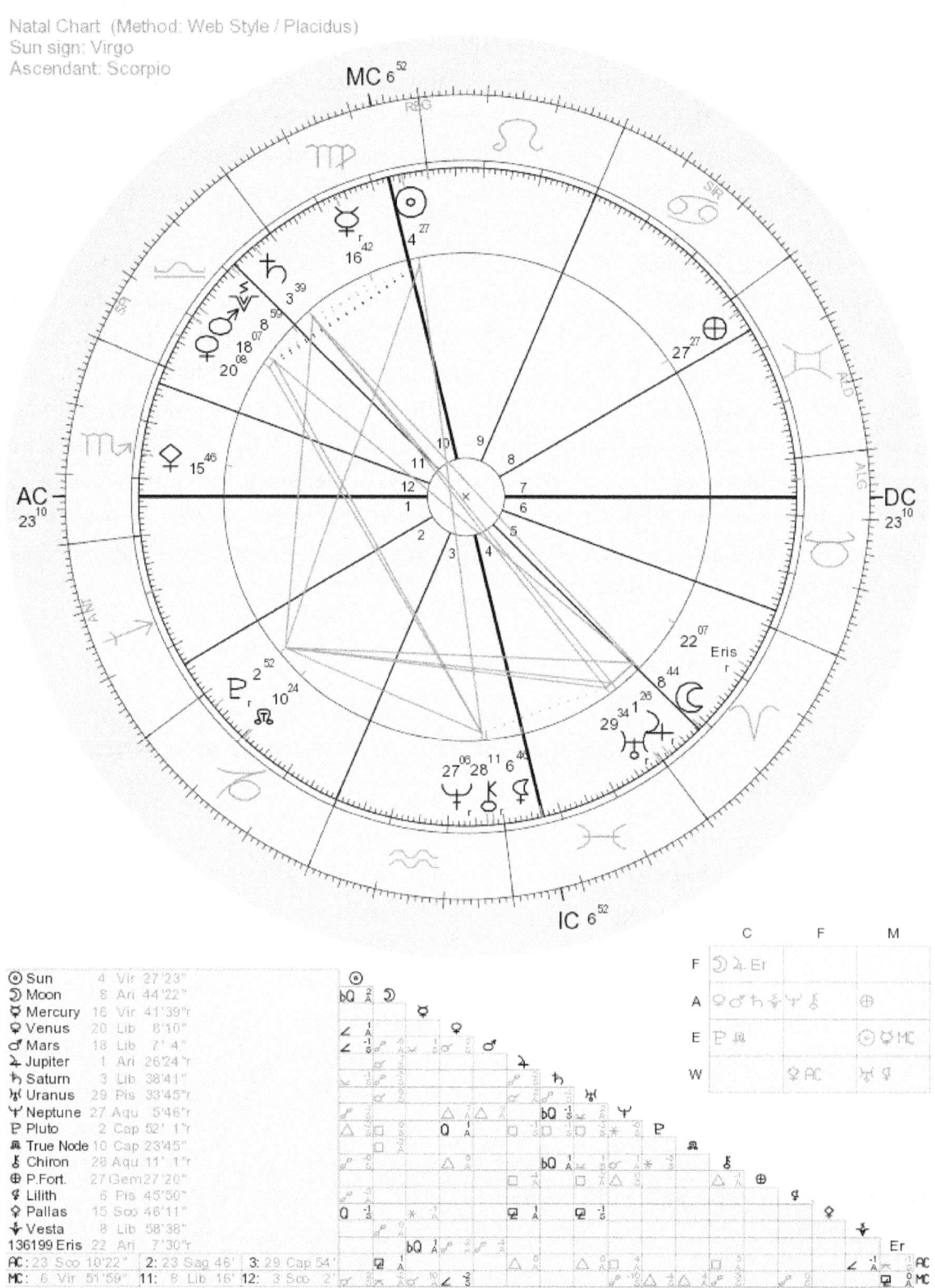

With the Pluto-Jupiter square from the 2nd to the 4th house, she's going to be forced to move against her will due to financial complications. End of story, really.

But obligingly, look to the 7th house of removal, or moving in with the friend. Algol is right there on the cusp, showing how much she *really* doesn't want to move in with her friend. The friend is the 11th house, ruled by Venus in rulership in Libra, but Via Combust. Ugh. Venus is also opposing Eris and the Moon will come up to oppose Venus as well. Double ugh. But she has no choice, because the friend is in the best possible position to host her, even though it's to her detriment (Mars in Libra) to move in with him because they have a tendency to quarrel due to their vastly different lifestyles (Taurus on the 6th house cusp with Venus in the 11th house).

The Moon in Aries, which co-rules the querent, disposits back to the weak Mars in the 11th house of her friend. Venus is quintiling Pluto, showing it's the best decision for her financially. Vesta, ruler of the home and hearth, is in the 11th house of friends, and the angles are changing from fixed to mutable. So like it or not, everything is pointing to her moving in with her friend. The Moon's last Ptolemaic aspect is a sextile to the retrograde Neptune-Chiron conjunction, with Neptune retrograde ruling the 4th house, indicating that good will come of the disappointing outcome. The last true aspect of the Moon before going void-of-course is a semi-sextile to retrograde Uranus in the 4th house of home, so at least the ending won't be an abrupt upset, and a delay will likely be involved.

The querent ended up staying slightly longer than the notice she originally gave her landlord, so she could slowly dissolve her tie and bid farewell to her boyfriend (Moon in 5th) being left behind. She reluctantly moved in with the friend.

A Foreclosure Question: You, Too, Can Overcome Debility and Combustion

The burst of the housing bubble in the United States late in the decade had many victims. Luckily, this person didn't turn out to be one of them. The person involved in the matter was a friend of mine, and I asked the horary question on his behalf, as the matter was causing him an enormous amount of stress and anxiety. I phrased it, "Will my friend be able to defeat the foreclosure situation he's facing?" because his house was slated to be sold on the county courthouse steps three weeks from the time of the question. (Figure 8.3)

100 Open Source Modern Horary Astrology

Figure 8.3: Can My Friend Defeat the Foreclosure He's Facing?

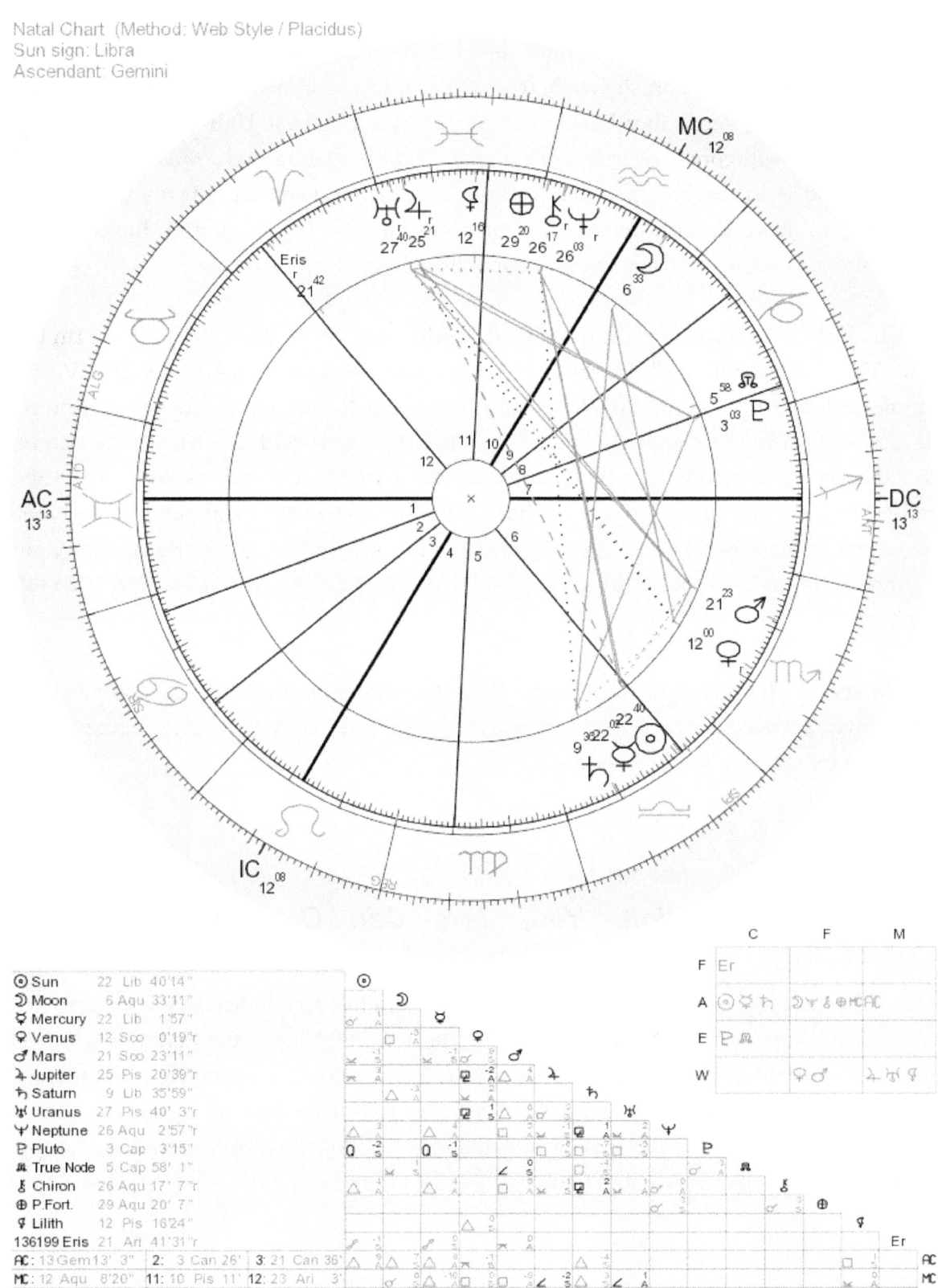

I ignored the general rule of derivative houses, which would require me to turn the chart to make the 11th house, ruling my friend, the 1st house. Instead, I chose to do something I do often, which is break traditional horary rules, this one a variant of decumbiture (which means lying down due to death or illness, used to represent a person not present), and use the 1st house for my friend. This is fine in charts where you're asking a question for or about someone else, but not specifically about your relationship or something occurring between you and that person.

So the 1st house represents my friend, ruled by Mercury since Gemini is rising. Saturn and the 10th house govern foreclosures (again, never be afraid to consult rulership books for ideas if you have doubts). The bank, holder of the mortgage is the 8th house, with Saturn and Capricorn, the planet and sign governing foreclosure ruling the 8th house. The chart is radical.

Mercury is combust the Sun, in fall by house, and Via Combust as well. Ouch. Mercury disposits to a seriously debilitated Venus, in her detriment by sign, in fall by house, and retrograde and intercepted on top of it. Talk about starting from way behind the eight ball! My friend was completely overwhelmed by the prospect of losing his home in three weeks, as the Sun rules the fourth house cusp of the home in question. Depression was setting in.

There was a slight glimmer of hope, though: Mercury and the Sun are both applying within three degrees to conjoin Spica, the benefic oasis in the Via Combust zone. Spica is just inside the 6th house cusp.

The Moon is in Aquarius, ruling freedom and litigation in the 9th house, and it's applying to trine Saturn, representing the bank and foreclosure. The Moon disposits to the retrograde Uranus-Jupiter conjunction in the 11th house, where Uranus is dignified. This indicates an unexpected lucky break, as originally hinted at by Spica.

Mercury, my friend's significator, is separating from Saturn, the bank, and forms no aspects with it. This is good, as no aspect means no action. Mercury is already partile conjunct the Sun, ruler of the 4th house, which literally means that the querent will stay in his home. The Moon will move up to trine Mercury and the Sun, affirming he'll stay put. The Moon will also eventually conjoin the retrograde Neptune-Chiron conjunction, which rules the 11th house of hopes and wishes while sitting in the 10th house of foreclosure. A miracle is at hand and a delay is almost certainly involved. The Moon's last true aspect is a semi-sextile to retrograde Uranus before it goes void-of-course. It is a second house-side semi-sextile, which is great for financial matters, so all of a sudden, things are looking pretty good indeed. And Uranus, the Moon's dispositor, was going to turn direct before the November 8th deadline, practically guaranteeing the foreclosure would not proceed as planned.

So what was the outcome? A week before I had asked the question, the bank involved in the foreclosure announced it would voluntarily suspend all foreclosures in all states after news broke out about "robo-signers" and other illegal fun and games with depositions and mortgage documents. This included all foreclosures in process, not just those in states requiring a judicial process. (The horary question involves a non-judicial state.) No one knew at the time of the question how long the moratorium would last, and there was speculation that it wouldn't be long, because the banks were losing too much money and their stock prices were plummeting. Three days after the time of the question, the bank announced foreclosures would resume in judicial states in spite of the investigations.[1] So it probably wouldn't be long before *all* foreclosure activity in *all* states, judicial process or not, fully resumed.

Saturn, representing the bank, rules the 8th house of illegal activity. Pluto is on the 12th house side of the 8th house cusp, and is in the bank's derived 12th house of hidden deals and financial shenanigans. Pluto quintiles the Sun-Mercury conjunction, showing the lucky break the bank's misdealings dealt to my friend.

Almost two full months after the horary question was asked, the bank announced it would resume *all* of the non-judicial foreclosures.[2] My friend remained in possession of the home for several more months before the bank finally foreclosed, and had long since moved to another residence. So as Spica inside the 6th house cusp hinted, the foreclosure didn't bring any ill affect to any of his day-to-day activities, and he did indeed prevail.

Practice Charts

On the following pages are four charts on which to try out your new horary skills. The first two charts are pretty simple and straightforward. The answers can be found in Appendix C.

Open Source Modern Horary Astrology 103

Chart 1: Should the querent move her residence to city X?

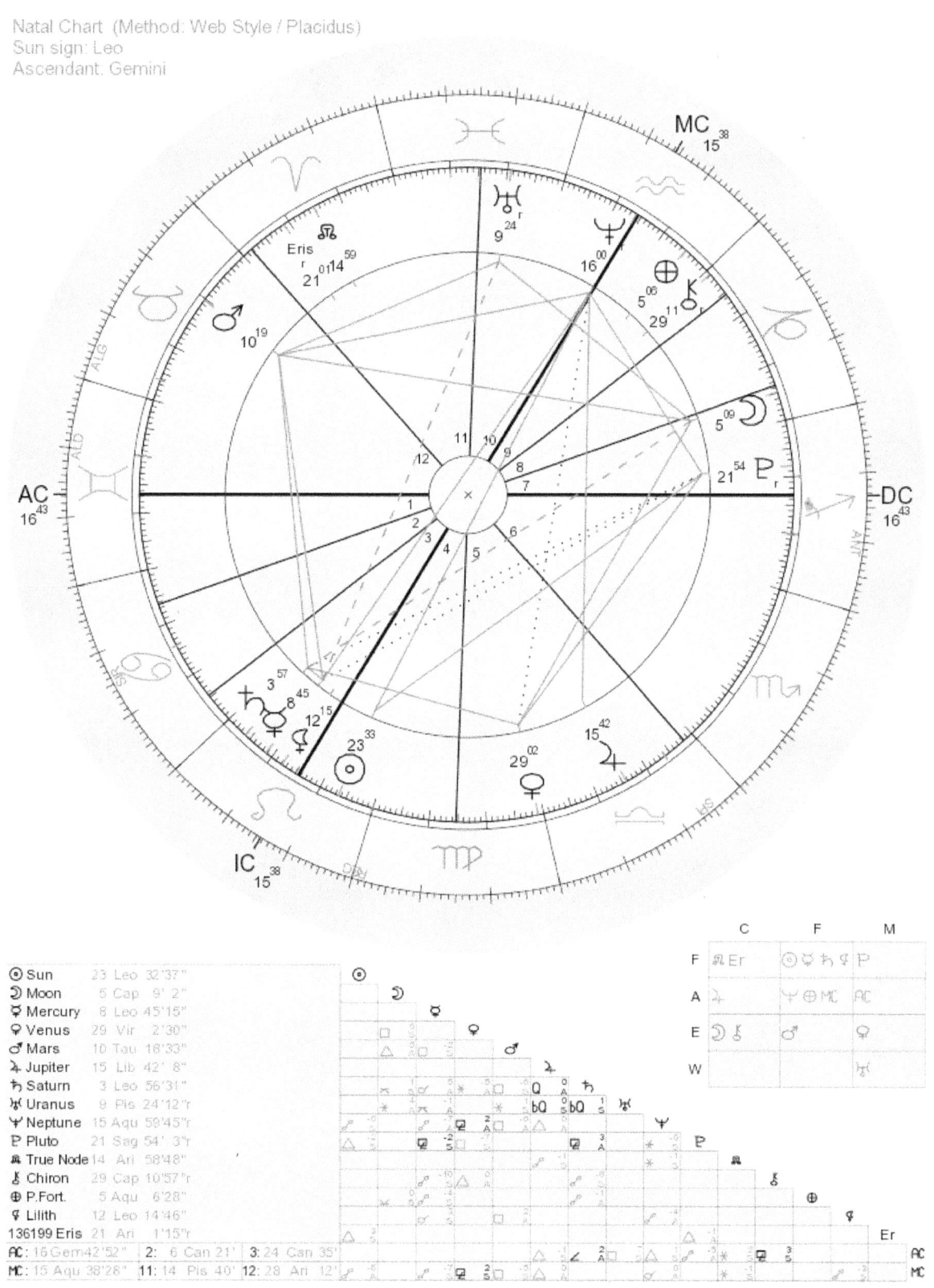

Chart 2: Should the querent pursue screenwriting?

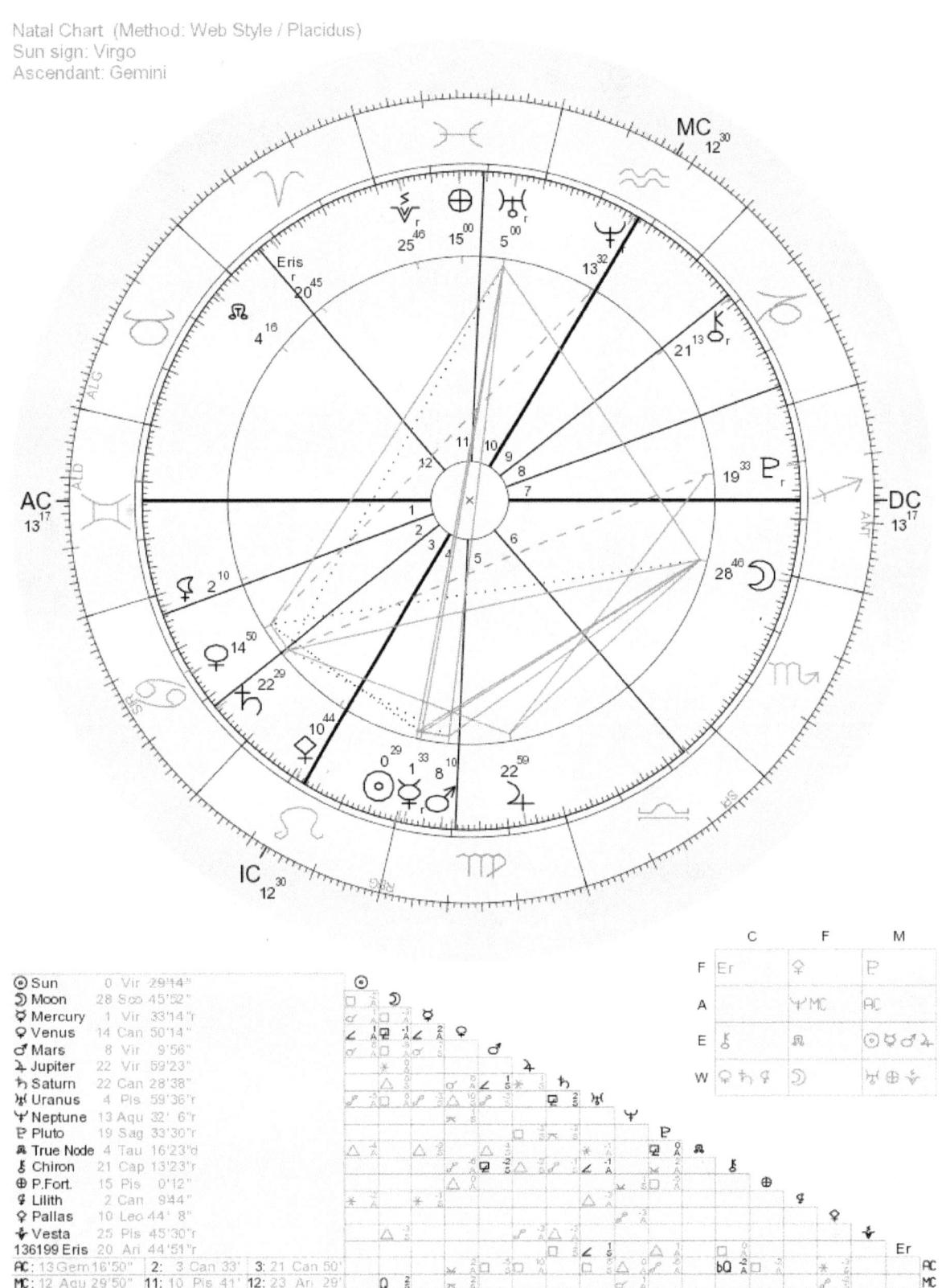

Chart 3: Will the querent get the job with the evil megacorporation?

(Hint: Use the 10th house for this, not the 6th, as it's a career position. Also, she is seeking placement with the evil megacorp via a recruiter.)

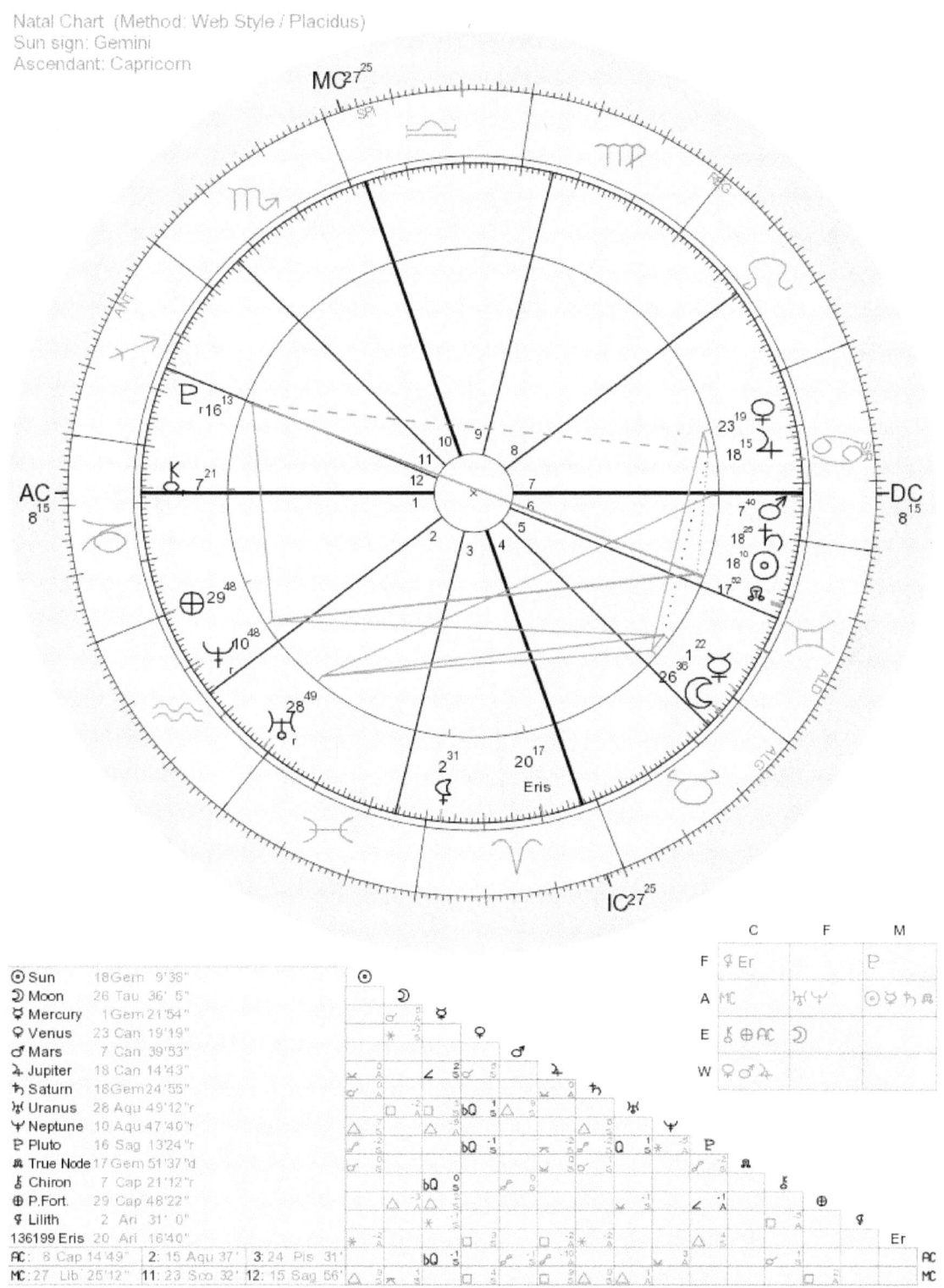

Chart 4: Should the querent rent a craft booth at the city's 4th of July event?

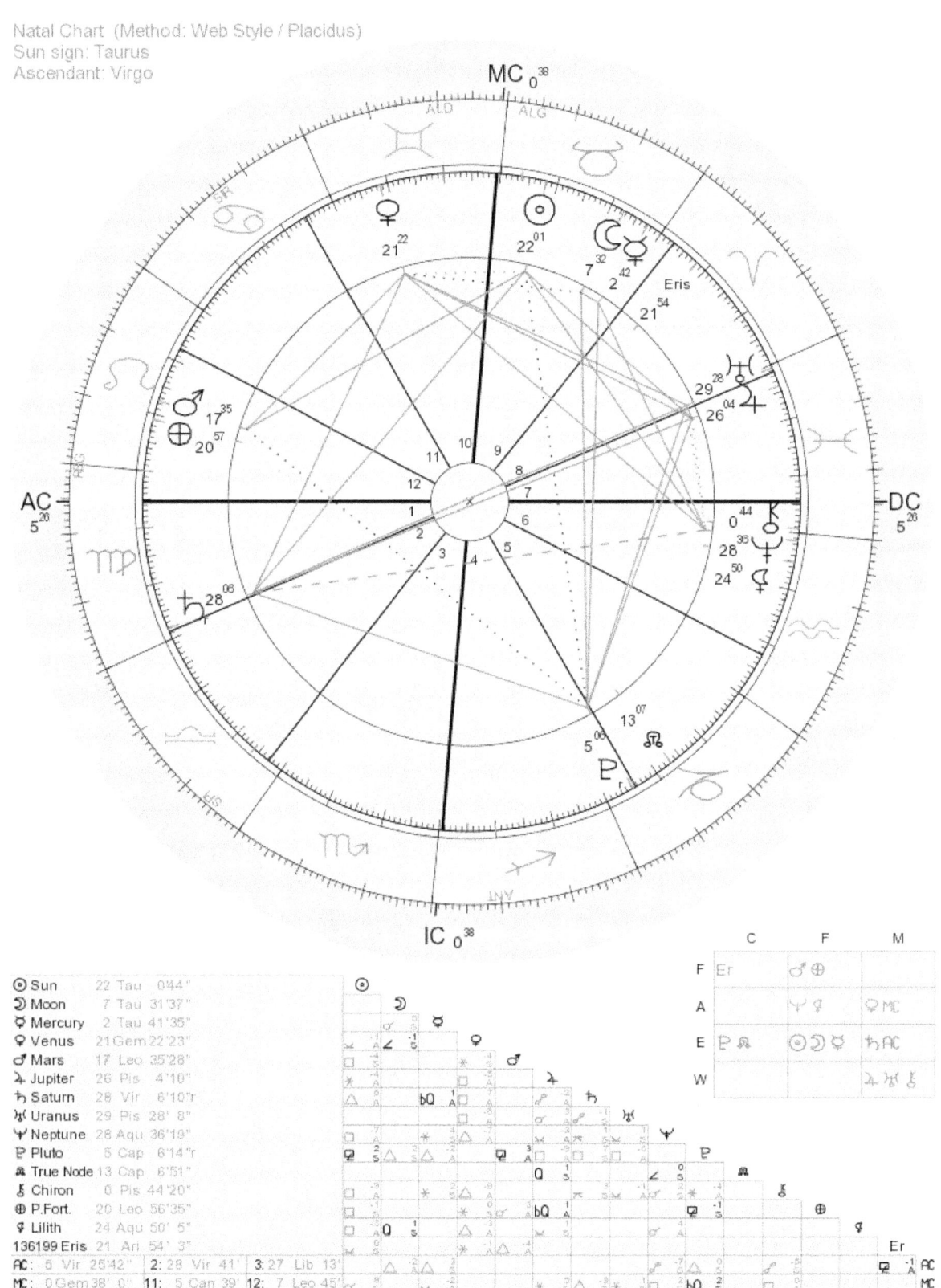

9 BEST PRACTICES

"Astrology is much too powerful to be trivialized, and astrologers must assume and embrace the responsibility we have to our clients and to our profession."[1]
— *astrologer Don McBroom*

Astrology has its limits and horary is no exception. The true power of astrology is unleashed when people don't expect it to do things that it cannot do; some things are simply beyond its scope. At the risk of overstatement, a chart can only reflect the reality of the querent's life—it cannot cure or fix anyone's life or make magic happen. Planets cannot do anything to or influence anyone—they can only symbolically represent.

Common sense and critical thinking skills do not go out the window when interpreting horary charts for querents. Be clear about astrology's limits and know when to refer out. For illnesses, doctors should be sought out; for divorces, lawyers; tax issues, an accountant; and stalking by exes, the police. It's astonishing how many people will consult psychics and astrologers instead. Also, avoid counseling—instead, refer out to a licensed mental health professional. Medical diagnosis with astrology, which can be stunningly accurate, can create serious liability issues for an astrologer if something goes awry. Only practicing physicians (M.D.'s, etc.) can diagnose and subsequently prescribe; the laws of the land are not superseded by horary charts.

What astrology *can* do, and very well at that, is bring insight and understanding to people and situations, and therefore create an avenue for healing or growth. When querents are emotionally distraught, they often lack the objectivity to clearly see and respond rationally to a situation. Part of the astrologer's job is to provide the objectivity the querent lacks.

Charts, like life, are not always black-and-white or absolute. Horary is not always about "yes" and "no" answers to questions if the chart doesn't indicate such—it's also about choices and options and understanding complexities and grey areas. The astrologer's role is to give the querent the clearest and most accurate information possible to make an informed decision. It is not to deny anyone their experience or give them advice on how to live their life.

"Our job isn't about being smart or right," says Michael Lutin. "People think we know stuff we don't know. We have to learn how to be real healers; be present for people while they suffer their pain. People use astrology to escape their pain."[2]

When the Astrologer Gets in the Way

Most horary astrologers are tremendously sincere in their efforts to help answer querents' inquiries. They want to help querents get clarity and objectivity about situations that are important to them. Unfortunately, astrologers and their beliefs can get in the way of helping the querent in a far worse manner than anything the mythical stricture about Saturn in the 7th house may be doing. Some astrologers won't listen when their querents try to correct information about details related to the question. There is always the possibility that you're misreading a symbol, so pay attention. You'll know the difference between misinterpretation and a querent trying to lobby you. Other astrologers will nitpick the way a question is worded, informing the querent that it won't yield a correct answer until it suits *their* understanding, rather than what the querent is actually thinking. A true professional may have their preferences, but they will not hassle and harangue the querent over how the question was asked, or what house system generated the chart, or any other petty issues. The chart contains the answers—the astrologer is just the middleman.

When interpreting horary charts, stick to the chart facts, and keep dogmas and spiritual beliefs *out* of the interpretation. Your beliefs and the querent's beliefs may be incompatible; there's no need to drag any of it into an interpretation. Sometimes the opposite situation will happen, and it will be the querent who will turn all cosmic on you while you are grounded in reality. Some people want a magic show that simply isn't there.

> "You don't know anything about God, the universe; you don't know anything about the soul, reincarnation, future lives, past lives. All that you know is simply hearsay. People have been chattering around you, and you are collecting all kinds of information that seems to be important to you. Why does it seem important? — It seems important because it covers your ignorance. It helps you to feel as if you know. But remember, it is a very big AS IF. You don't know, it is only AS IF."
>
> "All holy scriptures, all books on philosophy, all theology should be categorized into one category: as if. They are talking about every possible impossible thing they know nothing of! But they are articulate, imaginative intellectuals who can create systems out of nothing."[3]
>
> — *Osho*

"Quack astrology" is where there is little or no actual astrological application involved. Instead, the querent is bombarded with advice, beliefs, opinions, personal experiences, superstition, and New Age philosophy and platitudes. Sometimes, they won't even get that much. "I find it inexcusable for an astrology teacher or lecturer to impart their religious, political, sexual, or whatever personal beliefs to the students/audience without an astrological connection to what's being said," says astrologer Don McBroom. "If there is an astrological lesson to be learned, fine, but if we just want to express an editorial commentary, there are many other more appropriate forums to do so."[4] The same applies to one-on-one horary interpretations.

The goal in horary is objectivity, not more subjectivity. Instead, point the querent in the right direction based on the indicators in the horary chart. The best horary astrologers are almost invisible—they act as a bridge between the querent and the answer in the chart.

When talking with querents, avoid using astrological lingo, which will generate a blank stare from most of them upon hearing statements such as, "The lord of the quesited is in domicile in the 8th." Instead, use plain English (or whatever your native tongue) to explain your answers to the querent, such as: "Yes, your boyfriend will get the loan." By avoiding astrology lingo, you can even work with people who are skeptical or hostile toward astrology, because they won't know what you're using to provide them with information. I once ran an event chart behind-the-scenes for an older gentleman who is a hardcore Catholic and extremely hostile to astrology. He was going on vacation to Las Vegas with his two, thirty-something nephews, and the chart had hard aspects to Mars (querent) all over the place. I told him, "I hope you and your nephews agree in advance to your activities, otherwise you'll all end up fighting about it and ruin the trip." He just figured I understood the politics of family dynamics when I said that; he didn't know I was interpreting an event chart. Sure enough, when he got back from the trip, he informed me that the young nephews had wanted to spend all their time in casinos and strip clubs, while he had wanted to visit family living in the area. He and his nephews fought the entire time.

Give the querent useful background details, as well as a straight answer, even if the news is bad. While it's accurate to tell a querent, "Yes, your friend is lying," it's more helpful to say "Yes, your friend is lying because she is hiding a drug or alcohol problem." Providing as much specific and clear information as possible is the goal, but not to the point that the querent is overwhelmed with details or trivial minutiae. The conclusion, and whether it was right or wrong, is the most important piece of information the querent will remember long after the interpretation is over.

You Will Be Wrong

The last thing you want to do is tell a querent something absolute (e.g., "With Saturn in your fifth house, you will never have children.") that does not allow for the possibility that you are wrong or that things can change. Astrologers are not omnipotent gods—they're middlemen. Not only that, they're fallible. Astrologers are human beings subject to human error. Just like doctors, engineers, etc., astrologers can have a bad day or overlook something. So many possibilities in life can change things, causing charts to "backfire," with a completely different outcome than the one the astrologer predicted. When that happens (not if), go back and see if you missed or misread something in the chart. Retrace your steps. Have other astrologers look at it. See where you went wrong. Statistically, there is always going to be a percentage of charts that will come out differently than you predicted. Sometimes it's due to the astrologer's error. Sometimes, reality just changes and a different outcome happens for reasons you'll never know. Sometimes you have an off day. Sometimes the planets just win. It's called the law of averages and it's perfectly normal.

In the beginning, you're going to be wrong a lot as you learn to navigate your way through a horary chart, but don't be discouraged. Expect it, as skill comes with experience. After that, what kind of accuracy rate should you strive for? You may find yourself going in streaks, where you'll hit seven or eight straight, and then botch two in a row. The key is to provide consistently accurate answers at a level greater than chance. No one gets it right 100% of the time—not even people who have 50 or more years of horary experience. Astronomers, backed by science, make mistakes and flat-out get things wrong, so astrologers will, too. Practice to get good.

You Will Be Right

People often want to learn horary because of the genuine desire to help others. But despite your best and most accurate interpretations, people still won't listen. They will still go ahead and do what they want to do and completely ignore what you told them, both good and bad. This is to be expected. No one can ever really know why people still feel drawn to an experience or person clearly bad for them, or pass up a perfectly good opportunity throwing itself at their feet, or act completely against their own self-interest. Non-astrological people do this, too.

One reason people ask horary questions is because they sense or know a change is coming, but don't have all the facts or details in place to know exactly what or when. Fearing a possibly uncomfortable or painful situation that may upset their status quo and force an unwelcome change, they figure astrological foresight will allow them to try to alter or control the situation. Unfortunately, knowing the likely outcome rarely changes it or makes it any less unpleasant—at best it merely takes the surprise or shock out of it. Regardless of the intent, the astrologer's responsibility is to point the querent in the best direction possible based on the chart, and arm them with the most accurate information that will be useful, whether it's a relationship or other activity.

You Will Be Right, But for the Wrong Reasons

There will be times where you will misinterpret charts and still arrive at the right answer. Diana Stone's first foray into horary involved a correct answer to a nurse's "Am I pregnant?" question using a chart that was incorrectly calculated. It had been constructed by hand, way back in the days before computers and astrology software existed. The four major factors she used for judgment in the handwritten chart were completely missing from the "real" computer-generated chart she ran years later. And yet she got it right.[5]

Over the years, I've accidentally misderived houses and still described events or people perfectly. I've correctly answered questions in spite of misplaced asteroids and other objects by working from memory, instead of having the astrology software default them into the chart. I've even arrived at correct answers interpreting charts with the wrong date or time. Sometimes, in situations such as these, it's perfectly okay to be more lucky than good. It makes up for the times when you did everything right, but got it wrong.

Common Horary Myths

Below are a few of the most common misconceptions among horary practitioners about what can and can't be interpreted in a horary chart:

> 1) **A horary question can only be asked once,** *or* **the same horary question cannot be revisited again until the passage of six months, or a year, or whatever arbitrary time frame the astrologer's horary school taught them.**[6]

This is by far one of the biggest discrepancies among all horary practitioners. Do horary charts have expiration dates? The general rule of thumb taught by some horary schools is that the same question can't be asked twice, period. Other schools of thought state it can be, but only when the original circumstances have changed significantly. Naturally, neither will stop a querent from asking the same thing repeatedly, only phrased differently, over a relatively short period of time, and particularly if they didn't like the answer the first time around. This is to be expected.

Mark Twain allegedly said, "History doesn't repeat itself, but it does rhyme."[7] The same is true for horary charts when questions are asked repeatedly about the same situation after an answer has previously been given. Often, you'll end up with similar significators, and similar aspects, if not similar charts. This is because the acute anxiety triggering the slew of questions usually happens within a short period of time, such as a few days or a week, when the planets haven't moved more than a few degrees from where they were when the original question was asked.

Historically, William Lilly did not apply a time limit.[8] The answer to a horary question can last from a brief period of time to indefinitely, depending on the situation. Therefore, someone who goes apartment hunting for a week or two and keeps asking, "Should I rent the apartment I just looked at?" will get a reliable answer, because even though the same question is being asked, it's about different potential residences. If there are multiple job interviews for the same position spanned over a short period of time, the chart for each separate interview will be applicable and valid, even though the answer may have been completely revealed in the first chart. Or, a question such as "Will Bob find a job?" can be followed up two weeks later after a lead, when Bob lands an interview. It may have a slight variation, such as "Will Bob *get* the job?" but nonetheless, it's a similar question relating to Bob's basic employment status, and will return a valid answer.

2) A chart can only answer the question exactly as asked, and no further information can be gleaned.[9]

In Joan McEvers' horary text, she calls several questions asked at the same time about the same matter *compounded* questions, while she describes questions about different subjects gleaned from the same chart as *multiple* questions. Both types are valid and return reliable answers, and she provides case studies of each.[10]

Charts will sometimes limit the amount of information available because that's the reality of where the situation is at. Other times, charts will tell you as much as you are capable of finding. See Diana Stone's case study in Appendix A - Part III, titled "Horary 2—The Client Who Found Out More Than He Wanted to Know" for an example of the latter.

3) Questions about death cannot be answered.

Death is a fact of life and as a reality-based question, it can be answered just as readily as questions about pregnancy and birth. Taboos and morality belong to the astrologer, not the solar system, so don't let subjective, personal beliefs get in the way of helpful and accurate astrology. For an excellent, professional example of how to handle a death-related question, see Diana Stone's case study in Appendix A - Part III, titled "Horary 28—Will I be attending father's funeral in six months?"

4) There must be at least three confirmations of judgment before an accurate conclusion can be reached.

Life is not black and white, and charts do not always adhere to the astrologer's demands or ancient edicts. Some charts will give a *lot* more than three indications that an answer is yes or no, and some will barely give one or two. The astrologer has to accept the chart as it is, and be cognizant of either the limitations or the abundance of information contained within it, rather than trying to force the chart to fit arbitrary and subjective rules.

Staying on Track

Key things to remember when interpreting horary charts:

- Always focus on the most important goal of interpreting horary charts: HELP THE QUERENT!

- Protect the querent's privacy at all times. *Always* respect the confidentiality of your querent and your querent's data. One failure to follow that simple step can permanently ruin your reputation.

- Don't feed the skeptics by fishing for additional background information from querents. A properly asked question and the chart are all you need to set to work.

- Charts don't lie, but people sure do. Some querents will try to lobby you to their point of view of what outcome they want. Stand firm. "Heed what the chart says, not what the querent wants it to say or what the astrologer thinks it should say," notes Diana Stone.[11]

- In general, there are three types of querents: 1) Those who know the answer already, but just need outside confirmation to find peace or relief. 2) Those who know the answer already, don't like it, and want you to tell them something different. 3) Those who honestly don't know the answer. The third type is rare.

- If you get lost or stuck interpreting a chart, return to the core formula of S.A.M.E.: Significators + Aspects + Moon + and Extras = Conclusion. Midpoint trees can also help you refocus on the core of what's important in the chart. Midpoint trees also make excellent tiebreakers if all of the regular chart indicators are evenly split between pro and con.

- Always be on the lookout for new techniques you can adapt as your own, and not necessarily from horary, but from other branches as well (e.g., Vedic, Cosmobiology, etc.). Also, you do *not* have to use horary rules or one technique exclusively to interpret a horary chart correctly. You can combine interpretive techniques from sun sign, natal, progressions, etc., if it will help you synthesize the information. The more tools you have, the more options you will have available to you to dissect the chart correctly and confirm your answer.

- There's more than one way to find the same information in a chart. As such, there's more than one way to arrive at a correct answer. This is a major reason why all the various horary methodologies work.

- Consistently correct answers are the only proof of validity of technique or methodology you need, regardless of what you use to interpret a chart.

- There are no absolutes in horary astrology. Each chart is unique and may require a different approach to unlocking and unfolding its answers. The method to do so may vary from chart to chart.

- If something astrological exists scientifically, and you understand its meaning, and it works consistently and accurately, you can utilize it. There's no need to wait for a consensus of use.

- When in doubt, experiment. Think and research, or try a different approach to interpreting the chart than normal. You don't have to give an immediate and hasty (and likely incorrect) answer. Take your time and think things through.

- You can choose what objects you prefer to use in any given chart. However, don't pretend something doesn't exist (asteroids, TNOs, etc.) or deny scientific fact because it wasn't known in William Lilly's era and prior. As astronomy grows and changes, so does the astrology based on it.

- Don't try to dazzle the querent with a deep and profound answer to their predicament if there isn't one. When in doubt, stick to the chart facts, keep it simple and realistic, and you won't go wrong.

- It's okay to say tell the querent you don't know something. If you don't see it in the chart, say so. Some charts will only yield a limited amount of information, as sometimes even a chart has its limits. Also, if the matter diverges greatly from the original question, it may be necessary to ask a new question, and run a new horary chart, to answer it.

10 TOP TEN HORARY MISTAKES & HOW TO AVOID THEM

"People want to know the symptom and the healing. They don't want to learn astrology." [1]
— *astrologer Michael Lutin*

Horary can be tough enough for a beginner without making things even harder with these self-defeating but easily avoidable errors. Don't worry; I have committed every mistake on the list, often more than once, and lived to tell—and became a better horary astrologer because of it. But really, stop trying to read your own charts. You'll make yourself crazy that way.

1) **Giving advice to the querent.**

Querents must become the *solution* to their problems, not *more* of the problem. Nothing else will create change, either in themselves or in their lives. There are people who will spend a lot of time running from astrologer, to psychic to tarot reader, hoping someone, anyone, will give them "the answer," instead of channeling that freneticness toward resolving their problem. Giving advice to a querent by telling them what you think they should do with their lives based on your personal philosophy or experience only perpetuates that cycle. Don't fall for the trap.

Also, giving advice will set you up to be the perfect scapegoat when things invariably backfire: "You told me that love is the most important thing in the world, so I should go back to him! The abuse got even worse!", "You said the market was on a down-swing and I should buy gold! I lost a fortune!", "You told me to quit my job and wait for something I love to do to manifest! Now I'm totally broke with a year-long gap on my resumé!", "You told me he wasn't involved with someone else and that I should go for what I want! Now he won't even speak to me!", "You said that my health was fine and that herbs would help ease the pain! I'm scheduled to have a tumor removed next week!" These are easily preventable and avoidable headaches.

Horary astrology is designed to give facts and probabilities and likely outcomes connected to those facts, not advice, which is free for a reason. If the astrologer's advice was so wonderful, they'd be living it themselves, rather than preaching it to others. The querent does not need advice—the querent needs objectivity and facts to gain clarity in the matter so they can make their own decision and act accordingly. Laying out options, potential scenarios and likely outcomes is fine. Being honest and realistic is golden. Preaching to someone about what you think they should do with their life or relationship, or trying to solve their problems for them, is not. And until your own life is in order, giving advice and trying to solve others' problems can be a way to avoid one's own mental housekeeping.

WRONG: "I think you should do X based on my personal experience..."

RIGHT: "Based on the chart, if you do X, then Y will be your likely outcome. If you do A, then B will be your likely outcome."

2) Trying to interpret your own horary charts.

We all do this. Stop. Really. This is akin to trying to perform surgery on yourself. Almost no one has that level of detachment and objectivity when a matter concerns them. The greater the vested interest you have in the outcome, the greater the likelihood of inaccuracy. Anthony Louis puts it pointedly: "It is possible to see almost anything you want in a chart due to wishful thinking."[2]

Have a friend learn horary with you, so you can interpret and learn from each other. If not, some online astrology forums permit asking for an interpretation, but the answers you receive may vary considerably. Or you could hire a professional. Diana Stone wisely states, "If you are the astrologer doing your own chart, it falls along the same lines as the old saying, 'A lawyer representing himself has a fool for a client.'"[3]

3) Assigning incorrect houses or significators.

Your mastery of house rulership and the matters governed by the planets will determine your ease and success with horary. Because if you don't locate the question in the right houses, you're essentially finished before you start. Fortunately, it's very difficult to misplace significators if you let the chart lead you, and if you use rulership books and other sources for guidance until you have enough experience with similar types of questions. Therefore, study the meanings of the houses extremely in-depth. For example, the 6th house rules jobs while the 10th house rules careers. Working retail to put yourself through college would be a 6th house matter. Finding a position as Vice President of Marketing would be the 10th house. The 7th house is for committed relationships, the 5th house is for dates and romantic dalliances.

Sometimes the wording of the question itself can be misleading. A question such as "Should I buy the computer stock?" is a 5th house speculation matter, not a 2nd house purchasing or personal finance matter. The type of stock, computer or otherwise, is irrelevant. "Did he see my picture on Facebook?" is a first house matter (me=personal identity), not an 11th house (social networking) matter, because the core of the question is about "Did he notice me?" rather than the avenue of how or where. Focus on the core essence of the question, and not on the fringe details such as description or action.

Usually, significators are assigned by house first, then planets, although some schools of horary thought do it vice versa. Both methods are valid. Also, if the chart is radical, it will show you by significator placement within the chart where to focus. Let the chart lead you.

4)   Blindly applying rules and thereby strangling the message of a chart, without first getting an overview of what the chart is actually saying.

Some horary practitioners will cling too tightly to their methodologies, completely overlooking what's staring them right in the face. Traditional horary beginners in particular have an overweening knack for over-application of rules, simply because rules are the inherent core of their technique. This obscures the chart's message and causes conclusions to be drawn that aren't there, and missing what is actually right in front of them because it doesn't fit their rules. An incomplete or incorrect answer is usually not far behind.

To overcome this common horary mistake, refer back to Chapter 5 and the issue of interrogation versus dialogue. Keep the "Headlines, Details, Conclusions" concept from Chapter 6 in mind as well as the "S.A.M.E.: Significators + Aspects + Moon + Extras = Conclusion" formula. See what the significators are doing first and foremost, before looking at anything else. If there's a stricture or two, figure out why and then look at what they lead to. Look at what is relevant in the chart by seeing what is most obvious first, and *then* figure out which rules apply. Don't put the cart before the horse.

5)   Giving the Moon's aspects too much importance in the outcome of the chart.

As mentioned previously, Marc Edmund Jones described the horary Moon as "Pertinent, but trivial."[4] An exception is if the Moon is a primary significator (e.g., the ascendant is in Cancer); then it's as important as if the ascendant were ruled by any other planet. Otherwise, the Moon is a theme or tone to the action being played out by the relationships between the chart significators. A benefic Moon in an otherwise lousy chart can merely mean the querent will endure the failure of the matter relatively unscathed. A bad Moon in an otherwise good chart can indicate nasty vicissitudes at work prior to eventual triumph. The Moon's involvement, except when it's a primary significator, is a soundtrack to the action being played out on the chart's stage. It can and does act, but rarely as a leading lady.

6) Giving too much credence to minor factors or trivial minutiae, obscuring the big picture.

This is an issue of focus and perspective in a chart, and often involves trying to skew an answer. The aspects and relationships between significators are *always* primary. The traditional tools of Arabic Parts, critical degrees and fixed stars, etc., if you choose to use them, do not override the actions of the planets or other objects that orbit the Sun. Also, a non-significator making a nice (or awful) aspect in irrelevant houses is background noise that can distract immensely from the main storyline. Further, don't get lost in trivialities or details the querent already knows—they want you to tell them what's going to happen, not what's already happened. Keeping the S.A.M.E formula in mind from Chapter 6, focus on significators, aspects and the Moon *before* considering the extras or additional minutiae.

7) Saving the horary question to be asked at a time when the Moon or other planets are in good aspect.

This is something every horary practitioner tries at one point or another, essentially trying to skew a horary question into an electional chart. It will invariably backfire, as the chart will spit back late degrees, no aspects between significators, or some other negation. Diana Stone addresses the issue this way: "One of the most absolutely foolish situations is when another astrologer calls for a horary question and tries to time the question according to what they know is going on in the sky. I don't know how many times I have heard this: 'I shouldn't ask now because the Moon is void-of-course or Mercury is retrograde.' Explain to me the logic of that! If the idea is to manipulate the solar system to give a positive answer, I can do that for free. If you want an accurate answer, however, forget all about the planets and ask the question when the inspiration seizes you."[5]

8) Trying to judge a chart based on one isolated factor because it's "good" in order to skew an answer.

Avoid using only one isolated factor in a chart to render a conclusion. Horary is almost never that simple. Synthesize all the factors into a clear and cohesive answer. Going gaga over a benefic fixed star or other singular factor such as Jupiter in the 1st house or trining the Moon does NOT override everything else happening in the chart. It does not automatically make the answer a "yes," especially if the rest of the chart is an absolute train wreck. The chart must be considered as a whole —you can't cherry-pick only the "good" things in it and ignore the afflicted and malefic. Each factor is a part of the big picture and weighed accordingly.

This symptom is usually due to interpreting your own charts, or the querent heavily lobbying you. Don't clutch at straws by thinking that the Moon sextile Venus is going to override a Saturn-Pluto square between significators. The Moon-Venus sextile may simply mean the querent will survive the calamity only somewhat worse for wear, compared to the damage that could have otherwise been done. Be realistic, and see the chart as significators-within-a-whole.

9) **Using too wide orbs.**

The ancients used to judge aspects by sign rather than degrees (e.g., Saturn at 5 degrees Cancer was automatically an opposition to the Sun at 26 degrees Capricorn, a 21 degree difference that by modern standards is way too far out of orb to make a connection). In the age of computerized charts, and modern astrology in general, degrees and orbs are the gold standard. Twenty degrees of distance between applying Mars and Neptune does not a conjunction make. An orb of seven degrees is good, five is better, and three or less is best. For midpoints, the standard is two degrees or less.

10) **Following someone else's technique too closely, to the exclusion of one's own common sense.**

All horary charts are unique, so to try and paint them all using a broad brush is self-defeating. Learning a technique is important, but at some point you have to drop the training wheels and think for yourself. Giving credence to something because a supposed authority on horary created some arbitrary rules about it is not going to help you think your way out of a jam in a complex chart. If breaking rules in light of what the chart is telling you makes sense, do it. The people who insist on obedience to horary rules over common sense and reality want an astrology that is immutable and absolute. It isn't and never will be.

11 RELATIONSHIP-ORIENTED HORARY QUESTIONS

> *"So what do you do when what you had at the beginning is not there anymore? Do you wiggle out and dump the relationship? When you learn that there's another human being over there, one you cannot control or possess, one who has baggage that prohibits you from having the total closeness and fulfilling partnership you imagined you could have, what do you do?...It is the "to be or not to be" of relationships."* [1]
>
> — **astrologer Michael Lutin**

Relationship questions are far and away the most common type of horary question. They are usually either forensic or predictive as mentioned earlier, only an additional trait they tend to have in common is that they lean toward being "other" directed, as in wanting to know someone else's motivations. That way the querent can attempt to control the person or manipulate the situation. This is not a surprise, as non-astrological people do the exact same thing, just using other methods.

True to Aristotle's *Poetics*, relationship questions are about beginnings, middles and endings. They follow a pretty set arc, from "Will we get together?" to "Is he cheating on me?" to "Will we break up?" to "Will we get back together again?" And everything in between, such as, "Is he 'The One?'", "Does he still love me?", "What does she think of me?" or "Will she leave her husband for me?"

Because querents have an ultra-vested interest in the outcome, relationship questions can be dicey for the astrologer. Querents never get upset if you tell them not to take the trip to Paris, or not to buy the car or sell the house. They don't even fuss very much when you tell them they won't get the big promotion. But the minute you tell them they aren't going to get the relationship they think they deserve, watch the fireworks go off, and how it will make them even more determined to pursue the matter. Not to mention what an idiot *you* are, because everyone except you can see that the querent and quesited are total soulmates meant to be together forever.

Predictably, querents will almost never avoid entering a relationship based on the interpretation of a horary chart, no matter how dire things look. This is not surprising, either, as non-astrological people enter relationships that are no good for them all the time, thinking they can change or reform the other person who has a track record of being a complete dirtball. And maybe that's not wrong, considering that one never really knows what attracts two people into a relationship to begin with. Regardless, each time the querent's relationship takes a turn for the worse, the horary questions will come rolling in. One week it will be about what to do. The next week it will be about how does the other person feel, and what are they thinking. Then eventually it will be will he or she come back, or is the relationship truly over. And then when will the next one come along. Count on it like clockwork.

In applying significators and houses to relationship questions, the mis- and over-use of the 7th house is the most fundamental mistake made in relationship horary charts. The issue of using the 5th house or the 7th house is where modern horary practitioners diverge the most from the traditionalists because many people not only don't understand the history behind the use of the 7th house as a relationship house, but they also don't understand the fundamental structure of modern relationships, particularly in the West.

Traditionally or historically, people lived with their parents until they married, and the marriages were arranged more often than not. That's going from the 1st house of the individual's autonomy straight to the 7th house and a legally-bound, committed partnership.

These days, it's not nearly so black and white. The majority of people meet, start off as friends (11th house), date (5th house), and then if there is chemistry, the relationship moves into something more committed such as a marriage (7th house), but not always. The basic, contemporary relationship structure is clear: Begin in the 11th house of friends, move into the romantic 5th house, and then grow into the partnership of the 7th house. Sometimes it will skew, where people fall into bed first (5th house), and then figure out afterward that they like each other (11th house), and then maybe go on to a committed relationship such as marriage or living together (7th house), or not. As *Dategirl* columnist Judy McGuire states, "I've had great relationships that morphed out of friendships, and amazing friendships that started off as dates."[2]

Most Western relationships in modern times do not begin with the 7th house. Traditionally, William Lilly considered the 7th house to represent a "yoked" relationship (hence the term "getting hitched" in marriages). From a contemporary standpoint, Anthony Louis, in his text *Horary Astrology*, makes the 5th house/7th house distinction very clear: "The 5th house is for romances, courtships, love affairs/flings...the 5th house holds sway over love relationships that *do not* involve commitment, such as dates, boyfriends (or girlfriends), or mistresses."[3]

"The 7th house, as opposite of the 1st, shows other people who are on equal footing with the querent," explains Louis. "It rules all kinds of partnerships and unions, the marriage partner, committed (yoked) relationships, marriage as well as divorce, open enemies and opponents, and significant others."[4] So when a querent states that they've dated someone a couple of times, and a horary practitioner wants to use the 7th house for the question, essentially putting two dates in the same house and standing as a 40-year marriage, I want to tear my hair out.

"When the romance is over, the relationship starts," says Michael Lutin.[5] It's a perfect description of the transition from the 5th house to the 7th house, as anyone who has ever been in a serious relationship can attest. When the 5th house candy-and-roses phase is over, and the 7th house warts-and-all phase begins, things get interesting.

For horary questions about extramarital affairs, the 5th house is used, not the 7th house, for the reasons specified above, since the 7th house relationship is one that is legally bound. Querents will try to fantasize the 5th house into the 7th house, but it doesn't work that way.

Cultural differences will also affect your horary interpretations and house usage. When interpreting a chart for someone from a traditional culture (e.g., Iran, where arranged marriages are very common) use the 7th house. In modern Western relationships, look at the reality of the querent's life and relationship, and assign the appropriate house. If a couple has lived together for six years, but are not married, use the 7th house, since the relationship is well established. If a couple has only been together for a few months, use the 5th house.

The North and South Nodes are *huge* in relationship horary questions. The North Node, as Lutin describes in *Sunshines*, is the happiness you earn. The South Node is the happiness you steal.[6] Guess which one most of us tend toward.

The North Node shows what needs to be done or focused on to achieve the aim of the horary question. For example, if the North Node is in Aries in the first house, the person needs to focus on their independence and autonomy in the relationship in order for it to succeed. The South Node shows what the person's real agenda is based on their obsession with what they think they aren't getting. The South Node in Libra in the 7th house can show someone who gets over-attached in relationships and will cling to one that isn't working, or who feels that they need to be in one at all costs or else they aren't "normal." Or perhaps they have a fear of being alone. Look to the planets disposited by the Nodes, and the aspects they make, for additional motivational clues.

Also key in relationship charts are the dignities and dispositors of the significators. If they disposit harmoniously, meaning the planets they disposit to are dignified or well-aspected, those areas will be bona fide strengths in the relationship. If one or more of the significators disposit to debilitated or afflicted planets, those areas are where problems will arise. If only one significator is dignified, that person may be who the relationship revolves around. Or, as Lutin notes, "There's a top and a bottom in every relationship."[7] Dignities and dispositors will show who is which.

Reception is also a crucial part of relationship charts. In the relationship chart below, where the significators are in each other's fall and detriment, the two people are not well-matched or good for each other. On the other hand, well-recepted significators, even if poorly aspected, show a dedicated couple that can stick together and persevere through difficulty.

Saturn in the 7th house is *not* a stricture in a relationship chart, or any other horary chart for that matter. It's a message that will tell you a lot about the state of the relationship. If well-aspected, it can indicate a long and enduring bond. If afflicted, it can be the proverbial ball and chain, and make the person feel trapped or alone in a relationship. Saturn is exalted in the 7th house, and from a modern horary standpoint, it takes on a meaning similar to Saturn in Libra, namely:

- The object of desire is unavailable or already spoken for. (If Saturn is conjunct or aspecting the ruler of the 5th house, it can confirm this.)
- The querent will spend an enormous amount of time, energy, and focus pursuing someone they can't have.[8]
- The querent is trying to keep a relationship alive, or hanging on to one they are bored with.[9]
- The querent is trying to forget about or escape from someone they are stuck with and can't get rid of.[10]
- Retrograde Saturn in 7th indicates the other person either can't commit at this time, *or* will return in a different state or frame of mind regarding the relationship. It can also mean the person is unavailable or already spoken for, similar to its non-retrograde status.
- Balance needs to be restored and maintained in the relationship. If the querent is too attached to the relationship, separation is indicated. If the querent is not in a relationship, they may seek one out to avoid loneliness.[11]
- Saturn in the 7th can also be a quintessential relationship inhibitor, via delays or obstacles, *or* can indicate a deep, unbreakable, abiding bond of true love. Aspects, the Nodes, reception, dignity and debilitation will determine which.

Like any other object in a horary chart, outer planets play a personal role in relationship charts. Aspects between Venus and Pluto can indicate triangles and power plays in relationships, as well as a union between two people who have very little in common. Uranus in the 7th house can show a breakup. Neptune in the 7th can show idealization of a partner, or not seeing them for who they really are, invariably ending in disappointment.

The interaction between planets and other astronomical objects can provide a lot of background and subtext to a relationship question. The asteroids Vesta, Juno and Ceres are imperative in relationship charts. Vesta will show the level of dedication and devotion; Ceres will show the amount of emotional availability and investment; and Juno will show struggles due to inequality or infidelity in the relationship. Lilith can be helpful, too, in showing either where both parties need their own individual space within the partnership, or unconscious sabotage. The TNO Sedna should be used if the relationship question deals with issues of loneliness, isolation or abuse at the hands of men if the querent is a woman. Positive aspects to Sedna show the querent is better off alone. Harsh aspects involving a significator and Sedna can show anger and bitterness over a relationship, past or present. Eris in the 5th or 7th houses assures strife and discord between the couple.

When a relationship breaks up during Mercury retrograde, it can have essentially the same effect as trying to sever a limb with a dull butter knife: it is incredibly painful (from all the ruminations and second-guessing) and doesn't work. When Mercury goes direct, and particularly when it clears its shadow, the opportunity to reconcile will often present itself. It can also indicate a rebound that doesn't last.

If the horary chart shows a break-up during a full moon or lunar eclipse (both indicating separations), the relationship is pretty much finished, unless a multitude of other factors in the chart can overcome it. It will still leave lasting damage. A solar eclipse can inject new life into a relationship by burning away long-standing problems or amplifying what has been denied, but a crisis will be precipitated first.

So in addition to the general horary guidelines, in relationship charts, specifically focus on:

- Assigning the correct relationship house (11th, 5th or 7th) based on the reality of the querent's relationship, and not their idealization of it.
- Looking at the Nodes to see what the purposes and agendas are in the relationship. (Refer to *Sunshines* if necessary.)
- Checking the significators' aspects, dignities and dispositors to each other, as well as reception.
- Venus and Juno: Whether they are dignified or debilitated, their sign and house placement as well as reception, midpoints, aspects and dispositors.
- The special significance of Saturn in the 7th house of a relationship chart, or Saturn aspecting the ruler of the 5th house.
- Using pertinent asteroids and TNOs, and seeing what aspects or other connections they make to significators and to the rulers of the 11th, 5th and 7th houses.
- Checking midpoints to see if there's harsh or benign connections involving significators. Then check midpoints for Venus, Juno and the Moon.

A Typical "Will We Get Together?" Chart

Containing, of course, its corollary "And if so, how will things work out?"

In this chart (Figure 11.1), the female querent and male quesited don't know each other very well, but are on friendly terms at work. So this is clearly a 5th house romance and dating question, not a 7th house marriage and partnership question. Jupiter, the querent's ruler, is in the 6th house and in detriment both by sign and house. Interestingly, it signifies the moonlighting job (6th house) for a local sports team (Jupiter) where they met. Venus, ruler of the 5th, is retrograde and in detriment in Aries in the third house, showing that the two are not on the same wavelength, nor do they have a lot in common. Mars trines the Sun and sextiles Uranus, so they are more friendly than romantic, and it won't be long-lasting.

The Moon forms a grand trine with Jupiter and Neptune, so the querent has unrealistic expectations to say the least. The deal-killer though, is the Moon will quincunx Saturn in the 5th house, at Caput Algol nonetheless—she is out of her mind if she thinks this can work! There is no romantic possibility here, especially with Saturn in the dead degrees of Taurus and disposited by retrograde and detrimented Venus. The final nail in the coffin would have been the Sun-Eris conjunction with Juno in the 4th house of outcome, and dispositing to the querent's co-significator, Mars, in the 1st house, but this was not known at the time, as Eris hadn't been discovered yet. (It's always interesting to recover objects in charts retroactively for research purposes.)

The North Node is in the 7th house, dispositing to the Moon in Libra, which is applying to trine Jupiter, the querent's ruler. The Moon will apply to square the Nodes, indicating a "damned if you do, damned if you don't" proposition. The Moon also disposits to debilitated Venus. The last two aspects to the Moon before it goes void-of-course are the aforementioned quincunx to Saturn, and a sextile to Chiron in Sagittarius as the last true aspect. So it will hurt a bit from disappointment when it runs its course and falls apart.

The first date was lunch together, and it was a disaster. The querent described the conversation as "forced" and the event "uncomfortable" as they really didn't have much to talk about. She said it felt strange meeting outside of their familiar work environment.

Troopers that they are, they decided to try again and have dinner together two weeks later. It was an even worse disaster, as he told her he didn't usually go to nice restaurants or like spending lots of money on dates. (Moon quincunx Saturn, rulers of the 8th and 2nd houses of money, with Saturn in the 5th house of pleasure.) Needless to say, and thankfully for her, there were no further dates with the cheap and unromantic cad.

Figure 11.1: Will the Querent Get Together with Co-Worker?

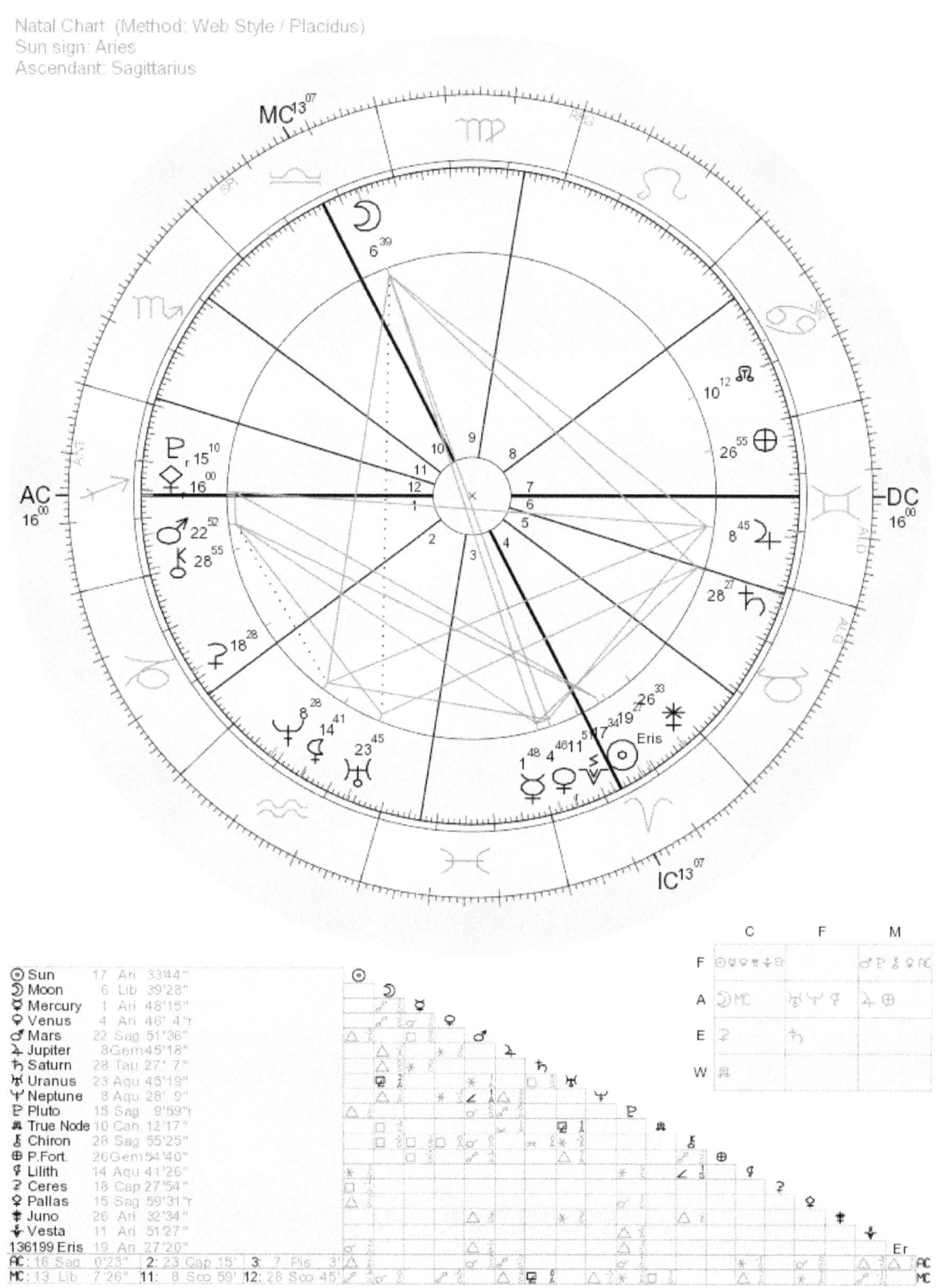

The Ultimate Breakup Chart

They write country music songs about charts like this.

The querent called her long-time boyfriend and told him that their relationship was over. After all was said and done, she retrieved the time of the call from her phone and erected a chart. She had a habit of forgiving him and taking him back in the past, and wanted to know if it was truly over this time, and asked me to take a look. (Figure 11.2)

It's *so* over.

All of the angles are at 29 degrees, a major crisis point of no return. Combined with the Sun in the 12th house ruling the 8th, there is literally no life left in the relationship. The Sun is applying to square Uranus, the breakup planet, which is sitting right at the 3rd house cusp with Eris in the 3rd house—an upsetting phone call indeed! The Moon's most recent aspect prior to the chart was an opposition to Venus, showing the separation. The Moon is also in a very wide, mutually separating trine to retrograde Mercury, her boyfriend's significator, showing their best days are long behind them.

Looking at the dignities and dispositors of the significators, the querent's Jupiter disposits to itself in rulership traditionally, meaning she sustained (the 2nd house is a succeedent house) the relationship through her generosity (particularly financial; again, 2nd house). But looking more deeply using the modern rulership, Jupiter disposits to Neptune in Aquarius, which disposits to and mutually recepts Uranus in Pisces, but Uranus is in fall in the 2nd house. She had no stability or reliability in the relationship and felt emotionally distant from him, as signified by vague Neptune and disruptive Uranus. They separated frequently for long durations during the course of the relationship. Why? Her boyfriend's significator, Mercury, disposits to a Via Combust Saturn, in turn dispositing to Venus in Scorpio, indicating he felt that the relationship was too much work and demanded more commitment than he was willing to give. Venus disposits to Pluto in Capricorn, which is intercepted in his derived 7th, meaning he controlled the relationship with emotional distance and limited their interactions to his convenience, thereby alienating her.

Proving Beverley Rostant's retrograde axiom from Chapter 5, which states, "A retrograde 7th house ruler may mean...in a relationship question, that the person can't commit at this time," the boyfriend, signified by Mercury, is retrograde at early degrees Capricorn, showing the demands he faces from a new job, leaving little time for the relationship. As signified by Mercury, he preferred to come and go in the relationship, rather than stay and settle down. Deriving the house to put him

Figure 11.2: The Ultimate Breakup Chart

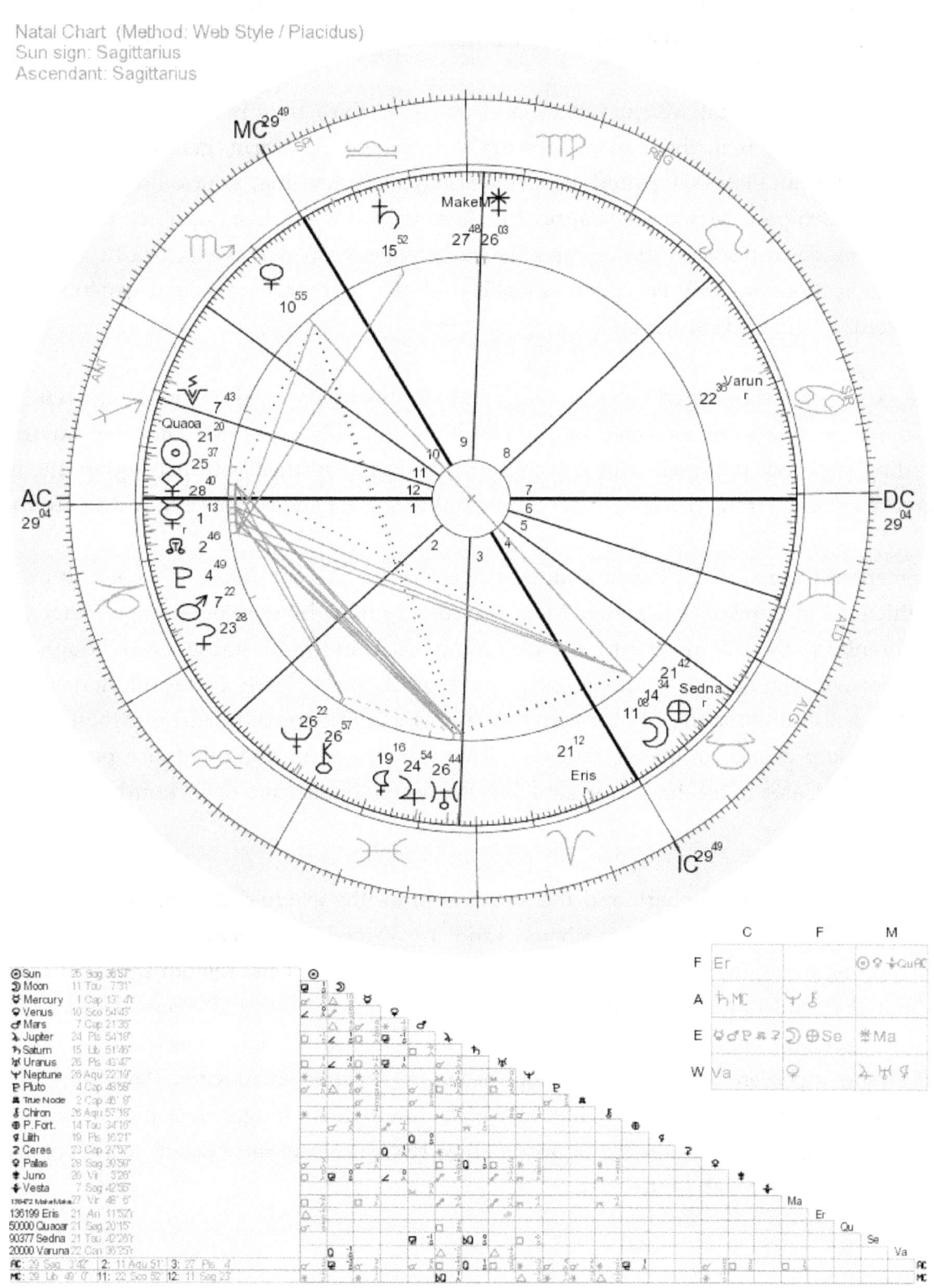

on the ascendant, the 7th house is loaded with complications that are impeding the relationship, including his Pluto in Capricorn dedication and loyalty to his teenagers from a previous marriage. (Scorpio on the cusp of derived 5th house with Vesta in the derived 5th house). Venus in detriment and Via Combust in his derived 4th house also affirms that this time, it really is the bitter end.

From a reception standpoint, Mercury, his significator, is in the sign of Jupiter's fall, and Jupiter, the querent's significator, is in the sign of Mercury's detriment. So warm, generous, idealizing and forgiving Jupiter in Pisces is paired up with stingy, withholding, controlling, inhibiting and uncommitted retrograde Mercury in Capricorn. There is clearly a lack of harmony; this is definitely not a match made in heaven. Jupiter rules the 12th house cusp with Vesta nearby, showing the querent's dedication was way beyond reasonable and her own forgiveness and generosity toward him contributed to her self-undoing.

Jupiter is conjunct and besieged between Lilith and Uranus in Pisces, showing the querent's revolt against the lousy treatment indicated by Jupiter ruling the 12th house. Mercury, her boyfriend, is retrograding back into detriment and will combust the Sun, and then both will square the Jupiter-Uranus conjunction. Fireworks, loss, misery, unhappiness, grief and sorrow abound all around.

The intercepted Capricorn 1st house stellium co-ruling the querent disposits to Saturn exalted in Libra, which is Via Combust *and* square Mars, the ruler of the 4th house of endings. What's helpful to the querent was the fact that Saturn is biquintiling Sedna in the 4th house, even though Sedna is a bit too close to Algol at the 5th house cusp for comfort. She's clearly better off alone so she can come to her senses and see the guy for who he really is, with no romantic ideals (Moon semisquare Jupiter), and stop chasing romantic fantasies. This is affirmed by the otherwise poorly aspected Jupiter sextiling Ceres in the 1st house, showing she needs to take care of and nurture herself from now on.

But the crown jewel of the chart, and the story, is Juno, the asteroid that represents committed relationships and problems within them. Juno in Virgo is quincunx the Neptune-Chiron conjunction, showing the pain involved in the disillusionment of the relationship and facing the reality that it would not be a permanent partnership as they'd originally hoped. Juno is highly afflicted in the chart, particularly through a T-square to the Sun-Pallas conjunction and midpoint, the ascendant, and Mercury, while opposing the Jupiter-Uranus conjunction. The T-square outlet leg is in the 6th house of day-to-day life, of which they will no longer be a part of each other's anymore. They have drifted apart and are leading two separate and entirely different lives, as shown by Gemini on the 6th house cusp.

There is no way out; the relationship is dead. Mars, her 4th house ruler, is applying to square Saturn, which is Mars' dispositor, and Venus is in detriment in his derivative 4th house of endings, sesquiquadrate Jupiter, her significator. Rest in peace.

The Moon in the 4th house is exalted by sign, dignified by house, and conjunct the Part of Fortune —ending the relationship was absolutely the best possible thing she could do. The Moon's last Ptolemaic aspect is a sextile to Uranus, while the Moon's last *true* aspect is a quincunx to Pallas in the 12th. The Uranus aspect played out as follows: Aquarius rules the 2nd house of moveable goods and Venus (Taurus Moon dispositor) is in the quesited's derived 4th house and ruling that house. The querent made a surprise visit to the quesited's home, and moved her stuff out. The Palladian adjustment was the acceptance that it really was the end and that the wise decision, though painful and sorrowful, was made and executed, and there would be no going back.

12 AN EVOLVING BODY OF WORK

"It's not about planets anymore, anyway." [1]
- Kathy Svitil, Lead Science Writer, Caltech

Astronomers are now expanding their knowledge of the solar system far faster than they can precisely define the objects that are being discovered.[2] Future discoveries will no doubt suggest new categories and further blur the boundaries of old ones.[3] The International Astronomical Union (IAU) may continue to reclassify objects as their knowledge advances, but that should only marginally affect astrologers. Though an object's precise astronomical definition is important to determine how to integrate a new discovery into astrological charts, the primary concern is the object's archetypical symbolism. And that is usually established via the mythological figure the object is named for.

What's in a Name?

According to NASA, once an object is discovered, it is given a provisional number (e.g., 2002 LM60 is now known as Quaoar; astronomers jokingly call these license plate numbers). Once it is permanently numbered (e.g., 50000 for Quaoar), it is eligible for naming. The International Astronomical Union (IAU) is responsible for the naming of astronomical objects, a mandate carried out for TNOs by its Committee on Small Body Nomenclature. This group has established several naming conventions for TNOs. All must be named for mythological characters. Objects in resonances with Neptune, like Pluto, are to be named for characters from underworld myths. Objects in low-inclination, low-eccentricity orbits, such as Quaoar, are named for characters from creation myths. Objects orbiting between Jupiter and Neptune are named for the hybrid Centaurs. A recent extension of this convention calls for using the names of other mythological hybrid creatures for objects that cross the orbits of both Neptune and Saturn.[4]

The IAU uses over 250 publications on mythology to source planetary names (See Appendix D). With many of the more familiar names from Greek and Roman mythologies already in use, there is now a cross-cultural expansion in IAU naming conventions beyond the Greco-Roman pantheon of creation and underworld naming conventions. Diverging from familiar Western myths allows for a more inclusive approach; to learn and understand the stories of other, sometimes distant and markedly different cultures. What's critical is to ensure that the meaning, symbolism and truth of those myths doesn't get lost in translation between cultures, since the symbolism is so primary for astrologers.

Due to sheer numbers, "Not all of the Kuiper belt objects known and numbered have names," says Mike Brown. "And I think most don't need them. It is okay to consign them to semi-anonymous license plate numbers if they are never really going to be thought about as more than one of the crowd. But a few special objects get studied and talked about and written about enough that need not so much just names, but also personalities."[5]

"Astrologers generally ascribe synchronicity and meaning to the name a planet is given," says astrologer Mitch Horowitz. "More than any other single factor, the founding myth behind how these planetary objects are named tends to color their perception in astrology."[6] More conscious than synchronous, astronomers put plenty of thought and research into naming the newly discovered objects. For example, dwarf planet 2007 OR10, known among its discovery team by its code name "Snow White," is still officially nameless as of this writing for one simple reason: "We have not yet proposed a real name for it, as we don't know enough to have a name with meaning," says its co-discoverer, Mike Brown.[7]

"We take naming objects in the solar system very carefully," adds Brown. "We've picked out the names for Quaoar (creation force of the Tongva tribe who live in Los Angeles), Orcus (the earlier Etruscan counterpart to Pluto, for an object that appears much like a twin of Pluto), Sedna (the Inuit goddess of the sea, for the coldest, most distant object at the time), and Eris (the Greek goddess of discord and strife, for the object that finally led to the demotion of Pluto). Each of these names came after considerable thought and debate, and each of them fit some characteristic of the body that made us feel that it was appropriate...Orcus and Sedna fit the character of the orbit of the body. Eris was so appropriate, it is enough to make me almost start believing in astrology. Quaoar was, we felt, a nice tribute to the fact that all mythological deities are not Greek or Roman. I enjoy, take seriously, and spend way too much time on this giving of names."[8]

TNOs: A New Astrological Way of Thinking

The TNOs are a whole new astrological arena that operates differently than the inner and outer solar system. And only now is the capacity being developed to understand and integrate something that is not even clearly understood by astronomers, let alone astrologers. Slowly and surely, the sense of order will reveal itself—but it won't be on our terms.

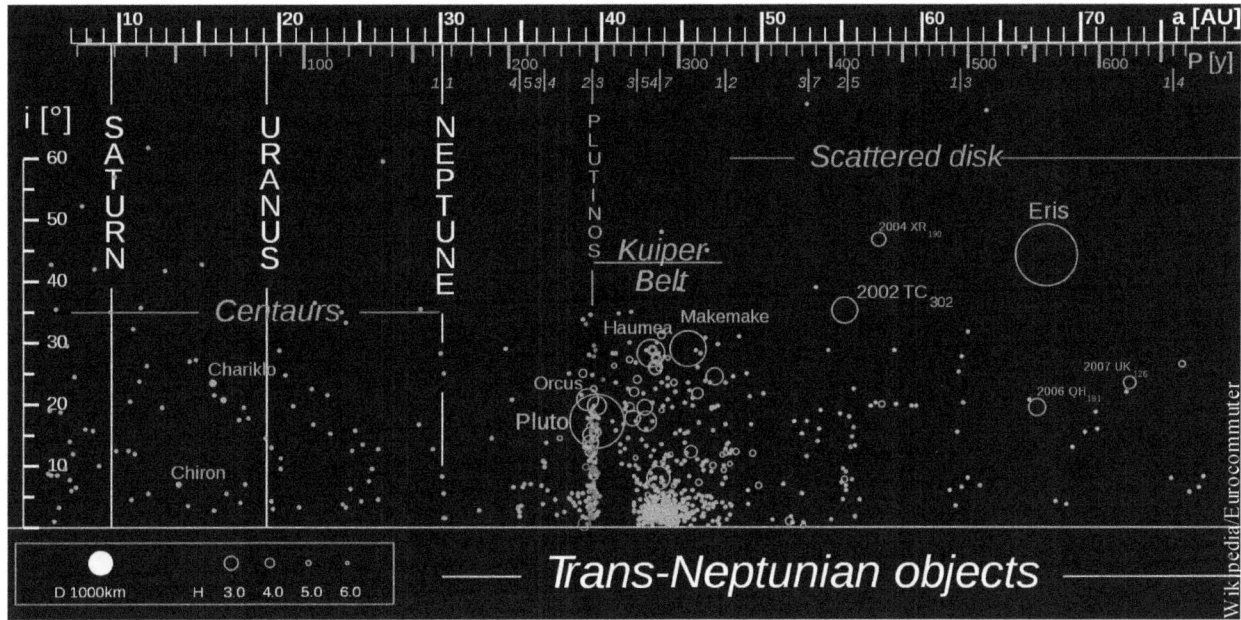

There are 20 named, non-Centaur TNOs in the solar system, with more eligible for and awaiting naming. TNOs are the last to be discovered, though they came first, at the birth of the Sun. They don't move far or quickly. Parked in one sign for centuries or a millennium, traditional horary concepts such as dignities, terms, faces, etc., are rendered completely meaningless. The TNOs are so far away physically, yet in the confines of a horoscope, they are every bit as pinpointedly personal as the inner and outer solar system planets. But the TNOs can't be thought of or utilized like the inner and outer solar system, because astrology cannot continue to be shoved into a one-size-fits-all Ptolemaic model. Like the astronomy it's based on, astrology must grow, change and evolve to accommodate new knowledge.

Asteroids and TNOs have demonstrated that objects do not need to rule or govern signs to be powerful and effective in either horary or natal charts. (Pluto, of course, being the leftover exception.) They have plenty of power and meaning in their own right, and assert it in particular via aspects, midpoints and house placement. The TNOs are an invitation to break all of the astrological rules because they are literally beyond them. "[The TNOs] show the orderly anarchy beyond Pluto," says Mike Brown.[9] Anarchy, from the Greek *anarchos*, means without leaders. This indicates the TNOs operate independently, without hierarchy, and with no need for rulerships—or rules for that matter. That's the stuff of the inner and outer solar system planets, not the trans-Neptunian solar system bodies. In their "orderly anarchy," the TNOs can still show strength or weakness, such as Eris does in Aries, her strongest placement according to her myth. How the TNOs connect and relate to the planets is very different than the way the planets relate among themselves. But despite their eccentricities, the TNOs integrate easily into horary interpretations, once their quirks are understood.

ASTROLOGICAL CHARACTERISTICS OF TNOs

- No glyphs yet.
- "Orderly anarchy"; symbolism matters most.
- Not collective, generational or transpersonal like Uranus, Neptune or Pluto have been ascribed; personal in specific, immutable ways.
- Changed astronomers' entire view of solar system and origins, and astrologers' ways of thinking about integration; do not fit into Ptolemaic astrological paradigms.
- Astrology software packages not yet advanced enough to integrate most of the current discoveries.
- No astrological ephemerides for TNOs centrally published yet, or integrated with standard Sun through Pluto ephemerides.
- Provide primary information on their own in a horary chart, not just supplemental or secondary detail to inner and outer solar system planets.
- Not like asteroids, nor entirely like planets. TNOs are a hybrid in that they are innumerable, larger than asteroids, and yet much smaller than planets, though they behave like planets and tend to have moons. Most TNOs are smaller than Earth's Moon (2,160 miles in diameter). Pluto, the largest known TNO, is only 1,466 miles in diameter, less than 1/4 of Earth's diameter.
- Don't reveal all of their full symbolism and application right away; not unusual as the ancients took centuries to piece together the complete symbolic meanings of the classical planets, fixed stars, etc.
- Can significantly overpower a significator, asteroid or inner/outer planet's stand-alone meaning, particularly if conjoined.
- TNOs rarely approach each other in human terms. House placement, and the interconnections via aspects and midpoints to asteroids and planets, activate and magnify them in a chart.
- Not cycle-oriented due to long and eccentric orbits. Many KBOs have "shockingly elongated" orbits like Sedna's.[10]
- TNOs don't combust the Sun in horary as inner/outer planets do. Instead, when close in orb to the Sun, the TNOs specific symbolism is intensely amplified. TNOs are as old as, and too far away from, the Sun for combustion to apply.
- Can be used for standalone interpretation, but are most optimized when connected to and used with the full solar system. TNOs are personal and pinpointedly specific in meaning on their own. They interconnect with the chart as a whole via aspect to significators, the Moon, midpoints, or asteroids, as well as house placement and dispositors.

- Except for Pluto, TNOs don't rule signs, or need to, in order to be meaningful or important. No dignities, and few debilities (i.e., retrogrades). Rulerships have no need or use in the trans-Neptunian solar system, as they symbolize entirely different astrological paradigms than the inner/outer solar system planets.
- Provide confirmation of judgment or outcome in horary.
- Many yet to be discovered due to current technology limitations.
- Long, often inclined or tilted, and elliptical orbits lift them off the ecliptic for long periods.
- Cross-cultural mythology and symbolism allows for greater inclusion, subtlety, nuance and richer detail within interpretations.
- There is a specific Native American symbolic link via Quaoar; a specific, symbolic South American link via Makemake; and a Hawaiian link via Haumea. These TNOs can be tied to horary questions with a geographic or cultural link to those places.

The new discoveries can easily be integrated into astrology in general and horary in particular. First become proficient with the inner and outer solar system planets (Sun through Neptune, and Pluto for old time's sake). Then, once you have that foundation and know what to look for in a chart, you can easily learn and add in the asteroids and TNOs. Certain TNOs may be more relevant to specific types of horary questions (i.e., relationships) than to others (finance). Like asteroids, they don't all have to be used at once, but the core group can be used regularly to provide primary information, deeper detail and assist with confirmation within your interpretations.

Using TNOs in Horary

Unlike natal astrology, with horary you don't have to wait more than half a century for an object like Sedna to transit a single sign to understand its meaning—combined with astronomical discovery research, horary's rapid resolutions make it easier to hone in on an object's use and meaning. Some astrologers take a conservative approach and want a long-term consensus of use, experience and interpretation for validation, based on decades (or longer) of observation. Depending on your skill level, this is not particularly necessary. Objects can be "recovered" in old horary case files where the outcome is known, and in event charts of well-documented historical events to examine cause and effect. (See Appendix G).

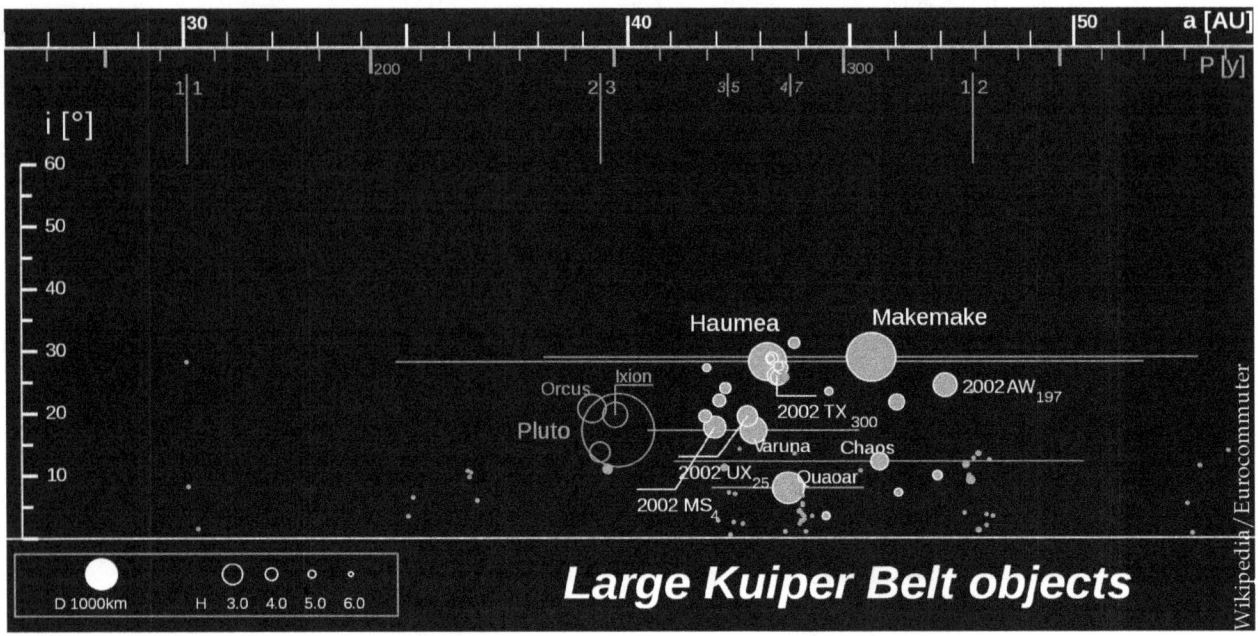

It's also possible to study the source myths once an object is named, contact and ask the discoverer for further clarity, read articles about the objects in newspapers, government space agency websites, astrophysics journals or other scientific magazines, or read the discovery white papers. All of these avenues provide enormous clues to the most accurate astrological symbolism and use. For example, due to Sedna's mysterious origins and elusiveness, her discovery team gave her the code name "Flying Dutchman" while compiling preliminary astronomical data about her. Upon their choosing the permanent name of Sedna, and comparing the two myths, the unintentional thematic similarities of isolation and an inability to return home contained within both are striking. And astrologically, in recovering Sedna in applicable natal charts and old horary case files where the outcome was long known, these themes resounded.

In using TNOs in horary, think bookended, simultaneous action: The planets (Sun through Neptune) lead from the front of the pack, while TNOs push from behind. The planets operate from the inside out, where the personal connects to the whole. TNOs work from the outside in, making the universal individual and personal. See what the TNOs are doing in their own right, then observe how it connects to what is happening in the rest of the chart. To do this, view them as standalone via house placement, then how or if they aspect other objects in the chart, particularly a significator. Then, check the aspects, midpoints and dispositors that connect them to the planets, and their influence on the specific situation. Finally, consider the Moon's aspects to them, as well as if the Moon's last true aspect involves a TNO.

Astronomers often don't have full and complete information on an object at the time of discovery or announcement, or even years later — they fill in the details as they become available through further research and study. Even several years after her discovery, Eris continues to give one of her co-discoverers fits, because she keeps defying his expectations of what she is, what she does, and how that affects the larger solar system: "Eris has gone from not really teaching us much new about the solar system, to potentially demanding that we throw out some of our most cherished assumptions." says Mike Brown.[11] Astrologically, it's no different.

Less than two decades since the Kuiper belt was discovered by astronomers, the TNOs are still a relatively new phenomenon to the astrological world. As a result, the symbolism and application below is only partially complete. This is not a problem, as traditional astrology took centuries to establish the classical planets' symbolic meanings. So even though the research is new and incomplete, there are specific details that are already known and proven. The keywords of symbolism available now will not be negated by the many that will come later with further research, integration, and widespread use. Using the TNOs provides primary information the planets alone can't, and synthesizes and affirms details in relation to the horary question. This keeps you from having to dig so deep to piece the story together. The TNOs, like asteroids, can determine, confirm, negate or underscore your conclusion. Following are the meanings of the larger known TNOs as gleaned from astronomical discovery research, natal, transit and progression work, and specific use obtained from recovery within old horary case files, as well as continued application within new horary questions.

* * * * *

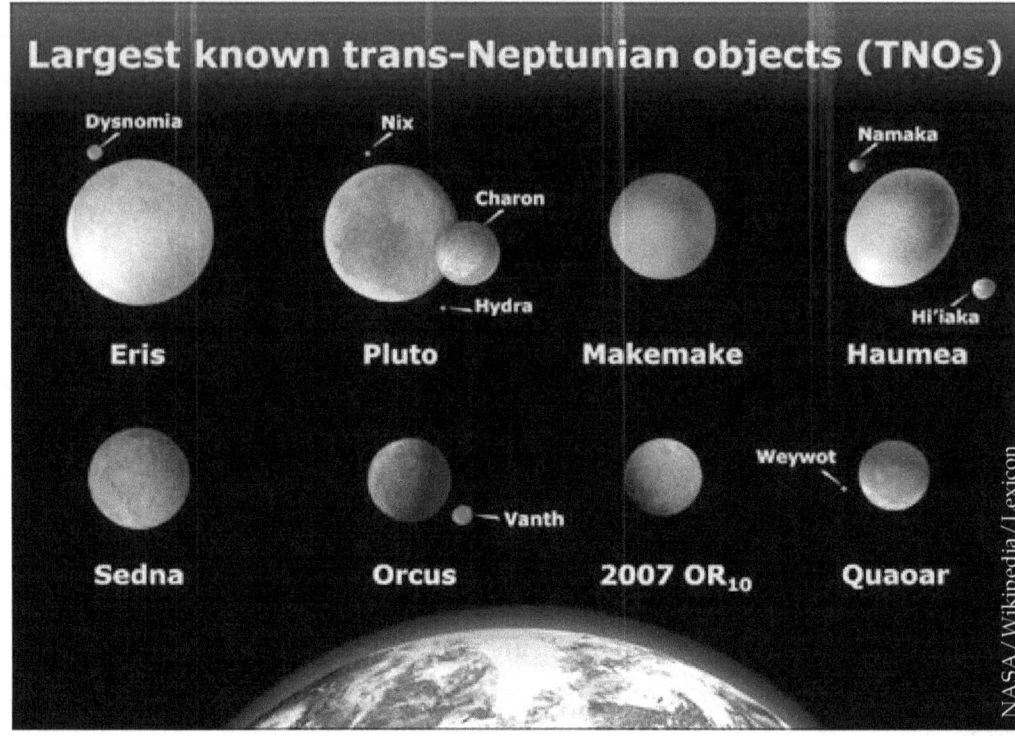

VARUNA

- **Cubewano (Classical KBO that orbits the Sun in circles; not controlled by orbital resonance with Neptune; does not cross Neptune's orbit)**
- **Orbital period: 283 years**
- **Discovered November 2000**

Varuna is named for the Hindu deity who presided over the waters of heaven and the ocean, as well as the guardian of immortality. He is often identified with Greek Poseidon and Roman Neptune, and is considered the god of oceans, rivers and rain. Varuna was a major Hindu deity until "replaced" by Indra. The myth states that Varuna upholds moral law and views and judges humanity and all the other gods, as he is omniscient, and therefore knows the complete truth of matters.[12]

In the divorce chart in Chapter 7, Varuna is conjunct the judge and the querent's significators in the 10th house, as well as Vesta, showing that the highest good and a fair settlement is assured. In the breakup chart in Chapter 11, Varuna is intercepted in the 7th house, quintiling its dispositor, the Moon in the 4th house. The integrity and respect was inhibited in the relationship at that point, further affirming it was time to end things (4th house).

As the Bette Midler song says, "God is watching us."[13] So is Varuna. In horary, look to Varuna for questions of truth, validity or integrity, such as "Is s/he lying?" or "Is this person the thief?" In the 3rd house, Varuna shows the truth and facts in a matter either by itself or via aspect to a significator or by disposition. If Varuna is conjunct Venus in the 9th in a relationship question, the querent will search for higher meaning through a personal relationship. If Varuna is in the 12th house, suffering as a result of telling the truth (e.g., a whistleblower) is possible, or that the truth of a situation may never be known.

QUAOAR

- **Cubewano (Classical KBO that orbits the Sun in circles; not controlled by orbital resonance with Neptune; does not cross Neptune's orbit)**
- **Discovered June 2002**
- **Orbital period: 286 years**
- **One moon: Weywot**

Pronounced KWAH-war, it is the first planetary name drawn from Native American traditions, rather than Greco-Roman antiquity. The Tongva are the native people of the area around Los Angeles, California, where the discovery of Quaoar was made, and it is named for the Tongva creator god.[14] Quaoar was the first TNO to be measured directly from Hubble Space Telescope images—it is about one billion miles farther than Pluto.[15]

Symbolically, Quaoar is the creative force that vanishes after its creation is complete. Astrologically, there is no harmful or malefic effect with Quaoar; its influence is benefic. Its symbolism is about the beginning and ending of matters, sometimes simultaneously. This is enormously informative when early degrees and late degrees of angles or significators aren't showing in the chart; it affirms and underscores it when they are. The old saying, "When one door closes, another one opens" is Quaoar at work. The house it's in shows where, and aspects and dispositors show whether it's a completion or a beginning.

Quaoar can be thought of as an astrological version of a sunset clause. It is a quick-shot of generative fuel for the beginning of any endeavor, and conversely, can show a fulfilled purpose and the end of a matter, based on the question rather than the degree of a sign. For example, in the divorce chart in Chapter 7, Quaoar is at 18 degrees of Sagittarius in the third house of documents. It was time to begin the divorce filing process (Quaoar in the 3rd) to destroy the marriage (Pluto in the 3rd with Quaoar). Quaoar can help offset the damage and destruction of Pluto by showing the "why" of a devastating or destructive event. It also can assist other KBOs in that manner.

In the breakup chart in Chapter 11, Quaoar is at 21 degrees of Sagittarius. It's part of a nasty T-square involving the querent's significator while conjunct the Sun (keep in mind TNOs are immune to combustion) in the 12th house, emphasizing the sorrowful ending as the life span of the relationship ended.

In addition to representing a vibrant beginning or a natural completion (or both), Quaoar can also show doing good in secret or from behind-the-scenes. Quaoar can also be used for U.S. Native American-related questions.

SEDNA

- **Detached object/scattered disc object (SDO)**
- **Discovered November 2003**
- **Orbital period: Estimated 12,000 years**
- **No Moons**

Sedna is too small, and its orbit too elliptical, for it to be considered a planet. It has been gravitationally battered around the outer solar system like a tennis ball.[16] Like Quaoar, Sedna represents another deviation from the Greco-Roman naming pantheon in favor of Native American traditions (Inuit). Its orbit never comes close to the planets in the solar system, and at its furthest point from the Sun, it can sit for centuries in a single sign. Thousands of years from now, when Sedna reaches its orbital elongation in the sign of Scorpio, it is estimated to remain there for roughly 1,500 years.[17]

Yale astronomer David L. Rabinowitz, a member of the Sedna discovery team, spoke of the intent behind the name:

> "The reason we chose the name Sedna is because the astronomical community has agreed that all the objects in the outer solar system should be named after characters from creation myths (or underworld figures if their orbits are coupled like Pluto's to Neptune). We might have chosen Greek or Roman gods, but they have all been used. So we looked at Inuit mythology. The Inuits are naturally familiar with the cold appropriate for distant planets. Sedna's association with the icy seas and sea creatures is also appropriate for the outer solar system since Uranus and Neptune are also associated with the ocean."[18]

"Myths like Sedna's demand we look at that which is bitter in life," says astrologer Mitch Horowitz. "Sedna is a goddess who harbors terrible wounds from anger and betrayal."[19] Sedna is "lonely and untouched," according to one of her three co-discoverers, Mike Brown.[20]

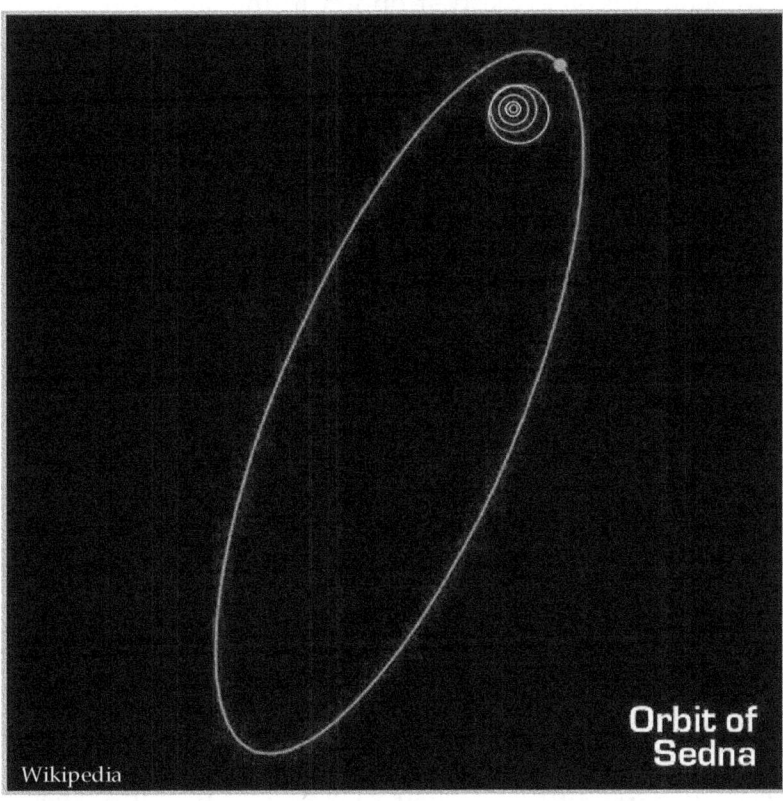

Fig. 12.4: The interior, round circles are the Sun-Pluto solar system. The outer loop is Sedna's orbit. The dot is her current position. See also: http://bit.ly/lbqRW6

Astrologically, Sedna is anti-relationship by nature, because of mishandling and mistrust, especially by those closest to her. She is angry, bitter and alone, and her aloneness is due to circumstances rather than choice. Sedna in a chart points to suffering endured at the hands of other people; the planets involved show in what ways. With Saturn in the 2nd, it will be due to lack of money; if opposing Venus, relationships. Sedna represents an abandoned outcast and a life damaged and ruined at the hands of other people, especially men, in a woman's chart. There are victims in this world, and Sedna is one of them. Sedna is powerless to fight back against her oppressors or have a say in her own fate. She symbolizes misery, loneliness, betrayal, abuse, and suffering. She is alone, forsaken, and can never go home. There is no New-Agey, positive thinking to explain away the suffering she's been dealt, or turn it into something triumphant, transcendental or heroic. Sedna is the un-Hollywood, unhappy ending. Her house placement, and aspects to other objects in the chart, show how the person copes, for better or for worse.

In horary, Sedna will depict loneliness in relationship charts. If well aspected, the loneliness and isolation can be put to good use or is the best option in the situation. In other types of horary questions, she'll amplify the bitterness and "raw deal" of a situation, or show "damaged goods." Use Sedna to represent child abuse and battered women in a horary chart, especially if the Moon and Ceres are involved. In a marriage election chart, keep Sedna out of angular houses, particularly the 4th and 7th, and preferably unaspected to significators. Sedna in the 4th house of real estate can indicate an abandoned or damaged building or property. Appropriately, her symbolism is at home in Pisces and the 12th house.

ORCUS

- **Resonant Kuiper Belt Object (Orbits twice around the Sun for every three solar orbits made by Neptune)**
- **Discovered February 2004**
- **Orbital period: 247 years**
- **One moon: Vanth**

This KBO is Pluto's doppelganger—its orbit is constrained to always be in the opposite phase of Pluto's orbit: Orcus is at aphelion (furthest distance away from the Sun) when Pluto is at perihelion (closest to the Sun) and vice versa. Because of this, Orcus has been called the anti-Pluto.[21]

According to one of Orcus' three co-discoverers, Mike Brown: "Several years ago, when searching for a name for what was then known only as 2004 DW, we decided to concentrate on the anti-Pluto aspect of the object's personality, and we came up with Orcus. In the version of the Orcus myth that I like to tell, Orcus was, essentially, the early Etruscan grim reaper, collecting the dead and bringing them to the underworld where another god, Pluto, ruled. As the Etruscan mythology was incorporated into Roman mythology and blended with Greek mythology, Orcus lost his separate identity and Pluto became the master of all of the functions of the dead. Orcus became in some ways simply an alternate name for Pluto, but it also remained a slightly more evil and punishing incarnation of Pluto. In that incarnation, the Latin word Orcus was the origin of words such as ogre and orc."[22]

"In my new mythological/astronomical view, Pluto, the Kuiper belt object, is now named after that earlier version of Pluto, before the Romans came along and swept everything together. And Orcus is his counterpart, destined to eventually be pushed aside by the rising Pluto. Orcus seemed a very appropriate name for this new object in the Kuiper belt." [23]

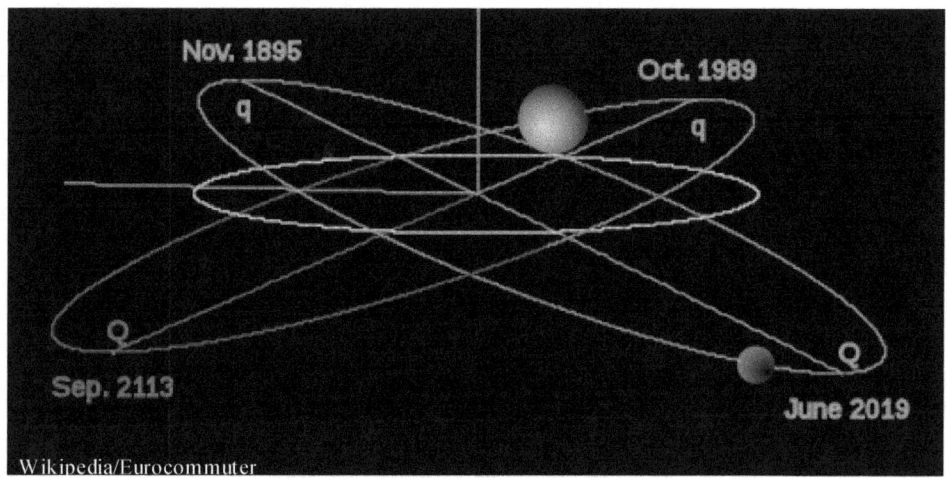

Fig. 12.5: Orbits of Orcus and Pluto as of April 2006
Orcus at far right; Pluto toward center; Neptune in center shown as a circle to represent the ecliptic. Perihelia (q) and Aphelia (Q) with dates of passage.

In a horary chart, use both Orcus and Pluto together rather than individually, and think of them as two sides of the same coin. Orcus is simultaneously overt when Pluto is covert, and vice versa; the houses they are located in will determine in what area. They represent the discovery and resolution of the dichotomy of intent (the stated goal) and outcome (the actual result, often in spite of the stated goal) in relation to the matter inquired about. In other words, they show the difference between what a querent says they want, and what they really want. Mundanely, Orcus and Pluto can show an intense and long-drawn-out rivalry or power struggle between two people, companies, or even nations.

In a political horary question about health care reform, angular Pluto in Capricorn in the 1st house is overt, while Orcus in Virgo in the cadent 9th house is covert. This signifies a clear disconnect between what the person is publicly espousing (Pluto in the 1st), versus what he actually believes (Orcus in the 9th). Conversely, in a relationship question, such as "Should I break up with my girlfriend?", Pluto in the succedent 5th house is covert, while Orcus in the angular 1st house is overt. Orcus in the 1st in Virgo may show the outward, practical and logical reasons why a split is desirable, such as moving away to college. But Pluto in the 5th is literally the dead giveaway, showing the querent's real intent is to sow some wild oats and outright cheat on his partner. Orcus and Pluto's relationship to the chart significators, Moon, dispositors, Juno and Venus' aspects to both Orcus and Pluto, as well as Juno and Venus' dispositors, would determine which scenario will prevail.

If either Orcus or Pluto are positively aspected with a significator, what one is destroying, the other is offering an alternative or way out. What one wants to keep buried, the other wants to dredge up. If harshly aspected, the two show the difficulty of taking the way out, or what's preventing it. House position and aspects reveal why, as well as midpoints. Transits of a significator to the Orcus-Pluto midpoint can catalyze unforeseen complications if the aspect is harsh, and power and tenacity if well-aspected.

HAUMEA

- **Dwarf planet**
- **Discovered December 2004**
- **Orbital period: 283 years**
- **Two moons: Hi'iaka and Namaka**

The dwarf planet Haumea is another TNO named outside of the Greco-Roman mythologies. Named for the matron goddess of Hawaii, Haumea is a goddess of fertility and childbirth, whose children broke off from different parts of her body. Splintered ice debris from an impact to Haumea is thought to have formed her two moons.[24] Haumea completes one rotation on its axis every four hours (fastest in the solar system), resulting in a bizarre, oblong, cigar-like shape. Haumea was shrouded in international controversy over which astronomy team was her rightful discoverer.[25]

In horary, Haumea is benefic and represents things that are fragmented, breaking apart, or splintering off to form something new. This can include things that are splintered or fractured (whether a relationship or circumstances); things in pieces but not scattered; quirkiness, as well as disputes or controversy over the origin or beginning of something. It is a creative fragmentation, rather than destructive one, similar to plant grafting or propagation. Haumea can also be used as a significator in Hawaii-related questions, such as, "Should we take the trip to Maui?" Haumea can also indicate a birth of either a person or matter under strange or controversial circumstances.

In the third house, Haumea represents missing pieces or facts in a situation; look to her aspects and dispositor to see exactly what. In the 8th house, she can show tax shelters spread all over the world, or an inheritance legacy split among many heirs (and the subsequent factions squabbling about it). In the 10th house, particularly with Saturn, Haumea can depict multiple corporate subsidiaries, and if squaring Pluto, their hidden assets.

If Haumea is connected to Quaoar by either aspect or midpoint, it indicates a profound emphasis toward a benevolent change and an entirely new set of circumstances or whole new way of life as a result of the breaking away. In the divorce election chart in Chapter 7, Haumea plays prominently, as she is conjunct the ascendant and sextiling Quaoar in Sagittarius in the 3rd house, indicating filing the legal documents (3rd house, Sagittarius) to facilitate the breakup (Haumea) easily (sextile) for the querent to rebuild his life anew (Pluto at zero Capricorn). But more importantly, the Haumea-Quaoar sextile eases the Moon-Venus quincunx to Quaoar, with Quaoar quincunxing the midpoint of the Moon-Venus conjunction, which required emotional adjustments to different strategies as new legal developments in the case unfolded (i.e., mediations rather than a trial) which would ultimately benefit the querent. The sextile gave the querent faith (Sagittarius) that things would work out well in the long run, despite the planetary skirmishes in the chart and difficulties inherent in the throes of a divorce.

Quaoar in turn, takes the sting out of the Moon-Venus square to Haumea, with Orcus at Regulus and sitting on the Moon-Venus/Haumea midpoint, showing the hugely beneficial and permanent life change he is making, and mitigating the pain via the support of friends (11th house). Based on the election chart, no matter what bumps in the road he hit, either personally or in the legal process, things would largely work in his favor, and a more fulfilling future lay ahead. From a personal standpoint, these configurations show that the querent was clearly finished with the marriage (Orcus and Quaoar) and had no regrets, but only positive and hopeful feelings about his decision and the future. He understood from the election chart that time and the process were on his side. (The entire chart could be interpreted accurately and tell the full story using just the TNOs alone, or the TNOs and only the Moon and Venus as significators, since they rule the querent.)

ERIS

- **Dwarf planet**
- **Discovered January 2005**
- **Orbital period: 556 years**
- **One Moon: Dysnomia**

"She wasn't the 10th planet as she was originally thought to be, but instead the killer of the 9th," says Mike Brown, one of Eris' three co-discoverers.[26] The Roman goddess of strife and discord, Eris caused Pluto's reclassification to dwarf planet status via IAU Resolutions B5 and B6 (See Appendix E). But she was hardly finished there. The controversy over the rightful discoverer of Haumea forced Brown's team to prematurely announce the discovery of Eris and Makemake on the same day to keep from getting scooped again. So she's had a direct impact on all of the named dwarf planets so far except Ceres.

Pluto was the biggest malefic astrologically until Eris' discovery—if she can get a planet reclassified, imagine the havoc she can wreak in a horary chart! Eris, the ancient consort of Mars, ignited the discord that started the Trojan War. Astrologically, Eris will always show where there's strife, discord and trouble; in other words, peace and harmony will be unattainable, as some sort of troublesome difficulty will be consistently lurking in the background to destabilize matters. Even nicely aspected, she's still going to cause problems. She will disrupt even the best-laid plans and intentions far more directly and personal than Mars, Uranus and Pluto combined (she doesn't need their help). Eris is strong in Aries, and almost overbearing when aspected with with Mars and Pluto, but is weak in Libra or with Venus and Jupiter. For example, Eris with Mars means serious damage will be inflicted and heads will roll in the matter as mayhem prevails. Eris with Venus shows no happiness will be found in a relationship, as the person signified will be impossible to please or prefer someone else entirely. Her location and aspects in a horary chart indicate where one will find trouble, quite literally. If well-aspected, the strife is still there, but as a "necessary evil" as part of achieving a larger goal. Use Eris in *all* horary charts, not just specific types of questions. And by all means, keep her out of the house-ruled matter in *all* electional charts.

MAKEMAKE

- **Dwarf planet**
- **Discovered March 2005**
- **Orbital period: 310 years**
- **No moons**

Pronounced MAH-kay MAH-kay, this dwarf planet was named for a creator god of Rapa Nui, the Chilean territory off the coast of South America better known as Easter Island. Pluto's discoverer, Clyde Tombaugh, could have discovered Makemake had it been located anywhere but where it was at the time of his observations—obscured by the dense background of stars of the Milky Way galaxy.[27] Instead, true to one of its symbolic keywords, it incubated until its discovery 75 years later.

Makemake is a powerful but subtle, subdued and somewhat obtuse archetype. It represents an incubation period prior to a new direction or beginning. It's the five steps backward before the ten steps forward. It's the delicate regrowth shortly after a forest fire. It's the space between the inhale and the exhale. It symbolizes a pause, or isolation, retreat or obscurity prior to growth and renewal, but not in a 12th house endings/confinement/sorrow way at all; it's more of a 5th-8th house, creativity brewing deeply and behind-the-scenes archetype. Makemake symbolizes transition, and also depicts situations that are fragile and delicate.

Just as houses can sometimes signify opposite qualities (e.g., the 7th house rules both marriage and divorce), Makemake does so as well. It symbolizes a wipeout, desolation or something heavily denuded where something once thrived (visualize strip mining or logging). It is the phase between Uranus or Pluto's violence and destruction, and Haumea or Quaoar's beginning. It can also show a situation where there is nothing to be gained. For example, Makemake conjunct Juno is a denuded relationship, with nothing left to it but emptiness (See the breakup chart in Chapter 11). In the divorce election chart in Chapter 7, Makemake is in the querent's 12th house and squaring Mars, the significator of his soon-to-be ex-wife. It literally symbolizes the legal (9th house) severance (Mars) of the empty, desolate marriage (Makemake), and the legal hassle of doing so. Makemake is also quincunxing Chiron in the chart, showing the querent's need to retreat and withdraw (Makemake in the 12th house) to heal (Chiron).

Makemake in the 6th house of a job chart can show unfulfilling work. Harshly aspecting the Moon in the 5th house can indicate an abortion or an empty, desolate childhood. Aspected to the Moon or Neptune, it can show a person living in a dead and distant past, reminiscing about a way of life that no longer exists. Aspected with Venus, it can show "the way things never were" in a relationship. Trining Mercury or Jupiter, a plethora of new ideas can flow forth. Makemake in the 2nd house can show a total financial wipeout, and the time it takes to retreat and come up with a new business plan. Via harsh aspects to the Moon, Makemake can show emotional emptiness from an ordeal. Harshly aspected with Saturn it can indicate desolation; in what manner will be symbolized by the house it occupies and the signs the two planets are in. Makemake opposing a significator in the 8th can show an unprofitable partnership. In a more mundane sense, it can also be linked to questions involving the Easter holiday, Chilean culture, or South America in general (e.g., "Should we travel to Peru this fall?").

CENTAURS: A Hybridized Experience

The Centaurs are asteroid-like bodies that orbit the Sun between Jupiter and Neptune, and represent an experience of conflicted duality. Most of life is not black and white or one-dimensional, and these archetypes reveal those gray areas of existence and experience in a horary chart.

Within the horary question posed, Centaurs often depict a dichotomy (i.e., two sides of the same coin) and a dynamic, often painful incongruency between two opposing qualities. For example, Chiron is a wounded healer. Pholus can show painful self-sacrifice for the greater good; Nessus, something that appears trustworthy but isn't, as well as vengeance under the guise of benevolence. Ixion can show where a person lets opportunity slip away from them because of their own improper behavior and passions out of control. The female Centaur, Chariklo, symbolizes anti-denial, or the willingness to look evenly at what's unpleasant for the sake of wisdom, to see or go where angels fear to tread, as well as a reluctant visionary.

For horary questions where there is an internal conflict of opposites (e.g., taking a job just to pay the bills or for security, when the true desire is to branch out as an entrepreneur), the Centaurs can help dissect the specifics of the cause—and show where to look for resolution.

Light Years Away: The Future of Horary & Astrology

In 2015, NASA's New Horizons satellite's five-year mission to the Kuiper belt will begin returning a wealth of data to astronomers, and possibly facilitate the discovery of more objects. It's time to prepare to adjust to and accommodate the new information accordingly. Eventually, new discoveries will be integrated into paradigms, both personal and collective, that aren't even established yet. This is not unusual—could people who grew up in an era of sending telegrams ever anticipate anything like cell phones and the Internet? So astrologers can be secure in knowing that more growth and revisions to theory, technique and interpretation are on the way. This is a blessing, not a curse.

Astronomical discoveries are only limited by the lack of sufficient technology to locate what's out there. After all, one can only see so far with a telescope from Earth, and orbiting telescopes such as Hubble and New Horizons have range and life-span limits. When the technologies improve, the discoveries will increase. And the more we discover and understand, the more astrology will subsequently integrate the new archetypes and symbolism. "The moment a new entity is observed or discovered, it enters the collective psyche," says astrologer Erin Sullivan. "The advent of a new planet…is always preceded by sudden advances in psychology and technology and followed by huge leaps in the social/global arena."[28]

To grow and evolve, astrologers will have to move the art toward the future and the unknown, and redefine and reinvent it accordingly. The future of astrology, horary or otherwise, will never be found in a dead and antiquated past, in long-forgotten texts. It's in a universe and solar system we have yet to know, reunited with its long-lost, runaway son, astronomy. The future of one is linked to new discoveries by the other.

Astrology's future circa the late 21st, and even 22nd centuries, will be something as yet unimaginable. In the near future though, as younger generations familiar with the full solar system take an interest in astrology, horoscopes linking the inner planets to the TNOs, and maybe objects in the Oort cloud eventually, will be the norm. What does that say about where humanity will be in consciousness when that happens? How will that alter interpretations? What will charts reflect when newly-discovered objects only move a few degrees (or less) in a lifetime, or even a generation? What happens when *multiple* generations possess a certain object in a specific sign or degree? Will that make house placement the most significant factor since it's the most changeable?

In horary charts, is it wise to use TNOs alone or with just a couple of significators and midpoints? Or does using the full solar system as a whole, rather than its individual pieces, yield the best answers? It's worth experimenting to find out. But we're not there yet. The software to generate the charts isn't there yet, but it will come in time. As we catch up. And as the astronomers catch us up.

"On the day of the discovery [of Haumea], we knew absolutely nothing..." says Mike Brown. "In the years since, we've learned a tremendous amount, and things were beginning to make sense. We had moved from exploration to explanation."[29] Astrologers would do the art, and their clients, a tremendous service to do likewise.

"The outer planets...Pluto, Chiron, Sedna, Eris and other bodies just being discovered, move slowly," says Michael Lutin. "They influence our personal evolution and move us in directions we often find it difficult, and even impossible, to comprehend. Their purpose is to awaken us to higher meaning, our purpose and our understanding of what we are here to learn and experience, which is sometimes a great big pain in the ass. It's not correct to think of planets or their influences as 'good' or 'bad.' It's all part of the trip through this world, which is sometimes a great big pain in the ass. But when the planets are aligned in more favorable configurations, oh, those moments of joy. It makes it all worth it."[30]

We're always looking for greater control in our daily lives, and yet we have less of it than we think.[31] In many ways we are still at the mercy of our reptilian brains, full of desire, competition and violence rather than cooperation and egalitarianism. Astrology can't change that. But as long as people look to astrology to find answers to help them cope with their pain, or encourage them to realize their greatest wishes and hopes, good and great astrologers will always be in need.

EPILOGUE - Beyond Astrology

Q: "A famous astrologer and composer, Dane Rudhyar, who was a friend of George Gurdjieff, said, 'The old idea of astrology—that experience happens to human beings—is not true. On the contrary, human beings happen to their experience.' My observation is that every astrologer who is courageous enough will find out that Gurdjieff is right when he says, 'Man is a machine.'"[1]

A: "George Gurdjieff is right when he says that man is a machine, but by MAN he means all those who are living unconsciously, who are not aware, who are not awake, who do not respond to reality but only react. Ninety-nine point nine percent of human beings come in the category of machines. With these machines, astrology is possible."

"In fact, predictions can be made, guarantees can be issued only about machines. A watch can be guaranteed for five years, a car can be guaranteed for a certain time because we know the capacity of the machine, how much it can work, how long it can go. Its scope is limited. And it cannot do anything on its own, it can only react to situations—which are almost predictable."

"If you are enlightened, then astrology cannot function for you. Then you can love, then you can do, then you can act, then you have a certain mastery over your own being. But unconscious, you are just moving hither and thither as the wind blows. And anybody who has studied human nature deeply...There are many astrological schools that have studied for centuries how the mechanical man works. They have come to certain conclusions, and their conclusions are almost always correct. If they are incorrect, that means the astrologer is not well prepared, his studies in human nature and unconscious behavior are not complete. But the moment you start becoming conscious, you start becoming really a human being—not a machine."[2]

— Osho
from "Destiny, Freedom and the Soul"

APPENDIX A – Modern Horary's Public Body of Evidence

PART I - Books on Symbolism & Meanings of the Outer Planets

Cosmic Trends	Philip Brown
Healing Pluto Problems	Donna Cunningham
Focus on Neptune	Virginia Elenbaas
Focus on Pluto	Virginia Elenbaas
The Book of Pluto: Turning Darkness to Wisdom with Astrology	Steven Forrest
Pluto, Volume I: The Evolutionary Journey of the Soul	Jeffery Wolf Green
The Astrological Neptune and the Quest for Redemption	Liz Greene
The Astrology of Fate [This book is about Pluto]	Liz Greene
The Outer Planets & Their Cycles: The Astrology of the Collective	Liz Greene
Hades Moon	Judy Hall
Revolutionary Spirit: Exploring the Astrological Uranus	Haydn Paul
Visionary Dreamer: Exploring the Astrological Neptune	Haydn Paul
Phoenix Rising: Exploring the Astrological Pluto	Haydn Paul
The Gods of Change: Pain, Crisis, and the Transits of Uranus, Neptune, and Pluto	Howard Sasportas
Prometheus the Awakener [This book is about Uranus]	Richard Tarnas
Alive & Well with Neptune, Transits of Heart & Soul	Bill Tierney
How To Personalize the Outer Planets: The Astrology of Uranus, Neptune & Pluto	Noel Tyl

PART II - Books About Modern Horary Astrology

A Modern Scientific Textbook on Horary Astrology with Authentic Charts and Predictions	Geraldine Davis
Art of Horary Astrology in Practice	Sylvia Delong
Contest Charts	Doris Chase Doane
Modern Horary Astrology	Doris Chase Doane
Cosmic Loom	Dennis Elwell
Simplified Horary Astrology	Ivy M. Goldstein-Jacobson
Handbook Of Horary Astrology	Karen Hamaker-Zondag
Electional Astrology: The Art of Timing	Joann Hampar
Horary Astrology: Practical Techniques for Problem Solving with a Primer of Symbolism	Marc Edmund Jones
Horary at Its Best	Alphee Lavoie
Horary Lectures	Alphee Lavoie
Lose this Book...and Find it with Horary	Alphee Lavoie
Horary Astrology	Alan Leo
Horary Astrology Plain & Simple	Anthony Louis
The Only Way to Learn Horary & Electional Astrology - Vol. VI	Marion March & Joan McEvers
Consultation Chart: A Guide to What It Is and How to Use It	Wanda Sellar
Horary Aspects & Techniques	Dona Shaw
Analysis and Prediction Vol. VIII, Case Studies in Prediction Horary and Electional Astrology	Noel Tyl

PART III - Modern Horary Case Studies

The majority of Diana Stone's online case studies are available at
http://www.astrologyguild.com/jupiterpage.htm
(Use your browser's "find" feature to search for her name on the page.)

Below is a brief index with URLs to specific cases.

Horary 1	A twist of fate. (http://www.astrologyguild.com/horaryfirst.htm)
Horary 2	The client who found out more than he wanted to know. (http://www.astrologyguild.com/horary2.htm)
Horary Letters	Regarding Horary 2 column. (http://www.astrologyguild.com/horaryletters.htm)
Horary 3	A woman asks: Should I buy the house? And what can happen when you ignore the answer. (http://www.astrologyguild.com/horary3.htm)
Horary 4	Should I see Dad...? (http://www.astrologyguild.com/horary4.htm)
Horary 5	Change doctors & Have hysterectomy? (http://www.astrologyguild.com/horary5.htm)
Horary 6	A 22year old question finally answered. (http://www.astrologyguild.com/horary6.htm)
Horary 7	Missing Book Where is it? (http://www.astrologyguild.com/horary7.htm)
Horary 8	Should I see the same Dentist? Sometimes we don't know why the answer is YES. (http://www.astrologyguild.com/horary8.htm)
Horary 9	There is no Horary 9; it was a miscalculation by the webmaster.
Horary 10	Will Maria be deported? (http://www.astrologyguild.com/horary10.htm)
Horary 11	Hire housekeepers? (http://www.astrologyguild.com/horary11.htm)
Horary 12	Continuing with Business involvement? (http://www.astrologyguild.com/horary12.htm)

Horary 13	Should I sign the lease? (http://www.astrologyguild.com/horary13.htm)
Horary 14	Horse Trainer Question. (http://www.astrologyguild.com/horary14.htm)
Horary 15	Is the Astrologer ever wrong? (http://www.astrologyguild.com/horary15.htm)
Horary 16	Whose chart is this anyway? (http://www.astrologyguild.com/horary16.htm)
Horary 17	Is Sally substantially guilty? A question of guilt or innocence. (http://www.astrologyguild.com/horary17.htm)
Horary 18	Should Mike buy the House? (http://www.astrologyguild.com/horary18.htm)
Horary 19	Collect Social Security? (http://www.astrologyguild.com/horary19.htm)
Horary 20	What is the outcome of visiting Bob in person? (http://www.astrologyguild.com/horary20.htm)
Horary 21	Buy a House? (http://www.astrologyguild.com/horary21.htm)
Horary 22	Should I sell this house? (http://www.astrologyguild.com/horary22.htm)
Horary 23	Will I ever get my old job back? (http://www.astrologyguild.com/horary23.htm)
Horary 24	Should we move to Helena to be near my daughter? (http://www.astrologyguild.com/horary24.htm)
Horary 25	Man asks: Should I pursue the relationship with Amelia? (http://www.astrologyguild.com/horary25.htm)
Horary 26	Should I rent the apartment? (http://www.astrologyguild.com/horary26.htm)
Horary 27	Will I be able to stay in contact with Roger? (http://www.astrologyguild.com/horary27.htm)
Horary 28	Will I be attending father's funeral in six months? (http://www.astrologyguild.com/horary28.htm)
Horary 29	Is the rumor true? (http://www.astrologyguild.com/horary29.htm)
Horary 30	David asks: Should I pursue a business relationship with XYZ Co.? (http://www.astrologyguild.com/horary30.htm)

The Author's Selected Modern Horary Case Study Transcripts

The following selection of case studies are real-time transcripts of querent interpretations with outcomes. This allows you to see the astrologer-querent interaction in its most raw form, warts and all. It's honest and authentic, more so than the carefully edited and polished case studies that are written up retroactively in horary texts after the outcome is already known.

In many cases, querents with astrological experience provided the chart and defaulted their preferences within.

Case Study #1:	Regulus & Spica can't overcome an opposition to Neptune.
Case Study #2:	Saturn in the 7th isn't a stricture against judgment in a relationship question—it's a wealth of information.
Case Study #3:	Pluto knows a shady car deal when it sees one.
Case Study #4:	Self-delusion over a bad living situation is narrowly averted by a Neptune-Uranus mutual reception.
Case Study #5:	A retrograde significator and outer planet T-square delay retirement.
Case Study #6:	A late degree ASC & Moon conjunct Uranus Rx causes high anxiety, but points to staying the course.
Case Study #7:	Use reality and geography when applying significators to a relocation chart.
Case Study #8:	Debilitated Venus opposing Sedna leaves a very bitter aftertaste in a long-dead relationship.
Case Study #9:	Career woes under the regime.
Case Study #10:	Pluto kills a business, while Venus brings a new opportunity.
Case Study #11:	When the astrologer totally and completely gets it WRONG!
Case Study #12:	The outer planets collude extensively to foil a house sale over the course of several months.
Case Study #13:	A Big Change looms at 29 degrees.

160 Open Source Modern Horary Astrology

Case Study #1: Regulus & Spica can't overcome an opposition to Neptune

Planets always trump fixed stars. Always.

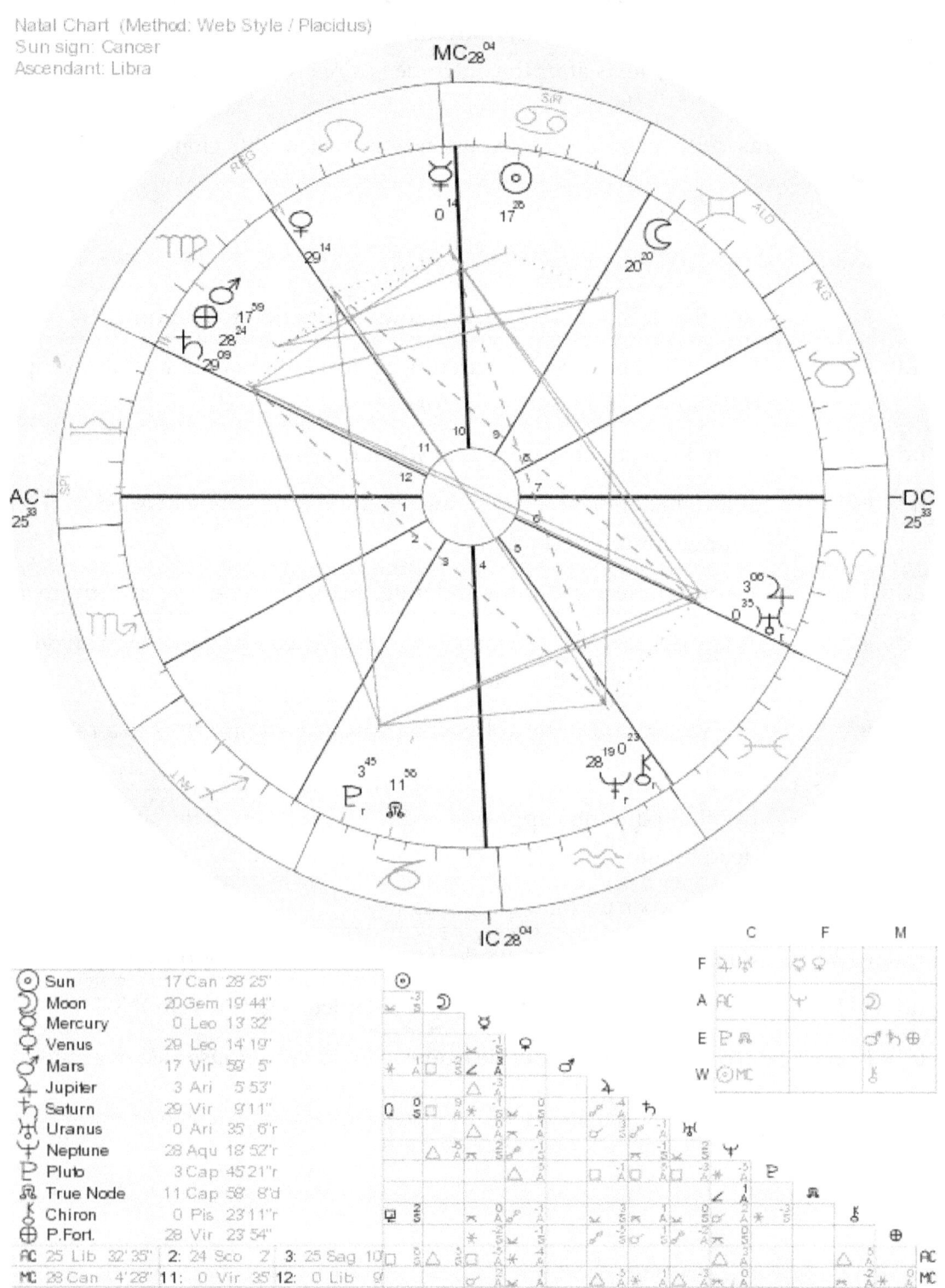

QUERENT: This afternoon I got phone call with a surprise job offer. I've never applied to this job and they got to me because of some languages that I speak and on first look this job seems exciting but I don't know much about it yet. I will give them call back later but first I wanted to see how it looked in the stars.

R.K. ALEXANDER: Be careful with this because although the benefic fixed stars are nice and wonderful, it's the planets who are the "stars" of the show. Fixed stars are the lipstick/nail polish at best—they aren't the entire outfit! They only add mild, minor color to what the planets are doing.

In this chart, yes, Venus, your ruler is at Regulus, but you have to note immediately that it is opposing Neptune in the 4th house of outcomes, showing that you aren't looking at the situation realistically. This is further emphasized by the fact that Mercury is in fall at 0° degrees Leo in the 10th/career, showing that you literally know almost nothing about the situation/offer (zero degrees) that you are wildly enthused (Leo) about. The Mercury trine to Uranus shows the unexpected call from literally out of the blue.

The Moon rules the career/10th and is in Gemini, indicating the linguistic skills. The only remaining aspects it makes before going void-of-course is a trine to Neptune in the 4th of outcome, and then a square to Saturn, ruler of the 4th house of outcome. (Your ruler Venus refranates into Virgo before the Moon can get to it, so things may fall through with the whole deal.)

The Moon's last aspect, the square to Saturn in your 11th house of hopes/wishes, may indicate that the more realistic you are about this and the more facts you find out about it (Saturn in Virgo, again, with Mercury in fall), the less glamorous (Neptune) the whole thing will be. Don't be led into a Moon/Neptune trap: something that looks to be more than it really is, or have false promises that get made and never kept. You might want to make sure the company is totally legit, and get everything in writing up front from them. They probably won't like that, and if they balk, that should raise some red flags for you. Again, Venus opposing Neptune at Regulus reinforces this and may mean that you'll be lucky (Regulus) to walk away from something that looks like more than it really is (Neptune).

With your ruler Venus refranating from the Moon and with the Moon's last aspect a square to Saturn ruling your 4th house, I think you will change your mind the more you find out about this deal and will walk away somewhat disappointed, having pre-built it up in your mind so much ahead of time before knowing the facts of the situation. The reality of what they are offering will not meet up with your hopes/wishes (11th) or fantasies (Neptune) of it, despite their attempts to convince you otherwise (Moon trine Neptune). In sum, look before you leap, be realistic, and get all of your facts and figures up front before moving forward with this.

They'll want you to be sure, but it's probably not in your best interests as they may pull a bait and switch on you (Neptune) by promising you things and once they have you, giving you a sour Saturn deal in reality once you're hooked (Saturn on the 12th house cusp).

But keep the enthusiasm—no wonder they called you.

QUERENT: You are spot on! It is exactly as you said and I will know more about this job on Monday so I will keep you posted. I have just one more beginner question...does this reading change if I currently have a job (even though as a contractor)?

R.K. ALEXANDER: No, the reading doesn't change even if you currently have a job, whether contractor or not (contractor employment is 6th house/Mercury). This is because the horary question you asked was specifically about the surprise job offer, and not about your current position.

However, your current position would be reflected in this chart. With Venus at the last degree of Leo, and Mercury at zero degrees and trining Uranus/Jupiter in the 6th, it looks like you are near the end of your current contract position (your ruler Venus at the last degree of Leo) and are ready for something new (zero degree Mercury/10th trining Uranus/Jupiter at early degrees of Aries, the beginning of the zodiac, and Uranus now retrograde.) Best wishes, don't worry, something better will roll along if this offer you asked the horary about doesn't work out. Your ruler Venus at Regulus is kind of protecting you in that way.

PS—Another reason for vigilance in pursuing this opportunity is that when you call the people back on Monday, you'll still be under the influence of the solar eclipse at 19° Cancer, meaning something is yet to be revealed (eclipse) that affects your security (Cancer).

OUTCOME

QUERENT: I wanted to update this...Yes, I did go last week to learn more about this job and yes I was disappointed...it is a contractor job with the same pay as now, much farther, more stress...so I guess I should have saved my gas and NO GO but my name stayed there so maybe, one day...something. So I think you were sooooo right. Thank you!

Case Study #2: Saturn in the 7th isn't a stricture against judgment in a relationship question—it's a wealth of information

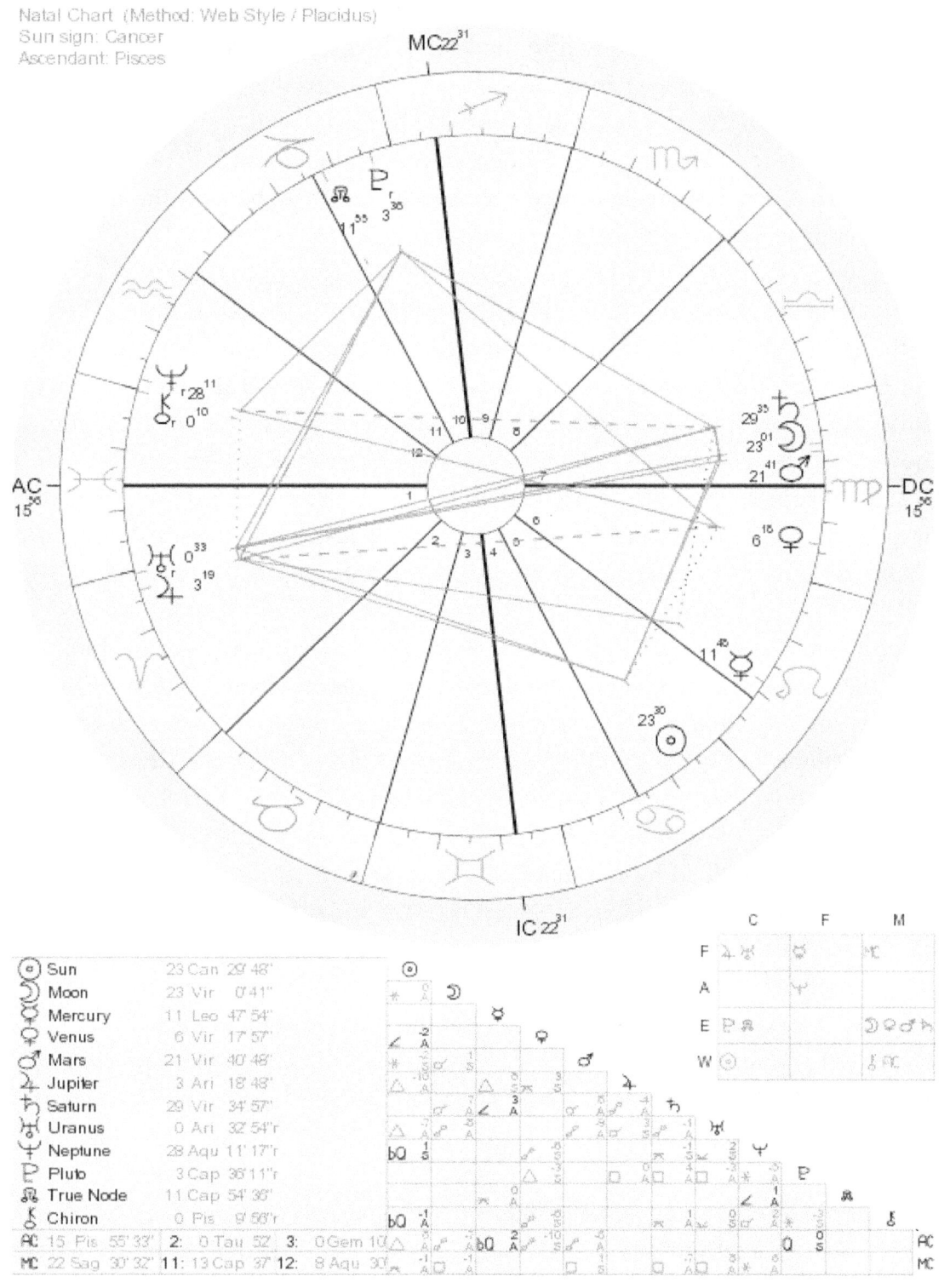

QUERENT: I have a crush on someone and I'm not sure if its all fantasy in my head or if it seems like its somewhat mutual...would like some advice on whether I should act on it.

R.K. ALEXANDER: Due to the wording of your question, I would use Neptune for you rather than Jupiter. This is a 5th house question in modern technique because it is of a romantic/crush nature, not a partnership/marriage nature. Sun in the fifth affirms this.

So you are Neptune and the object of your desire is the Moon. (Even if you used the Jupiter/Mercury traditional rulerships, there's not much help there because the trine you mention is rapidly separating at 8 degrees already.)

Using the moderns, Neptune/you in the 12th in Aquarius, and Aquarius on the 12th cusp, and Uranus in the 1st seems to indicate that this is more of an impulse item. Moon in Virgo/the other person is applying to form a quincunx to your ruler/Neptune. Moon is also conjoining Saturn, ruler of the 12th traditionally and 11th modern. It shows your hopes and wishes (modern), but the twelfth shows your apprehensions about asking as well as your lack of clarity of feelings. Mercury, ruling the signs Saturn and the Moon are in, is in fall in Leo, further muddying the waters about what you're really feeling here and trying to achieve. It also rules the 4th house of outcome. Nutshell: Your thoughts and feelings about the person are not congruent and clear.

Moon is applying to sextile the Sun in the 5th, so if you approach, it may look favorable at first and approaching the person will be benign. I think the lack of clarity about your feelings will kick in with the Moon-Neptune quincunx, and then when the Moon conjoins Saturn at the dead degree of Virgo, you may think the better of things (Virgo), see the reality of the situation (Saturn) and change your mind about the person (late degrees about to switch signs). So I don't think the chart is "bad" as you mentioned. I just think the lack of clarity about your feelings, fears, and what you are really looking for are amplified by the chart. It may be an experience you need to go through to clarify your feelings about what you are looking for (11th) and this person you have your eye on is the vehicle for it. But the Moon-Neptune quincunx and Moon-Saturn conjunction, especially the Moon-Saturn conjunction, seems to indicate to me to show some restraint (Saturn) and re-think/analyze (Virgo) your feelings, motivations and the situation a bit more.

PS—Saturn in the 7th can indicate the other person is unavailable/spoken for, too. Saturn conjunct the ruler of the 5th (Moon) can affirm this.

QUERENT: Wow, if one was skeptical about horary...you just changed their mind completely! This is like looking straight into my brain. Haha! I am very confused about my feelings, not just about him but in general. I've definitely worried about changing my mind once I initiate things...I also haven't initiated things because I have the biggest fear of hearing the 'spoken for' thing too! So it was very ironic that you mentioned that!

Perhaps I might briefly step up and throw out some bait for him to make a move. I do want to do something so that I can gain some clarity as you said...but letting it go is also a form of clarity for me. Arg! This is why I ask...my brain takes me in circles!

Thank you so much for your very insightful response! It is amazing!

OUTCOME

QUERENT: Well, I found out today that he is spoken for! Isn't that something! That Saturn sure did point that out! You are amazing! Now that I know he is attached, my feelings really have cleared up over him...it really was just a 'fantasy' idea....hmmm, interesting.

R.K. ALEXANDER: Truthfully, the first half of your question contained the answer. The Pisces ASC/Neptune 12th just affirmed it.

166 Open Source Modern Horary Astrology

Case Study #3: Pluto knows a shady car deal when it sees one

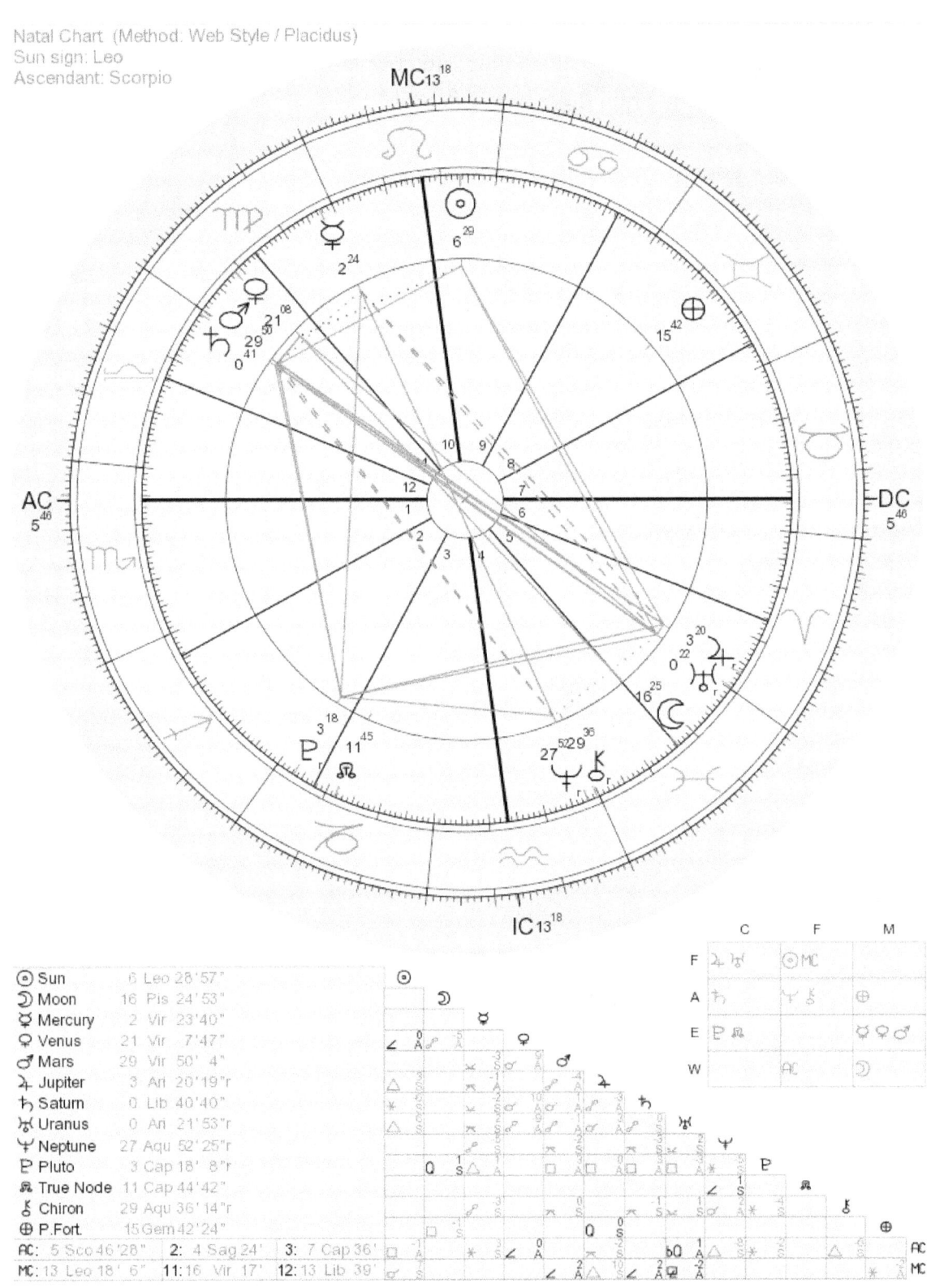

QUERENT: Just saw an ad for the type of car I've been looking for, it is much older model that I am fond of. I'm a bit anxious to move on it , but don't want to make a mistake. Will this car be a mess of repairs, and is the dealer honest and fair?

R.K. ALEXANDER: I think you would have a SEVERE (Scorpio ASC) case of buyer's remorse after you buy the car. The Ascendant Via Combust shows the anxiety already.

The car is the 3rd house and Mercury rules cars. Saturn is exalted in Libra in the 11th house of hopes and wishes, showing that the car is older than you prefer but you have high hopes for it. Mercury/the car is in rulership and is going to trine your modern ASC ruler Pluto in the 2nd house. The car salesman is 7th house/Taurus, with Venus in fall in Virgo, disposited by Mercury, meaning he's in a weak position that favors you getting a good deal. I don't think he's dishonest, as much as desperate to sell. I also think he'll fold like a house of cards if you use that Scorpio to interrogate the living daylights out of him with deeply detailed questions (Scorpio) about the quality and "health" of the car (Virgo). You'll also have to negotiate though, affirmed by Jupiter/2nd house ruler (inflated price) opposing Saturn in Libra (negotiation).

That's pretty much where the good news ends and the rest of the chart goes off a cliff. I'm actually hoping your traditional ruler ASC/Mars, at the dead degree of Virgo, means that the car is already sold and too late for you to buy! Mars is going to move into detriment and conjoin Saturn/the car, indicating buyers remorse if you use Mars as your traditional ruler. If you use modern Pluto, you get a Mars/Pluto square, which equals expensive repairs. Saturn/the car is opposing Uranus, indicating the car will be unreliable and frustrating. Both are T-squaring Pluto, meaning expensive repairs. Mars and Saturn squaring Pluto in the 2nd indicate you will be walking into substantial (Jupiter/2nd house ruler) financial repairs on the car. Finally, Saturn in Libra disposited by Venus in fall has Venus ruling the 12th house cusp of sorrow, self-undoing, and regret.

Buyer's remorse and problems are also indicated because three of the main significators here—Saturn/car, Pluto/you, Mars/you traditional—are all involved in the T-square. Moon in Pisces in 4th house of outcome is about to oppose Venus in Fall, leading to disappointment and sorrow. Neptune in the 4th quincunxing the Mars-Saturn conjunction affirms your disillusionment. Saturn traditional and Uranus modern ruling the 4th house cusp in opposition to each other affirms a non-happy ending. Saturn's exaltation to me is negated and overwhelmed by all the affliction to it.

Moon also recently formed an opposition to Mercury just prior to the chart, and makes me wonder if the previous owner wanted to dump it because of its hidden problems (Pisces)—ask the dealer to run a Carfax report and see if they're willing to provide service records. I think Moon in Pisces/ASC applying trine is affirming your intuition (Pisces) in the suspicions (Scorpio ASC) embedded in the words you chose for the question you asked. You know something's off. Scorpio paranoia isn't always bad.

I strongly recommend you heed your intuition (Moon/Pisces) and pass this one up and wait for a better time—and vehicle.

OUTCOME

QUERENT: Well I saw the car at the dealers house, and when I asked what dealership he is affiliated with he mentioned the town it was in. When I pressed for more info about this dealership, he mentioned the whereabouts of this place, but never would divulge a name. When I asked if he would mind my taking it for my mechanic to view, he said he did not want to do this because it would take some time, and he did not want the dealer plate out for very long in case he needed to let someone else test drive a car. Sounds funny to me!

It is an older car (18 years), so of course some $$ is expected to be spent in restoration, but my concern was if the transmission or some other pricey repair would befall me. Yeah, this sounded too dodgy, I have a mechanic one town over who could sum up the mechanical condition of this car in less than an hour, and this 'dealer' would not consent to this.

R.K. ALEXANDER: SERIOUSLY?!?!?! "I want to sell you a car, but I won't tell you my dealership's name, you can't drive it, and you can't have a mechanic look at it." I can't imagine bigger red flags! Apparently the dealer (Libra/12th cusp) has plenty to hide! Most salesmen would be throwing themselves and tons of information at your feet in this economy! Now I'm wondering if the damned thing is stolen...Don't walk away from this deal—RUN! Fast!

Open Source Modern Horary Astrology 169

Case Study #4: Self-delusion over a bad living situation is narrowly averted by a Uranus-Neptune mutual reception

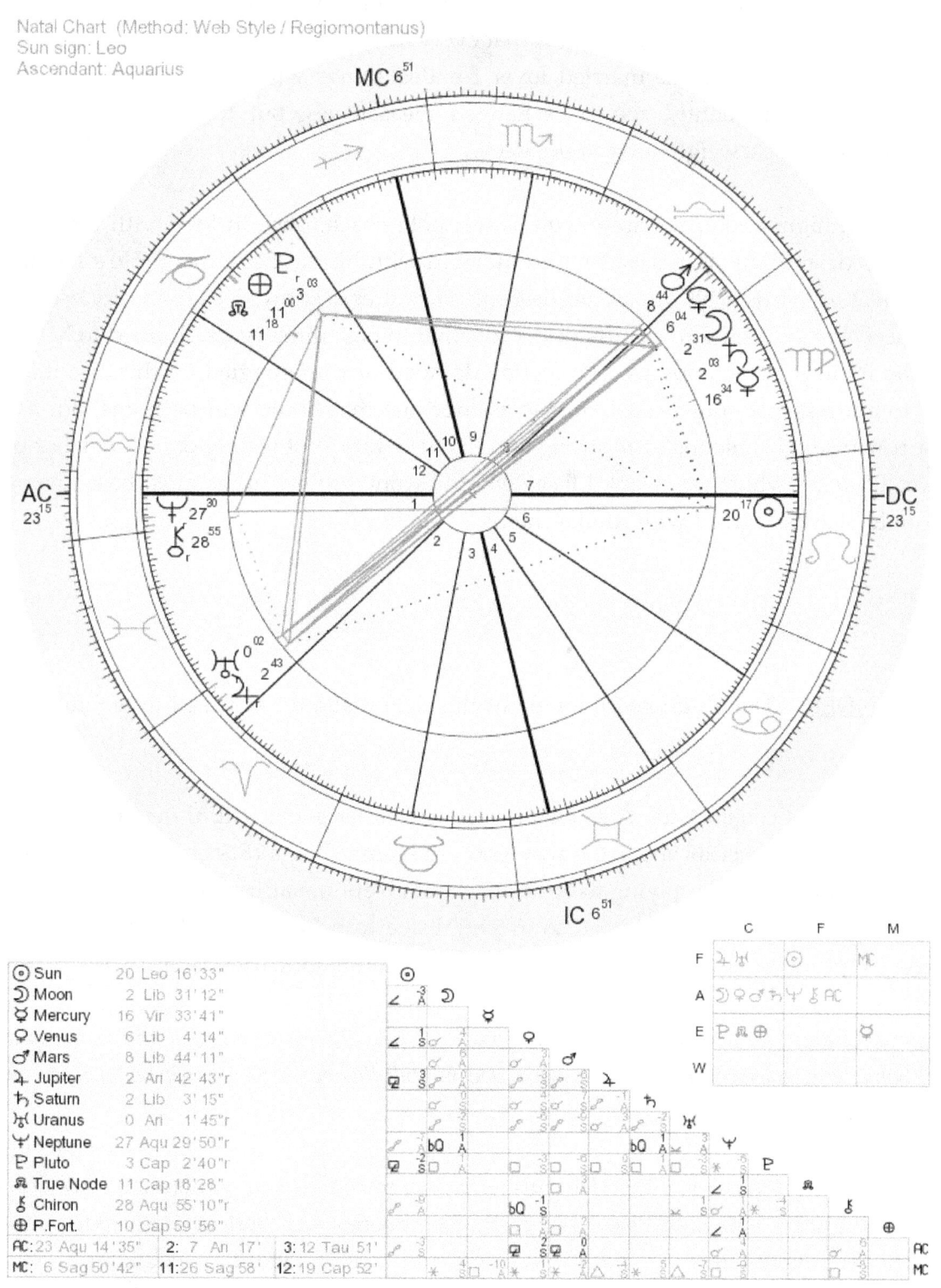

QUERENT: My current living arrangement is not dreadful, but is wearing me down. the old guy I rent from is starting to act a bit strange—forgetful—and it seems to me, more and more sarcastic towards me, which he has never been in the past. Additionally, I want to get out of this neighborhood. The place I've been offered to share is closer to work and not as sketchy as where I am living now. Also, and quite important, is that every day I go to or from my place, I have to cross the small intersection where the married lover I ended things with a few months back, owns a business. I see him frequently, we've exchanged pleasantries, but there is still an unhealthy attraction that feels like a weight around my neck.

My friend from high school, a man—swim/water polo coach, once in love with him, no longer. Affinity exists despite the past, asked me to move in with him in September. He's moving into a nice apartment which is a bit pricey, needs help on rent and knows I'm living in less-than-good circumstances. We've been through the ringer together in past three years. Seemed to have worked through the BS in past few months. Not feeling deluded or rose-goggled on this. See it as a good situation to address both our needs. He has assured me that home will be home, not a place of drama or romance. My antenna's are strong and I believe him. Not feeling delusional, but practical. I told him, "You see whom you want, I'll see whom I want, but my home must be a haven. Do not trespass on it." He has agreed with similar intent.

Can it work?

R.K. ALEXANDER: There's an awful lot about this deal that ain't kosher. I urge you to seriously reconsider.

Retrograde Neptune conjunct the ASC tells me there's either some willful denial on your part or something drastically unclear about the way you are seeing things (Pisces intercepted in the 1st). The Sun as traditional ruler applying to opposition with Neptune affirms that things aren't quite as orderly and compartmental and agreed to as you'd like to believe, with "believe" being the key word here. (Neptune in Aquarius indicates the desire for a romantic friendship.)

Your ruler is Uranus retrograde, and today it goes back into Pisces, forming a mutual reception with Neptune. Something unexpected is going to make you rethink this deal and see if it really truly represents your best interest/1st house.

Your "friend" is Jupiter, ruler of the 11th. Jupiter is also retrograde, and conjunct You/Uranus, but Uranus will refranate back into Pisces before the conjunction can perfect. Since both Jupiter and Uranus will eventually retrograde back into Pisces and conjoin (about a week after Mercury goes direct next month), further emphasizing that Neptune/ASC conjunction, you both may convince yourselves this is a great idea. Pluto in the 11th house also makes me wonder about your friend's motives, as Pluto is squaring your ruler and the Moon. The T-square outlet leg is in...you guessed it —the 5th house of romance.

Something tells me the two of you still have romantic feelings for each other and aren't quite being honest about it (Neptune/you, Mercury intercepted him and Jupiter disposited by Mars in Libra), either with yourselves or each other.

Mercury retrograde is the least of your worries. Mercury is intercepted in rulership in the 7th, meaning your friend could be telling you what you want to hear to get you to make the move. Mercury in rulership and Pluto in the 11th literally means he's the one calling all the shots, so all the talk about "must be my haven, etc." is just talk going in one ear and out the other with him—with the interception, it just looks subtle. He promises no drama (Neptune) or romance (Leo), but I guarantee you, those issues will be front and center (Sun opposing Neptune).

Moon ruler of the 6th of day-to-day living just conjoined Saturn, ruler of the 12th of self-undoing. It will oppose your friend/Jupiter, and it's possible if you press the issue, the truth (Jupiter) may come out about what's really going on. This isn't necessarily a bad thing—it may let you guys openly and honestly discuss your real feelings and motives, which Pluto is going to force the issue on anyway. Who knows? Maybe you want to be romantic again with each other, that's not so bad. It's just you have to be clear if you want your living situation tied up in that.

Moon is soon to conjoin Venus, ruler of the 3rd and the 8th, so I wonder if a woman will come along with news of a better housing offer that puts you in a position of power (Venus in rulership/Libra), rather than at the Pluto mercy of your friend. Mercury as ruler of the 4th does not favor you *at all* in this situation. You may want to be romantic with him, but maybe find another place to live while doing it so you're not under his control.

Moon will eventually sextile the Sun and trine Neptune before void-of-course, so you'll come out okay. I think you can do better than this deal if you truly don't want a relationship tied in with your housing sitch. Let the Mercury retrograde delay work in your favor to fact-find further and re-visit the realities of the situation as they are, and not as you hope or wish (Neptune) it might be.

QUERENT: I trust myself enough right now to know that I will not engage in any sexual or romantic mingling with him if I were to move in, but do have concerns of him betraying the "haven" clause. This is my biggest concern. All of the discussion of "romantic" I've read makes me wonder if he's the one with an agenda along those lines. It's not too late for me to back out, but again, I have no other alternatives in place right now and I am just feeling trapped here where I am right now.

R.K. ALEXANDER: Absolutely no one is questioning any single one of your motives for moving. They are all very good ones and you probably really do need to make a move in your residence sooner rather than later. But the whole reason you asked this specific question is because deep down with Capricorn/Saturn on the 12th cusp, you know something is fundamentally (Saturn) wrong with this specific scenario. Hence the Uranian anxiety. With Neptune retrograde on the ASC, there's always a catch, unseen at the time, and so hopelessly obvious later.

The issue at question here is about moving in with an ex. Your biggest fears are that there will be romance (Leo) and drama (Neptune) in a place you prefer to have as a haven free of that. This chart is screaming at the top of its lungs via intercepted Mercury in the 7th/ruler of the 4th that you will have that in spades and it will not be wise to combine your residence with this man.

You may not have other alternatives right now—Venus is besieged between two malefics right now, so of course you're going to feel between the devil and the deep blue sea. But feelings aren't facts.

All you have to do is wait. You don't need to make a decision or move this very minute. Wait and see what happens, wait and explore other options i.e., let the retrogrades work in your favor. You have time and you have options (Saturn exalted in Libra). You're just not seeing them now because Uranus at a critical degree cardinal is giving you the false impression that if you don't act now you'll lose your chance, when the truth is that if you act rashly and impulsively (Uranus/Aries) you are going to have severe consequences to your actions (T-square).

Pluto square Venus indicates a triangle, so your friend he's toyed with may be involved. But Pluto is also in mutual application to a nasty square to your traditional ruler Saturn, which means you are setting yourself up to get a cold hard dose of reality in a very painful manner. Not to mention Saturn is in opposition to your modern ruler Uranus and the whole thing is in a nasty cardinal T-square anyway. Bad news all around.

The Moon, with its sextile to the Sun and trine to the Moon, is going to be your "out" and your saving grace. It's the only thing in the chart working in your favor.

OUTCOME

QUERENT: Thanks for the warning earlier. Last night a wicked truth was revealed by him—and I told him no dice. I really needed to read the things that you had offered to shake me out of my Neptune coma. HE IS DEALING COCAINE! He told me, "Ah, come on, babe, you're a chick from the bricks (we come from the same part of town)...you know how it is."

Now, I'm laughing—truly feeling okay about sticking it out in this dump for a bit longer. The albatross on the corner I spoke of is kids play compared to the possibility of dealing with the monkey that's on this man's back. Thanking the angels profusely...

174 Open Source Modern Horary Astrology

Case Study #5: A retrograde significator and outer planet T-square delay retirement

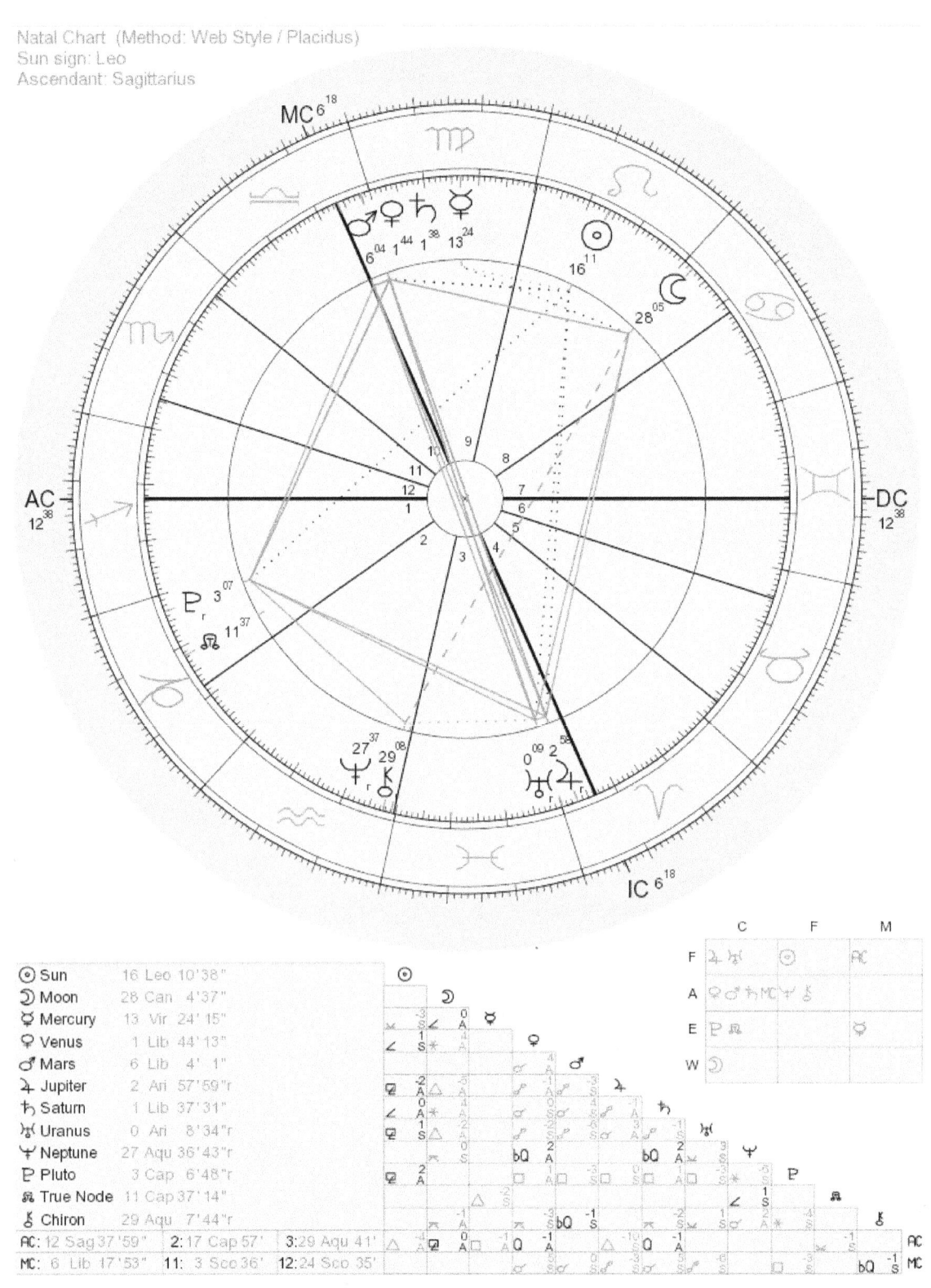

QUERENT: I am a student of horary and have cast a chart for the question, "When will I retire and begin to draw a pension?"

Querent significator Jupiter applying opposition to question significator Saturn (retirement) by 1 degree 20 minutes. Cardinal signs, cadent houses, does that mean one month and a week, or two on the timing? The Moon is void-of-course in the 8th house, which is okay since the question is when, not if, plus, the 8th is pensions and it is with the Sun in that house, and the event is in fact imminent. If I am looking at the 'end of the matter' do I look at Mars (ruler IC)?

R.K. ALEXANDER: Moon void-of-course in rulership in the 8th and the Sun in rulership in there as well is fine as you mentioned—it means the money is literally in the bank and easily available. Late Moon means you're coming to the end...

Your ruler is retrograde and in a nasty outer planet T-square. This indicates to me there will be some sort of delay due to things being out of your control. The outlet leg is the 7th house, so I wonder if a significant other or someone else is having a say in the when it happens.

Your ruler is opposing your employer's ruler (Venus in rulership) by mutual application, so they may have a strong say in when you get to retire. Jupiter and Mars in detriment (4th house/end of matter) are actually separating from opposition with four degrees between them, and so it could mean ephemeris time (when Jupiter hits 6 Aries next year/2011) rather than the four degrees horary modal time (days/weeks/months). Moon also changes sign and trines Jupiter in four degrees as well.

With the retrograde/T-square/void-of-course Moon and mutable ASC, for me it's not very clear (Moon's last aspect is a quincunx Neptune) to give you an EXACT time. But I don't think it's in weeks, I think it will take longer.

OUTCOME

QUERENT: This is true, the retirement/pension is imminent, no question. There is a delay due to my partner but completely out of our control. As far as employer input or say in retirement: This is true in a way, although it is certainly by choice as well. Jupiter goes to 6° Aries in February 2011, which is approximately the time that my current assignment ends. Your reply was amazing.

Case Study #6: A late degree ASC & Moon conjunct Uranus Rx causes high anxiety, but points to staying the course

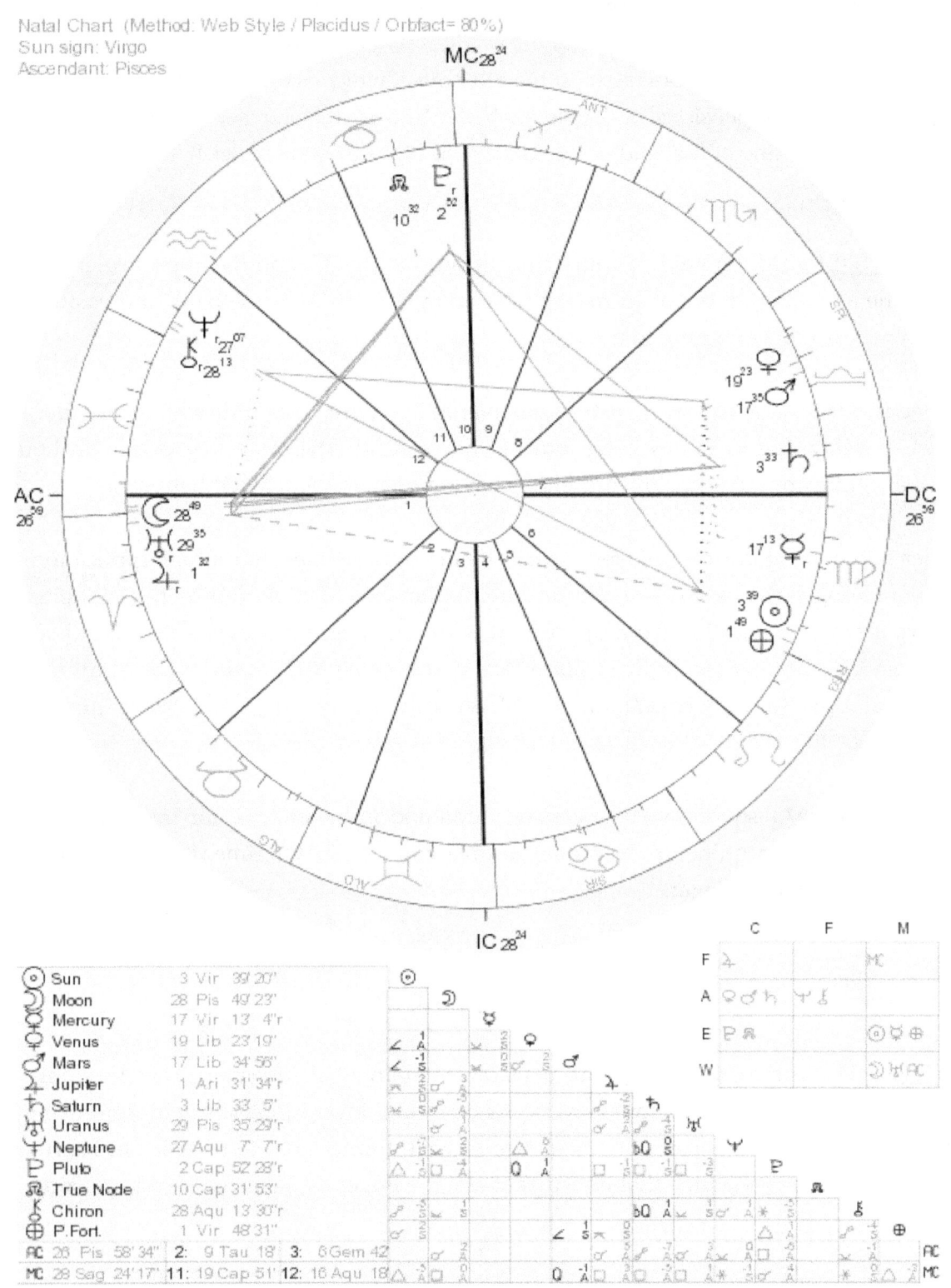

QUERENT: I have been looking for a job for a while, I am employed but need new job with benefits, plus a better salary. I have been in several interviews and it seems that finally I have a shot in getting a great job (I am being considered by two companies), with all I want and need. Problem is I need to go through another interview and then start to work right away. I am going away for two weeks for medical reasons; I need a bladder surgery and I will be evaluated during this trip, plus I will have a complete check-up, which I cannot afford at home, as my current job does not offer health insurance.

I am freaking out and have no idea of what to do...I am not very impartial when reading a chart to myself. I could change the plane tickets , but it will cost me plenty—almost what I paid for them to begin with. PLEASE HELP! No idea of what to do. Thanks!

R.K. ALEXANDER: Late degree Moon/ASC, continue with your plans as they are and take the trip and do the surgery. With the Sun in the 6th conjunct the Part of Fortune trining retrograde Pluto in the 10th/career, let the delays work in your favor since they probably won't hire as fast as they are saying they are (mutable angles, Mercury retrograde dignified in 6th as ruler of the 4th/outcome).

Your ruler Neptune retrograde is conjunct Chiron in the 12th, where Neptune is dignified, designating you need the medical attention more than the job right now. Neptune is also mutually recepted with Uranus retrograde, and Jupiter, traditional ruler of Pisces, is retrograde as well and will soon return to Pisces. These are benefic things, just slowed down. So try to slow down and take one step at a time, which is using the retrogrades in your favor.

I know that Moon-Uranus conjunction is making you hyper-anxious, but that's the nature of the beast and you can overcome it. Relax and proceed as originally planned.

QUERENT: Thanks so much for your input—I really appreciate you taking the time to look at the chart. I am calming down...I am going ahead with my trip. Got a call today and one of the companies scheduled an interview for Monday. I did not hear from the other one, but I called them and offered to be re-interviewed before the trip. That is all I can do for now.

R.K. ALEXANDER: With Neptune/you dignified by house and the Sun as ruler of the 6th in the 6th conjunct the Part of Fortune and trine retrograde Pluto in the 10th...AND with Mercury in rulership by sign and house in the sixth but retrograde...AND with Jupiter retrograde in 1st as your traditional ruler and ruler of the MC...If you explain the situation to them if they or anyone else makes an offer to you, they should be just fine with it and willing to wait (retrogrades). Just communicate the situation to them (Mercury rulership).

OUTCOME

QUERENT: I did not change the trip and both jobs were waiting for me.

Open Source Modern Horary Astrology 179

Case Study #7: Use reality and geography when applying significators to a relocation chart

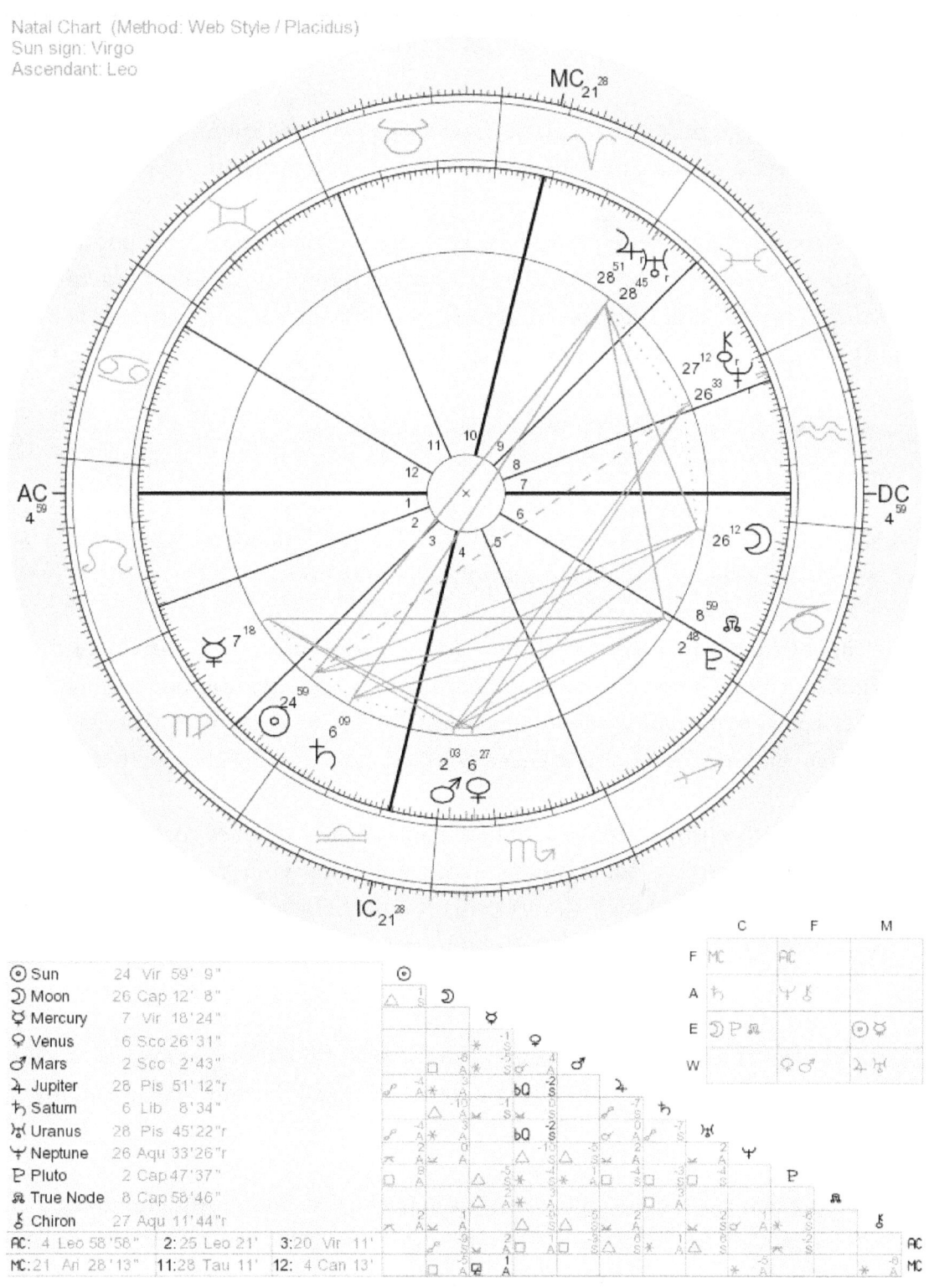

QUERENT: I need some help to clarify the right significator. My home town is A and recently I decided to move to town B. But I have doubts if this move is the right choice for me. I don't know where my life perspectives will be better at; in home town A or in town B? So I erected a chart while I was visiting town B.

My questions are:

1. What house is the significator for town A, which is my home town? Will it be the 4th house?
2. What house is the significator for town B? Where I was at when I posed the question and erected the chart?
3. Will it be the 4th house, since I already was at town B when I posed the question? Will it be the house opposite the 4th house (that is 10th), as an opponent to my home town A and shown by house 4? Will it be the 7th house, as a derived house (the fourth house after the home town cusp IC)? Will it be something else?

Very confused...Also, any idea about the answer of my dilemma?

R.K. ALEXANDER: Fourth house=current residence/Town A, 7th house=where you'd be moving to/Town B, since it's the derived 4th house from the radix 4th house.

Venus in detriment rules where you are at now (no wonder you want to leave), and Uranus Rx conjunct Jupiter Rx rules where you're going; hence the uncertainty, unpredictability, but also the excitement over a new opportunity. Moon will sextile the Jupiter-Uranus conjunction before void-of-course, so it may take awhile for you to get established in the new location with the retrogrades.

Moon in Capricorn is in detriment on the 12th house side of the 7th house cusp/new home and also giving you fears, apprehension, and cautions about uprooting your roots and surrendering the comfortable, familiar and established (Capricorn). Neptune Rx in Aquarius—dispositing to and mutually recepted with Uranus—is in the 7th house representing the new home, adding to your confusion and anxiety. Literally, take a leap of faith!

QUERENT: Thank you for your reply, you explained with brilliant accuracy your methodology. You were extremely clarifying, and honestly, you described 100% the way I feel about my dilemma! Thank you once more.

And I want to add that since my significator Sun is in the 3rd house, my intentions for moving away are obvious enough. Also, the change of residence is indicated on the chart by the opposition that Sun is going to form with the conjuction of Uranus/Jupiter, isn't it so? Besides, the Moon is ready to enter the 7th house (like me, as I'm ready to move to town B). So, I think you, too, agree that moving to town B is a wiser choice for me than staying back in home town A.

And one more theoretical question: Do you believe that the fact I was in town B (during a visit) when I asked the question should mean that 4th house is town B? Or is it irrelevant? Does the 4th house signify the permanent residence? (And the temporary residence during a visit is significated by 3rd house?)

R.K. ALEXANDER: It absolutely does not matter which town you were in when you asked the question. The question was about which town was better to move to, not anything about where you were physically standing at the time when you asked it. The 4th house is *always* your current residence, regardless of whether you are asking the question in Montserrat or Mongolia. And the 7th house is the house of "removals," or, where you would remove yourself to via leaving the 4th house residence. Where you asked the question is irrelevant. People travel all the time and ask horary questions; it has no bearing on the question itself. You still live where you normally live when you're not on the road.

QUERENT: That helps more than you can imagine! Thank you so much!

Case Study #8: Debilitated Venus opposing Sedna leaves a very bitter aftertaste in a long-dead relationship

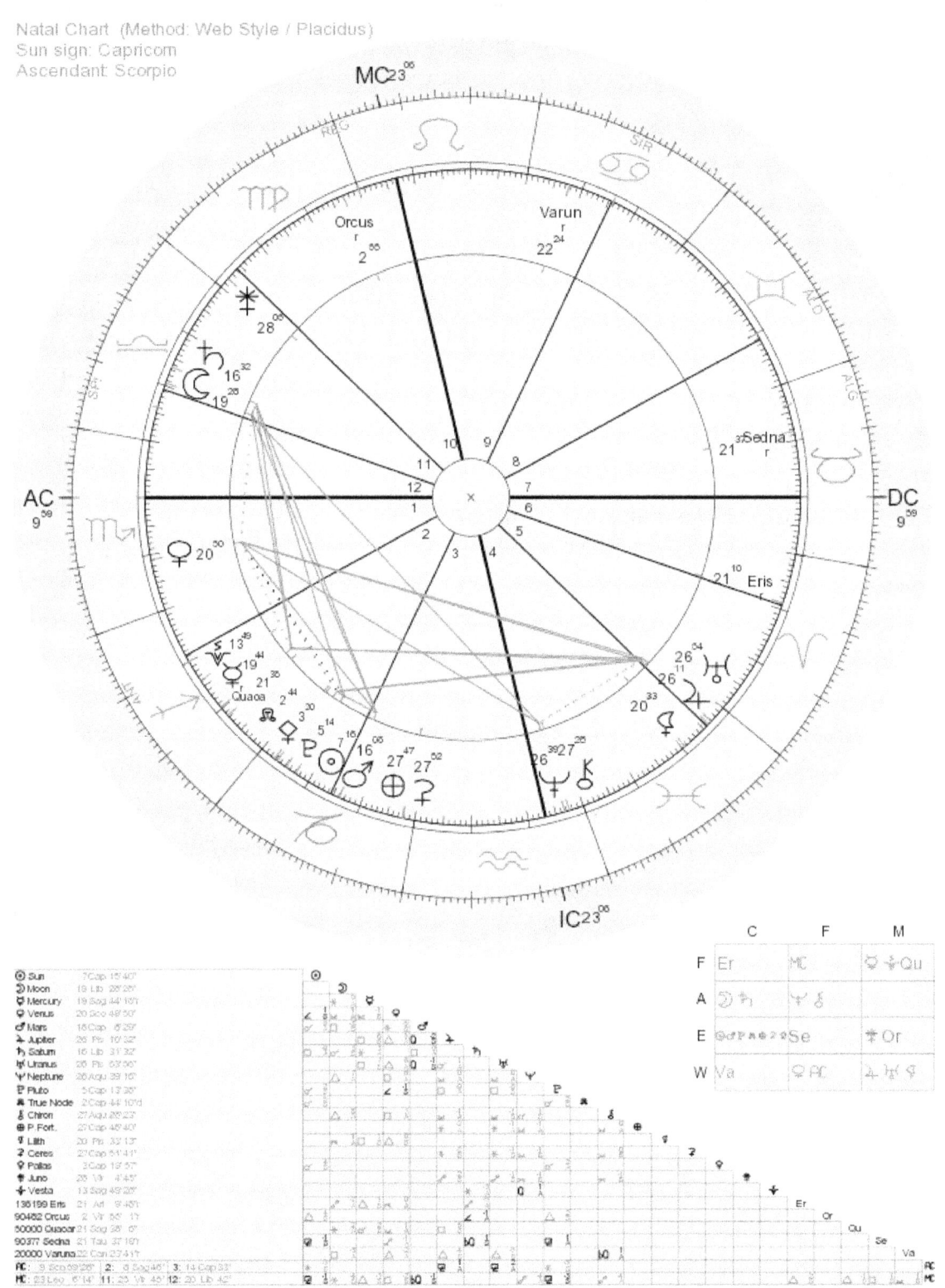

QUERENT: This is about an ex-boyfriend of mine, a long-distance love who still lives half a world away. It was hard to find closure on this story, and although I am not thinking about restarting this relationship again, I am still wondering if we will ever see each other again. I am Mars, he is Moon, as far as I know about horary so far. And I sure don't know much. There is contact between Mars and Moon, so is that a yes?

R.K. ALEXANDER: Short answer to this is no. Note that Saturn, ruler of the 3rd house of contact/connections/communication is partile squaring Mars. Moon is conjunct Saturn in the 12th, a reminiscence about springs past. Neptune is in the 4th, too, so it's more wishful thinking (air sign) than reality. This is good, since Venus is in double detriment in the first house, showing it wasn't the best possible relationship for you. Sometimes we remember things the way they never were and romanticize them in order to feel better about it.

PS—Nodes in 2nd/8th axis with Gemini and Mercury Rx shows there wasn't much security to be found in the relationship.

QUERENT: Thank you...I was not thinking or hoping to rekindle the relationship, just wondering if we would see each other again as friends maybe. But I guess the chart is pretty definite. Is this something that could change over time or because of different circumstances? Hope dies last, I guess. Oh, and is there a meaning to Spica so close to the Moon?

R.K. ALEXANDER Something about the relationship you had with him left a very bitter feeling behind with him (Sedna in the 7th opposing Venus in the 1st), so he's not feeling very fond about you or what happened. As far as friendship, Venus is applying to trine the Jupiter-Uranus conjunction (with Uranus detrimented by house), showing there'd have to be some sort of forgiveness (Pisces) and reconciliation before that door of friendship could open. Saturn Via Combust and as ruler of the 3rd is stationing retrograde in the 11th house of friendship, which doesn't help your cause. Both Moon and Saturn disposit to a detrimented Venus; again, not a pleasant situation.

Never is a long time, but perhaps the Moon-Saturn conjunction in an air sign and air house will encourage you to think long and hard about the situation, what happened, and why something from so long ago is still affecting you today.

PS—Spica can only describe, it cannot act, so at the Moon it is giving you benevolent feelings and pleasant memories about what was, but it is in the 12th and your feelings may be rosier than the reality actually was.

QUERENT: Thanks, it just always amazes me how accurate horary really is. There must be bitter feelings for him, I would hope it's more because of the circumstances of the relationship coming to an end. It was a long-distance relationship all along, and although we tried to change this, it just never worked out. It put more hardship on him to try for us to be together, and he definitely must have felt let down by me. I did my best back then, only it was not enough.

We are in contact online and by text messages, because we are business partners now, doing some import/export, but I really cannot tell what he really feels for me now. We never talk about what happened anymore, and that is part of why I am still thinking about it. I can't seem to find enough closure, because I can't talk about it, and also it was not a case of us just not loving each other anymore, more of being just worn out by the circumstances and the problems.

Well, I know now that it won't happen, at least not soon, but who knows, maybe one fine day in the future our business will bring us to meet again. It's just funny, I remember that the last question I asked myself when we parted was already that one, will I never see him again now. I am probably looking back with rose-colored glasses now, cause it was just never easy, but it's not that I can't get over it at all.

R.K. ALEXANDER: With Uranus in the 5th and all the Aquarius and Pisces mutual reception stuff, and Chiron conjunct Neptune in Aquarius, the sign of friendship, all you can do is extend an olive branch if you sincerely want to heal this, and if that's what it will take to bring closure for you —but there's a catch: You'd have to be completely detached from the outcome (Uranus). You're doing this more for you than for him, and you'll have to get to a mental state of where you have nothing to lose by his response or lack of response—it's all about you telling the truth for yourself moreso than him about what happened and creating clarity within your own being.

For every out you have in this chart to try to mend the fence, there's something afflicted there to block it. That may be the reason for the stationing Saturn ruling the 3rd, meaning it's going to take awhile for you to get to this phase/stage of self-honesty, detachment and let-go. But that's okay, because time/Saturn would be on your side.

You well know it's better to mend a fence late than never at all (Saturn exalted in Libra). And this chart isn't really about "never," it's about things that went awry and were left undone and then buried. And with Jupiter and Uranus at the end of forgiving Pisces, and Neptune conjunct Chiron (a wound that will hurt before it heals), you have the opportunity to make things right. Best of luck to you in whatever you decide.

QUERENT: Wow, that was a lot to swallow...many thanks. Well, it will take some time until I could be completely detached from the outcome, that's for sure. Although I don't want the relationship to start again, I am far from being objective about it. So it makes a lot of sense that it would take a long time. But the funny thing is, this really reminds me of the time when we started that business. That was shortly after our breakup, I was struggling to stay in contact with him and he was very reluctant about it. Then suddenly this business idea developed, and it was just too promising to just forget about it, but of course I was not sure if it would be a good idea for us to be entangled in business together. So I asked an astrologer about it. And I don't even know if she used horary or natal charts, but whatever she used, she gave me *very* similar advice. That the business would only work out and be good for us if I was extremely honest with him and told him about my motives. So that's what I did; I called him and told him about my ideas, and that I did it to try out a business, to help him out, but also to stay in contact with him without expecting more from him than just the contact. I was almost sure he would hang up on me after hearing this, but he agreed to try the business idea, and it worked out much better than I had expected, especially for him, which really makes me happy. So I will think about this more (I think about it anyway, whether I want it or not) and we will see what happens.

You are amazing. Some of your sentences are so accurate that I realized things only after reading them, although, believe me, this has been on my mind for a long time! Your astrological skills are a true blessing. Thanks.

Case Study #9: Career woes under the regime

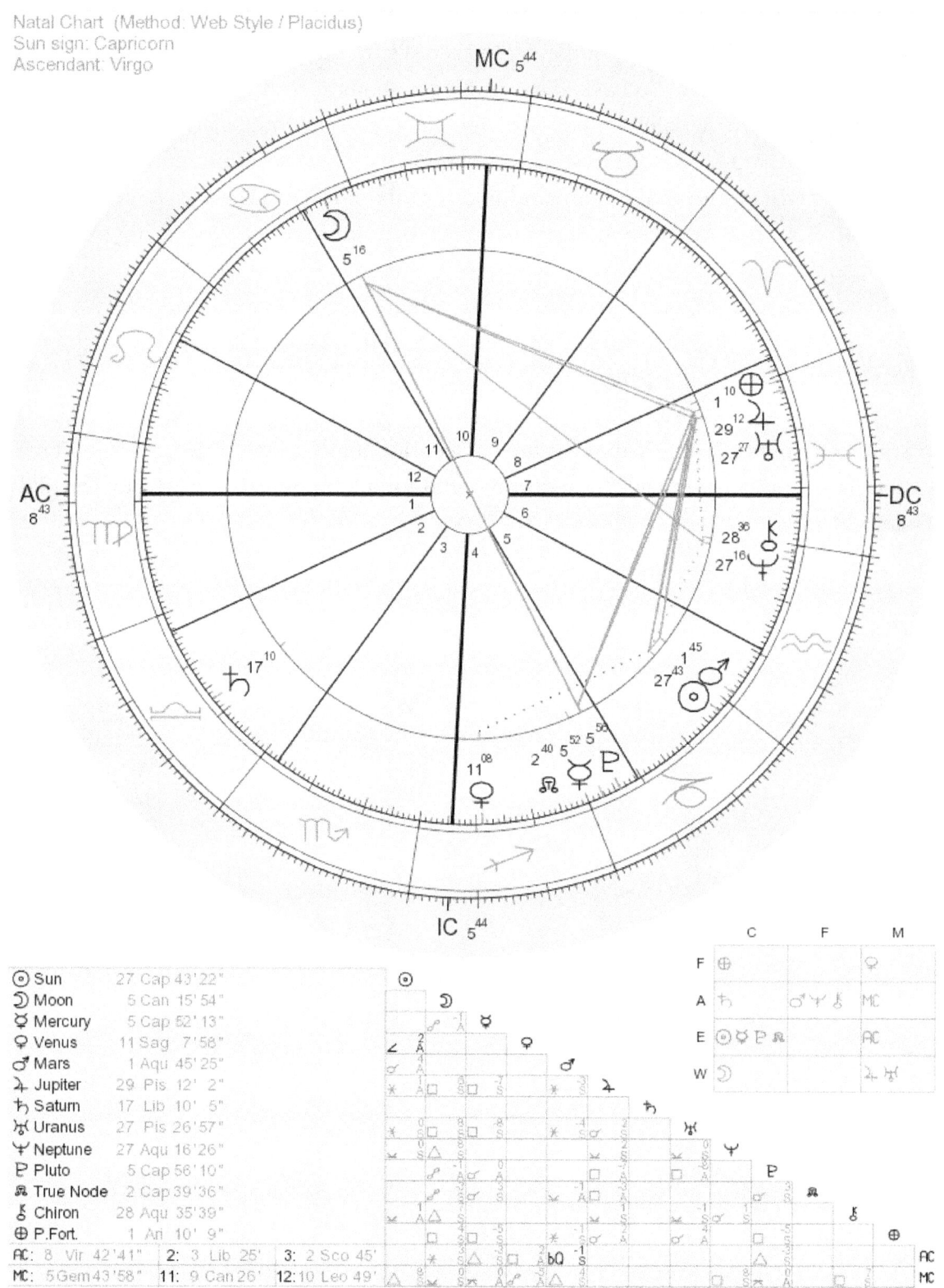

QUERENT: Recently I had a severe disappointment about a project I've been passionate about. I have no idea about what direction to take now on my job. Does my chart indicate a positive direction going forth in my career? Do you see indications about my health and romantic life from this chart?

R.K. ALEXANDER: To say you're feeling crushed by the regime, feeling steamrolled and dealing with killer politics in the situation is an understatement. At this point, you can't *buy* recognition for your efforts. You're being undermined by politics and political intrigue and it's cutting you to the core and making you doubt and second-guess yourself and feeding your insecurities in the most woeful of ways. (Just because you're paranoid *doesn't* mean they're not out to get you.)

There is going to be some unfortunate financial fallout as a result of the situation. This incident was a culmination of long-standing structural issues; it didn't just happen overnight. For the most part, it is completely out of your control and you will be forced to make some decisions and adjustments in your career to get back on track. This is going to take awhile, and things are going to get worse before they get better. You are going to have to get by on a bit of faith that things will work out in the long run (the Moon is early and has a lot of aspects to go through) rather than forcing action to make the changes. The changes will bring the fight to you and force you in the direction you're supposed to go.

For right now, negotiation is key. Lick your wounds and try to weather the turbulence for awhile as best as you can. The pain and confusion will linger a bit, and force another adjustment later on. There will be help later on from a sympathetic friend who sees what's going on and will assist you. It will seem like a last-minute miracle you'll never see coming, so again have faith while putting on your game face (even though you feel like you're crumbling inside) while not letting the bastards get you down and see you sweat.

Deal with this avalanche first, since it's so front and center, before worrying about health and relationships. Do that via another horary question at another time; one does not go berry-picking when a tornado is bearing down on them! Venus in Sadge and Jupiter-Uranus in the 7th show you need your freedom and friendship right now more than a relationship. There is too much unsettled in your life right now for a relationship.

QUERENT: This is an amazing response. It is incredibly helpful and insightful. Your comments frame my situation so accurately. If I didn't know better, I'd think you were one of my colleagues! Your response motivates me to learn horary so I can provide insight for a lost wanderer.

188   Open Source Modern Horary Astrology

Case Study #10: Pluto kills a business, while Venus brings a new opportunity

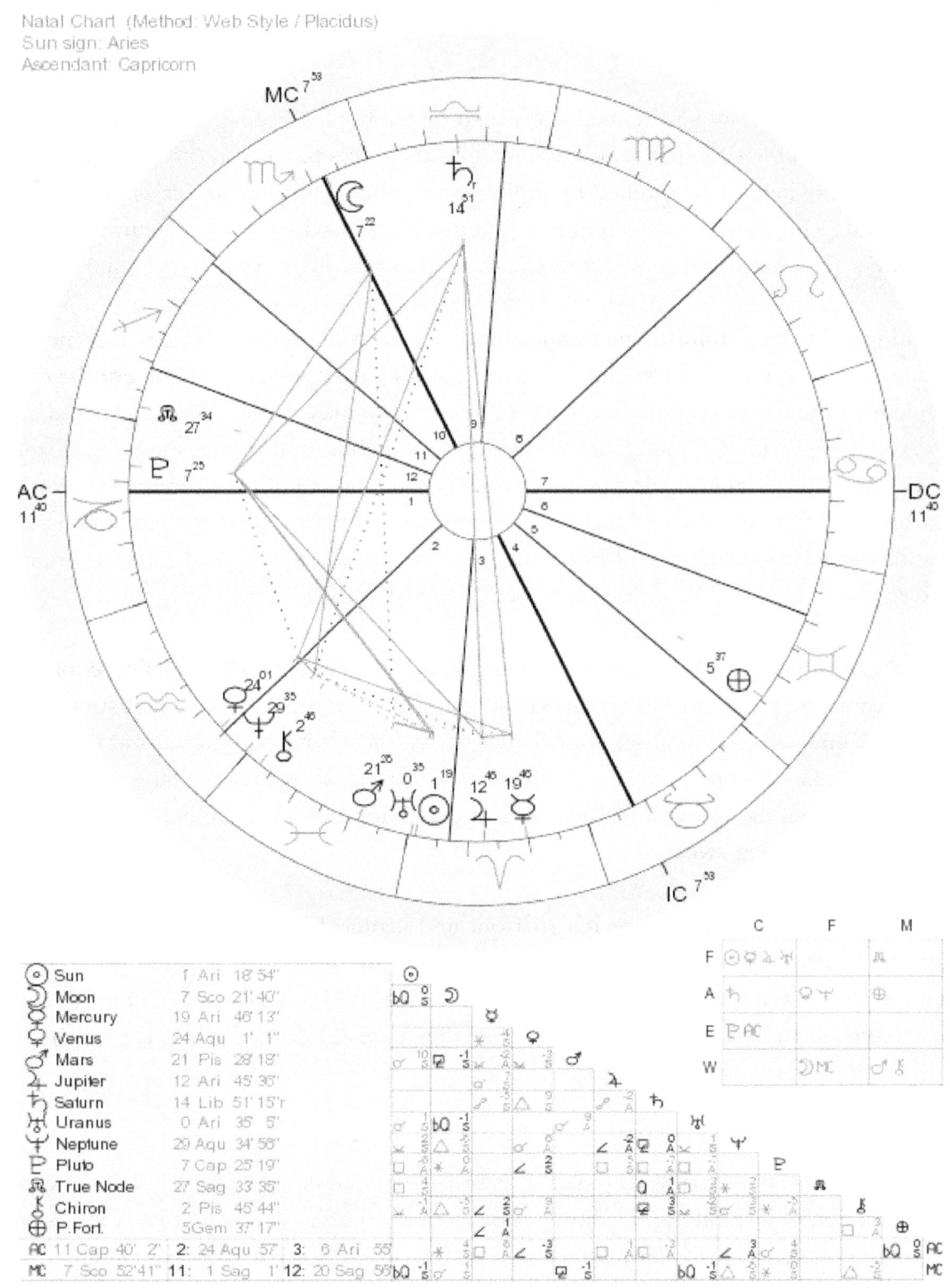

QUERENT: I started a business venture about six months ago. Things have not been working out. I've been trying to stay optimistic and keep trying as it is not in my nature to quit so easily, although this has been causing me a lot of stress and financial burden. I want to know if my investment will finally pay off some time in the near future, or if it's time for me to give it up and move on?

I'm not sure how to read the chart as I don't know which house to give my business... if it's the 10th, it is Scorpio-ruled by Pluto in 12th, an unfortunate house, and Moon conjunct MC in Scorpio says to me death and the end of something. Does this sound right?

R.K. ALEXANDER: The business is the 10th house, and the income from the business is the 11th house (2nd house from the 10th). If you don't place the question in the proper houses, you're finished before you start.

The Sun's applying square to Pluto is pretty much the kiss of death. The Moon in fall in Scorpio on the 12th house side of the business's first house is a final nail in the coffin as well. Since it's sextiling Pluto, you pretty much know the answer already.

Saturn Via Combust and retrograde in your 9th and the business's 12th isn't helping your cause either. It is the ruler of the business's 4th house of endings (radix 1st), which Pluto is on the 12th house side of. The ASC and Pluto are heavily afflicted, and the MC is only making separating aspects.

Venus, ruler of *your* 4th, is in late degrees and due to conjunct Neptune shortly, indicating dissolution. She'll then move into her sign of exaltation, so you will find something else better to move on to. But you have to let this go first. I think you'll find it a relief.

OUTCOME

QUERENT: I've decided this business I'm involved in right now I do need to let go of. However, I've just recently been made an offer to become involved in another venture. I'm hoping this will work out better, being Venus moving into her exaltation. I still am in the hole at this point and need to take care of that. We'll see. Thank you for your help.

190   Open Source Modern Horary Astrology

Case Study #11: When the astrologer totally and completely gets it WRONG!

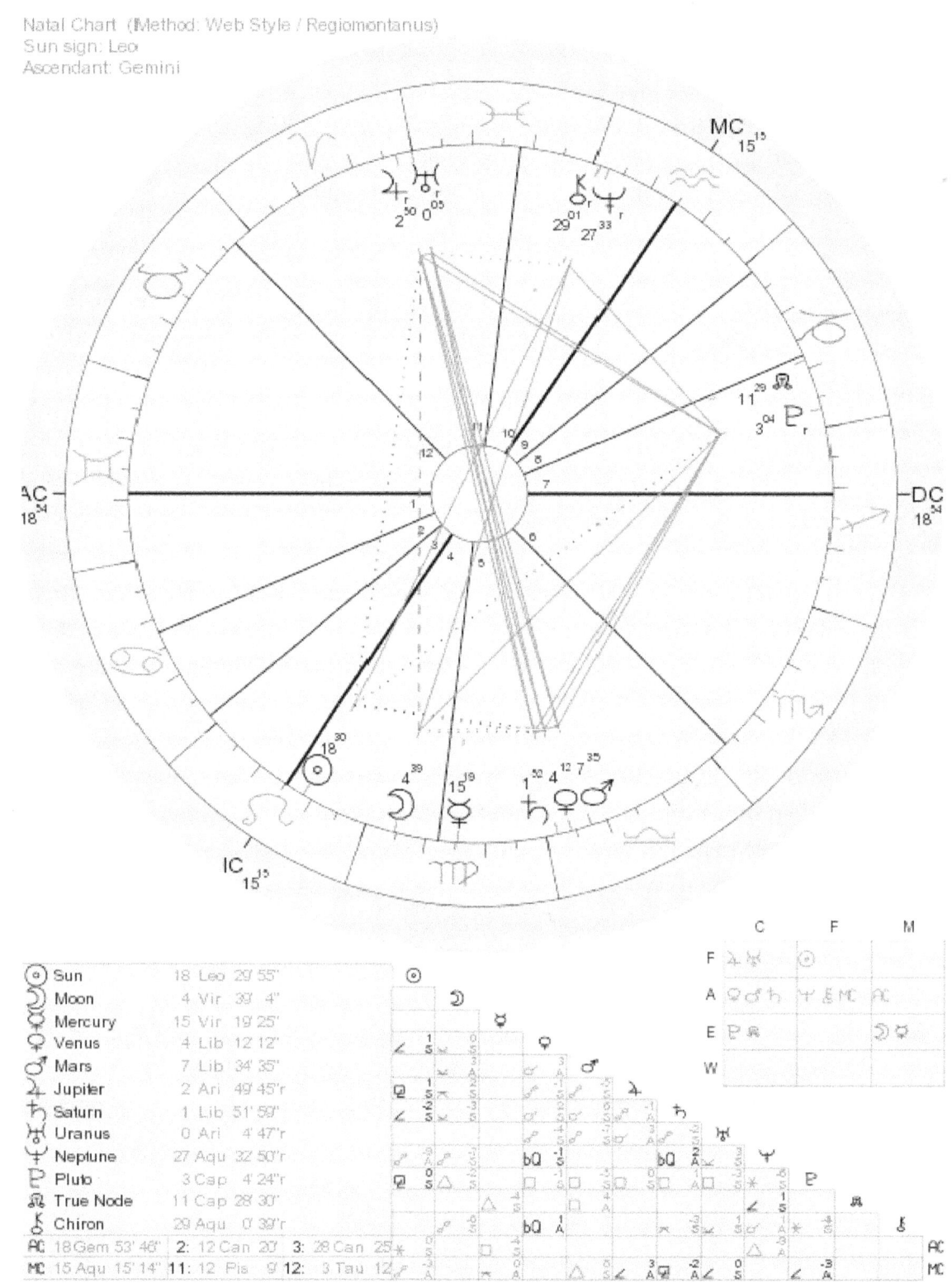

QUERENT: I am traveling around. I think I maybe pregnant and that changes things for me. Dad is excited. I find out tomorrow. My question: Am I having a baby?

R.K. ALEXANDER: With your ruler Mercury in rulership in the 5th house of children...and the Moon's next applying major aspect a conjunction to your ruler in the 5th before going VOC while the Moon is in dignity in the 4th and ruling the 3rd house of news/communication...and the Sun, ruler of children in rulership in the 4th house of outcome...and FAMILY...LET ME BE THE FIRST TO CONGRATULATE YOU!!!

QUERENT: I went to the clinic today only to find out my first morning urine was no good (not in fridge). So I did a home pregnancy test, but it came out negative—my urine could be too diluted. The doctor said it could come out negative as it's still kinda early. So I wait for the results from the clinic or try again in another week. I would be under a month.

R.K. ALEXANDER: Moon conjoins Mercury in a rough timeframe of 11 days. Meanwhile, I'll just consider my winning streak in jeopardy until then...(2007 New England Patriots, I think I feel your pain...)

OUTCOME

QUERENT: Turns out I am not pregnant. What about the significance of the T-squares? Saturn in 5th (as well as Neptune) do not bode well for pregnancy. Thanks for your input, but I still wonder about the squares and oppositions in terms of astrological language.

R.K. ALEXANDER: Neptune is in the 10th, not the 5th, so I'm not sure what you're referring to there. Yes, Saturn is in the 5th, but exalted, so it shouldn't have been a hindrance except for as you mentioned, a possible connection to the T-squares. It would have represented a grounding of the relationship and a turn of a more serious tone from romance to partnership with your man being so close to Venus/Mars. To me the T-squares in this chart would have symbolized the ultimate change in your way of life as a result of being pregnant, rather than a negation, due to the outlet leg of the T-square being in the 1st house/you.

The key thing for me is your significators and house cusps were strong and unaffected by the outer planet T-square (indicating events beyond your control). The chart and cusps had the market cornered on the so-called personal planets (Mercury in rulership) and the Moon in a fertile sign coming to conjunction in the fifth. Neptune to me is too far away orb-wise for the Sun opposition. Moon had recently trined Pluto in the 7th as a permanent change for the better with your partner as a result.

Sometimes we just get it flat-out wrong. Only God is infallible. Still, if we're right 7 to 9 times out of ten, you're doing better than chance—and the odds favor you.

You'll probably have kids...just not this time.

Case Study #12: The outer planets collude extensively to foil a house sale over the course of several months

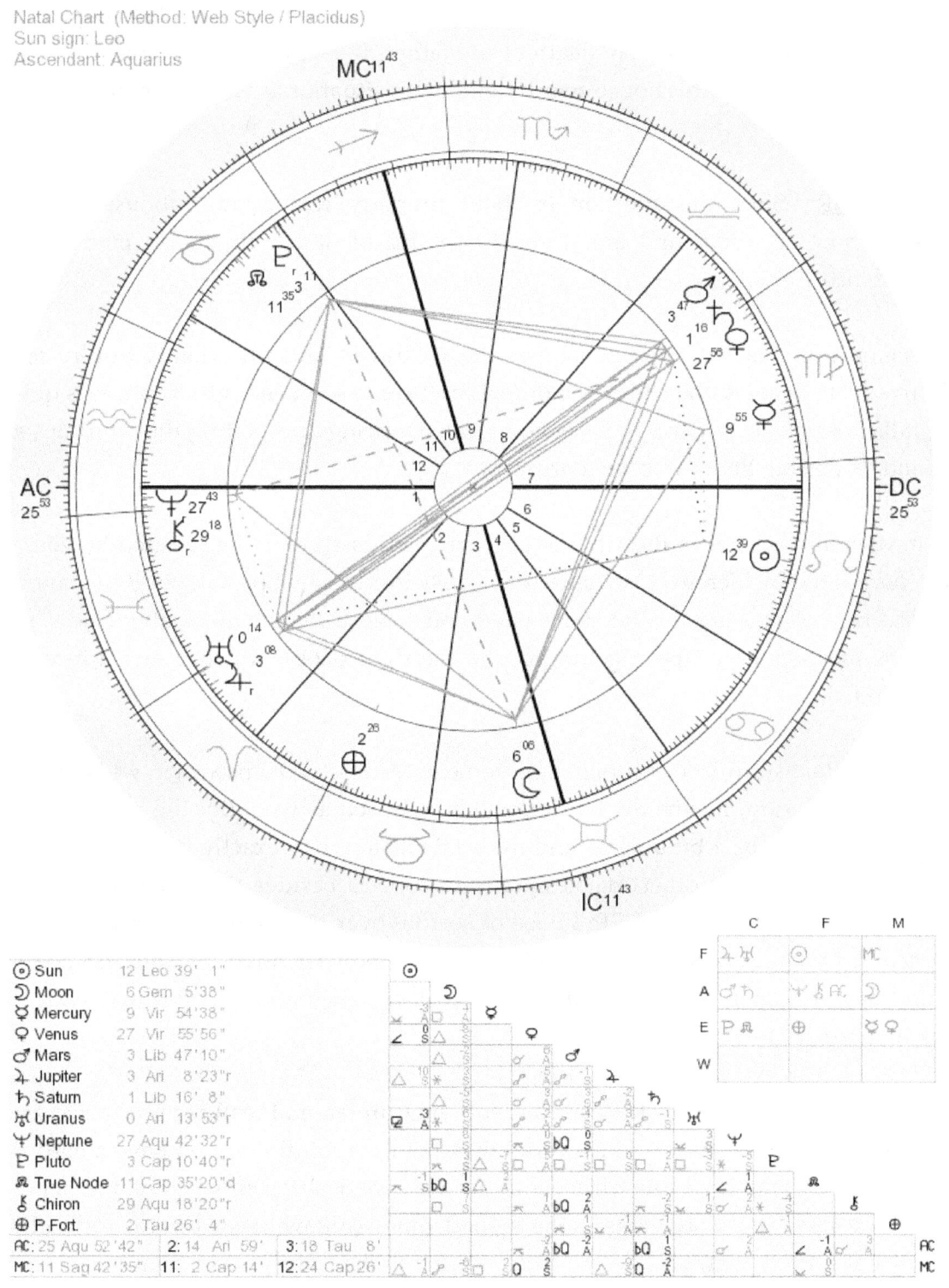

PART I

QUERENT: We have been trying to sell our house on and off for over 5 years. Let me add that this house is part of my late father's trust (so this can be put into the category of trusts and inheritance) and the "we" is my stepmother and I. We're both ready to close that chapter in our life, as it is directly linked to the untimely death of my father. It's still very emotional for us and I can say I am so very weary. Will this house ever be sold? This situation is very difficult on all levels.

R.K. ALEXANDER: Since the question is about property/real estate/a house you now own (regardless of how acquired) and are trying to get rid of, it's a 4th house matter, not an 8th house/inheritance.

Neptune rising and conjunct the ASC shows the weariness and uncertainty you're feeling and facing. In fixed late degrees, the end of the ordeal can't come soon enough! Neptune is quincunxing Venus in fall, ruler of the 8th and 3rd, which means financing and getting the word out about the property and its desirability have been a problem.

Mercury in rulership is ruler of the 4th/the property, and is about to be squared by your co-ruler, the Moon, disposited by Mercury. Not sure if you're using an agent or not, but if you are, it doesn't look like the two of you are on the same page and have different ideas about how to sell the property. The message hasn't been getting out to the right people, or they aren't receiving it the way you intended.

I'm hoping with the Saturn-Venus conjunction some new ideas and a new plan will arise. As Venus moves away from Saturn, maybe the burden will be released as well. But the best I can tell you is things are still going to be a bit unclear and uncertain as to when exactly it will sell. Mercury/the property is not making any other major significant aspects besides the Moon's applying square (difficulty), and Saturn (ruling the 12th house of sorrow over the circumstances of the inheritance via conjunction to Venus) and Uranus, traditional and modern rulers of your ASC are in early degrees and deadlocked in opposition, trying to break the stagnation. Unfortunately, it looks like more wait and see.

QUERENT: Thank you so kindly for your in-depth interpretation. I really appreciate it! Everything you say does make perfect sense and it's certainly what I was afraid of. I do have a hard time with the agent, but my stepmother is the trustee and I'm the beneficiary so my stepmother tends to have more clout in certain situations. This is the second time we have used the realtor and I am not pleased, but I also think that, yes, we are truly dealing with issues greater than ourselves with the market the way it is in our area. Our house could not be any cheaper, but we're up against so many foreclosures and short sales.

I had the feeling the feeling that this will be another year to forget as far as selling the house. My father has been gone ten years, so we've had this house for this long. I'm sure you can see why I'm so weary! Plus, I have to say, this past week I am re-living grief with my father's passing—grief I haven't felt in quite some time. What you have said about Venus, Saturn and Uranus makes sense.

I will do my best to breathe and take it one day at a time. Our time will come, even if it is hard to believe! Thank you!

R.K. ALEXANDER: With all of the outer planets in play in the chart that represent or co-rule you (Neptune, and the Saturn-Uranus opposition making a square Pluto in the house of hopes/wishes), it is absolutely and completely out of your control (especially since your stepmom is calling the shots—addressed below), and so you'll definitely have to find a way to make peace with that. With Aquarius rising, and Uranus in an early critical degree in the 1st house with Jupiter, the Uranian influence is undeniable—the house will likely sell when you last/least expect it to (Uranus). Two royal fixed stars, Antares and Aldebaran, are conjunct the 4th and 10th house angles, additionally signifying the greater meaning to it all and that it will all end well eventually.

Uranus is going to retrograde back into Pisces and stay there until the end of the year, so you'll have some soul-searching to do. It's almost like there's two separate issues at work here: The Saturn mundane sale of the physical property, and then all the emotional baggage attached to it due to the circumstances you obtained the property under, namely, the death of your father. It's as if the sale is secondary and the emotional processing and dealing with the loss are primary; the house is just the catalyst to provoke the emotional issues. This is affirmed by the Saturn-Uranus opposition with Saturn ruling the 12th house of loss/sorrow/buried emotion. The opposition to Uranus is trying to force the issue(s) to the surface so they can be looked at evenly (Saturn/Libra) confronted head-on (Uranus/Aries) and then released. All easier said than done.

Neptune conjunct the ASC = Ya gotta believe—it's the best way to survive the fact that you feel powerless with no control. With Neptune conjoining Chiron, it's also the desire for a painkiller to deal with it all. Like the rocks at the seashore that dissolve into sand over millennia, Neptune dissolves things slowly. Your ASC is in later degrees as is Neptune, and Neptune is going to peek into its rulership in Pisces for a few months next spring, so I think things will be different by then and you'll catch a quick glimpse of light at the end of the tunnel before it retrogrades back into Aquarius. Things are definitely in the homestretch, and I don't think you'll be spending another ten years dealing with this.

Jupiter/your stepmom is heavily afflicted in the chart, so her optimism, ideals and surely some denial may be flying in the face of the realistic and practical [Saturn] way things should be handled to get the house sold. It could be that unconsciously, with Mars in fall in Libra and squaring Pluto on her Scorpio derivative 12th, she hangs onto your father by hanging onto the property, and so subconsciously undermines things that would sell it because it would mean letting go forever. Again, Antares and Aldebaran come into play here since Antares is in your stepmom's sign, and Aldebaran is in the sign of the house/property. Until she has some sort of awakening, things will probably stay status quo.

Moon will trine Neptune before going void-of-course with a square to Venus, so in a way, what you're really asking is not so much when will the house be sold, but when will the pain affiliated with the unresolved emotional issues caused by your father's death and ownership of the house subside. Even if the house sold tomorrow, those issues would still be there needing to be looked at. The Moon/Neptune trine indicates to me that you'll find peace with the situation first, and then what the house does or doesn't do will be irrelevant.

This will not be an overnight process, as ten years into it you already know, so like you already said, be patient (Saturn exalted Libra), take it one day at a time, and focus on the real issue being provoked by the house, and then watch what happens.

PS — Each time the Saturn/Pluto/Uranus-Jupiter T-square gets activated, particularly by transits in early degrees of Cardinal signs, these issues will be revisited.

QUERENT: Your words have meant a great deal to me. I feel much more calm and at peace with this understanding. It all makes perfect sense. I tend to joke that the house will sell when we least expect it! But you are so right about the the finances being secondary to having the chapter of my father's passing closed once and for all!

Open Source Modern Horary Astrology 197

Part II

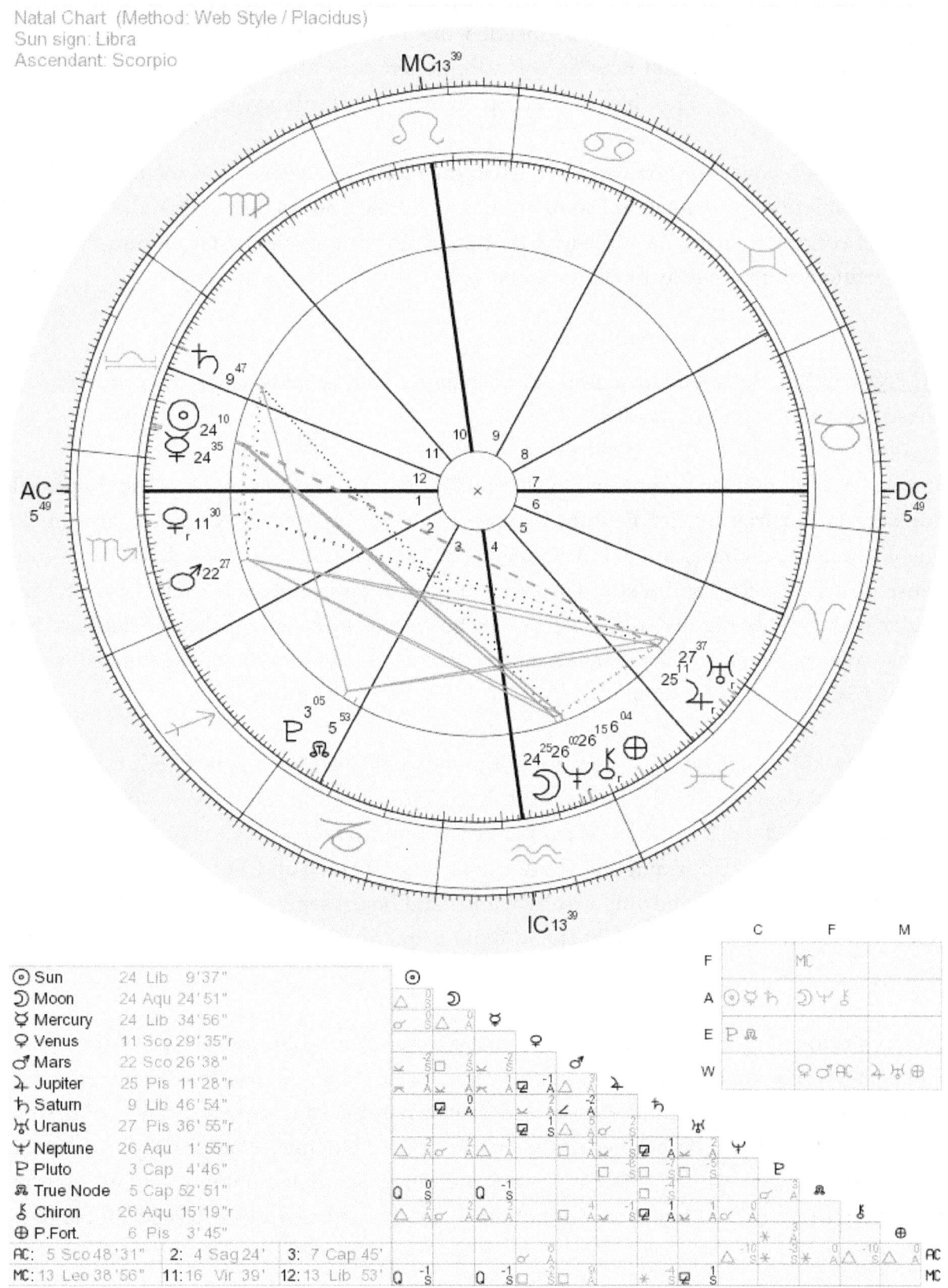

PART II - TWO MONTHS LATER

QUERENT: Well here it is, two offers! I heeded the advice given in your interpretation (thank you, thank you, thank you!) and now out of extreme left field after never receiving one offer in several years, we have two. Plus they showed up on my Dad's birthday.

So of course, the obvious question would be—will the offers be accepted and the house sold? I feel like that since my first interpretation I went ahead and let the powers that be "handle" the situation and let go of control. So have the afflictions that were affecting us the first go around been lifted? Are we charting through muddy or clear waters?

R.K. ALEXANDER: Since circumstances have changed substantially since the original question was asked, the chart is perfectly radical.

Hmmmm...I'm not optimistic about this—yet. The ASC is early and Via Combust, so there's a lot of high anxiety and a trial by fire in front of you yet. Venus is Rx, Via Combust and in double detriment by sign and house, so the buyers may change their minds or reneg. Uranus is ruling the 4th house of the property, and it's in detriment in the 5th and retrograde. Mars, your traditional ASC ruler is in double dignity in the 1st house, but is squaring the 4th house stellium. Saturn, traditional ruler of the 4th is sesquiquadrate the 4th house stellium and then semi-square Mars, traditional ASC ruler. (Had enough yet?)

So let's see-saw the other way for a minute—Pluto is the modern ruler of the ASC, especially since this is a financial deal (sale of the house) at its core. Pluto is in an applying sextile to the Part of Fortune in the 4th. Moon is in rulership by house. The Sun-Mercury Via Combust/combustion is at Spica in the 12th house and trining the 4th house stellium. Saturn and Venus are semi-sextile (but it's a 12th house semi-sextile and you'd really want a 2nd house semisextile), Part of Fortune is trine the ASC, Mars is free of the Via Combust and Mars is in applying trine to the modern house ruler Uranus.

Pluto is in detriment by house (2nd—your finances) and on the 12th house side of the 3rd house cusp of facts/contractual agreements. Uranus/the house is sesquiquadrate Venus/the buyers. Modernly, Pluto/You and Uranus/the house are in a separating square, which makes sense, because you've been trying to get free of the burden for a long time. Traditionally, Saturn/House and Mars/You are semi-square, and Saturn and the Moon sesquiquadrate, which are aspects that create friction, irritation and agitation, kind of like being pecked to death by ducks (apologies, Tim Cahill).

So what does it all mean?

The full moon later in the week at the dead degrees of Aries-Libra (you bet I use transits in horary) will fall around the same time as Mars' square to Neptune in the 4th. Full Moons are usually a culmination of things, especially at the end of a sign (29 Aries), so while it *looks* like this is the beginning of the end, I'm not so convinced. It's the retrogrades of Neptune and Uranus (and to a lesser extent, Venus) that are giving me the doubts about the deal.

When the Moon conjoins Neptune Rx, it can indicate disillusionment and disappointment with an outcome that isn't what you expected (Aquarius). Moon-Neptune also indicates high hopes that may not be realistic (Saturn sesquiquadrate Neptune). Uranus-Jupiter Rx indicates the offers may fall short of expectations, affirmed by Mercury/ruling the buyer's financing quincunx Jupiter/your 2nd house ruler. There may need to be a price adjustment, but you shouldn't have to give the farm away.

Mars will trine the Jupiter-Uranus conjunction later, so a better deal/offer will come along eventually—and again, like the first chart, unexpectedly. Let the retrogrades and the fixed angles to work in your favor and don't let the combust Sun-Mercury conjunction in cardinal signs make you feel you have to take action on this yesterday—you've waited ten years, for god's sake, you don't need to try to rush it to dump the property now. With Sun-Mercury at Spica combust/Via Combust trine the 4th house stellium, some good will come of it all even if these deals fall through.

I think you're getting closer to selling, but you're not quite there yet. Be *very* patient and make sure the money is realistic and in your favor. Don't be desperate to dump or in a hurry to sell. I think this has a bit of a way to go yet and you'll experience some delays and snafus.

QUERENT: Thanks again for coming to my aid! You're right with continuing to be patient particularly since we've lasted this long. The only thing that would make me a little jumpy is the inheritance tax that will be rearing its ugly head again in 2011. I really need to get my tookus in gear and talk with a tax specialist.

The thing that we're all worried about that could turn the offer on its ear is the house inspection. The house is 60 years old and while we've done some work to it, we're worried it may have some wear and tear that is unbeknownst to us. I'm pretty much waiting for this to end the deal, at least with the offer from the couple...but maybe not from the offer for investment property. We'll see.

I think the corker will be the splitting of money between myself and my stepmother once the house sells. That is where I foresee the disagreements, friction, etc. I get the feeling we both have different ideas.

If nothing else, all this sure woke me up from a slumber about this house. I seriously had forgotten about it over the last month until the phone was tossed into my sleeping face over the weekend. I'll just continue to hang in there and move my anxiety toward my schooling again.

OOOOOOOOOOOOOOOOOOOH!!!!!!!!!!!!! All I can do is laugh because just as I finished replying, I hopped over to my email and saw the headline from my stepmother, "The buyer pulled out of the deal." And there we go. On to Offer 2...

R.K. ALEXANDER: Sometimes it sucks being right.

With Uranus at the end of Pisces, as you just saw, if you count your chickens, they are sure *not* to hatch (Lutin). So don't worry about splitting money with your stepmom until the deal actually is finalized, and for god's sake, *never* discuss it while Venus is Rx in Scorpio! Wait wait wait wait wait until Venus goes direct, clears her shadow, and then moves into generous Sadge in January. The more you discuss up front, the less unpleasant surprises you'll face later. But you have to bide your time for now, because with half the sky retrograde, people change their minds and reneg as you just saw. The Nodes at Pluto don't help much either because people tend to want to welch on deals.

The retrogrades may be giving you a "test run" to see what kind of problems you'll be facing later when the deal actually happens, so you can resolve as much of it in advance as possible. As I mentioned previously, some good will come of all this, even if the deals fall through.

Re: the house inspection, Uranus retrograde and in detriment in the 5th house makes me think there's something wrong that you'd never suspect. There's something "stressed" about the property.

Taxes are ruled by Scorpio and the 8th, and the Moon is ruling your 9th/schooling, so your current course of action is wise. It's a cliche, but this is a marathon, not a sprint, as you know better than anyone. This new chart doesn't change that.

Hang in there and good luck!

QUERENT: I definitely want to heed your advice and what you described. I'm trying really hard to wait, wait, wait as I know you're right about Venus retrograde. But the latest surprise was that my stepmother has stated she wants to buy the house from the estate and give me my half. That way she takes over the title and I'm free and clear. Free and clear...right? RIGHT?!

We put the kibosh on the second offer because the more we looked into it, the more suspicious it became. It would have been a case of "giving the house away" which at this point would have been ridiculous. This whole deal caused a great rift between my stepmom and the realtor, but I've been waiting for that to come for years. I never liked our realtor.

Anyway, so what I was saying about waiting, I still am okay with it but my stepmother can't. Or won't. She wants to secure a loan ASAP, which I don't blame her with the interest rates being what they are. But I'm just waiting for something to rear its ugly head…ugh. I feel like we are still okay to negotiate a price, mainly because we will be gleaning it from current information and whatever the bank assesses. No big deal there. The situation "seems" like it can be very positive, but…I see where the "combustion" may build up. Oy. I'm waiting to be pecked to death by ducks.

R.K. ALEXANDER: The combustion relates to your stepmother (10th house/Sun) and it's in your 12th house of self-undoing (her derivative third of contracts with Venus Rx on the cusp and in the 4th—problems no matter which way you turn). Don't let her overwhelm you (combustion) into a deal. The terms would definitely *not* favor you and I don't think the banks would go for it, either (her derived 8th/Pisces cusp).

Stay fixed and firm (Scorpio). If you really believe your stepmom's offer will leave you free and clear, I have a bridge in Brooklyn I'd like to sell you! With the Sun-Neptune trine, your stepmom is completely over-idealizing the situation! With your stepmom's ruler in fall and Via combust, (regardless of Spica—trying to get rich quick) her ideas are not going to help anything in the situation. Alienating the realtor is not a good idea either, since it's not like your stepmom has been generating any leads on her own all these years. But the realtor is also looking out for her own interests, rather than yours (Venus Rx, double detriment).

I would not be surprised for this to go dormant again for awhile. I still think it was a test run for to show you in advance what problems you'll likely face when the deal eventually does happen, so you can prepare in advance behind the scenes (12th house).

QUERENT: My stepmom backed out. The realtor is back and we just dropped the price ever so slightly. And now the house will just go onto the back burner until next year.

I have to say, you were absolutely spot-on! She did over-idealize and I stood steadfast. My whip has been cracked on both she and the realtor, I'm not going to remain passive any longer. It will all be done soon enough and we now know exactly the issues we will have to deal with once we find the rightful new owner.

202 Open Source Modern Horary Astrology

Part III

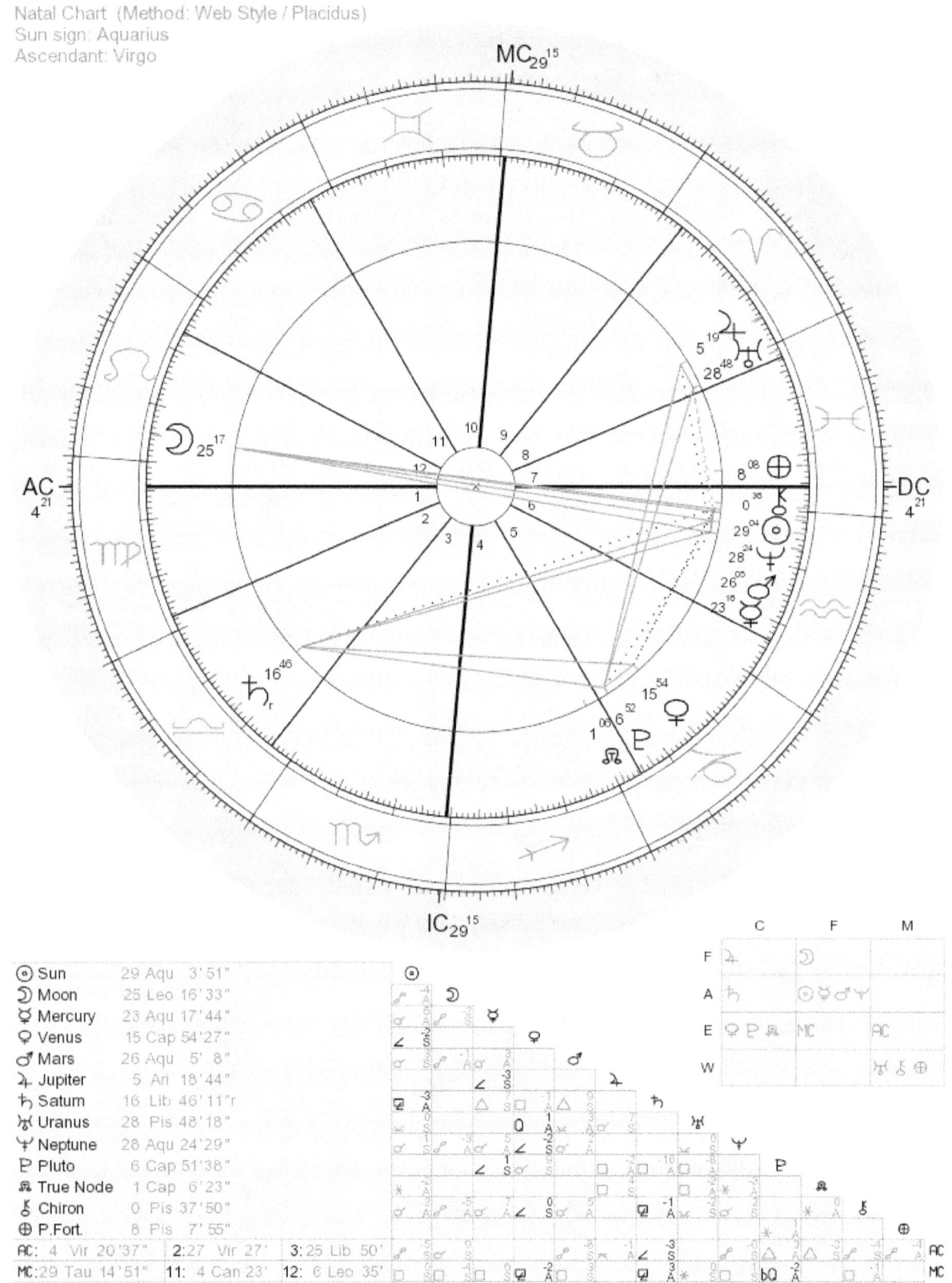

Natal Chart (Method: Web Style / Placidus)
Sun sign: Aquarius
Ascendant: Virgo

PART III -- FOUR MONTHS LATER (SIX AND A HALF MONTHS SINCE PART I)

QUERENT: Well, I'm here to say as of 4 p.m. today the house has SOLD!

After a surprise offer, a few counter offers and a runaround with the lender, the house is no longer ours. So now that the issue of whether the house will be sold has been answered, another has popped up: Will the trust that involves me and my stepmother be settled without dispute? In other words, will we be able to the split the money made from the sale without any major misunderstandings between us? It's a concern now because it has been a concern in the past (which has been brought up before). Thanks!

P.S. I brought the chart up and freaked, LOL! So much red. But I've heard about something called cazimi with the Sun. Is that happening here? Please let it be a good thing!

R.K. ALEXANDER: Good gawd, I'm glad your ordeal in selling the house is over—years since the ordeal began, but six months since the original discussion, not bad! However, now you have a new ordeal to look forward to...they say the final furlong is always the hardest, mmm?

Conflict abounds in this chart. Jupiter is in the 8th house of the trust and about to square Pluto, ruler of complications. Mercury/you, is exalted by sign and dignified by house, but you're sitting right on that Jupiter-Pluto midpoint. Talk about the hot seat! Mars, Jupiter's dispositor and ruler of the 9th house of legal issues, is going to conjoin Neptune, ruler of the trust (8th house). A skirmish will ensue, when the Moon moves up to oppose the Mars-Neptune midpoint very shortly (as in a couple of weeks).

Sun-Neptune are combust rather than cazimi, since the Sun is more than 17 minutes of arc from Neptune. The Sun is in detriment and at a dead degree, ruling the 12th house of ordeals, fears and mistrust, and disposits your Moon, which will oppose it before void-of-course. The situation is at the end of its rope, out of gas, and all the emotional baggage (Moon/Leo/12th) from the years of ordeal is ready to be dropped and let go of. (Neptune rules dissolution.) With Chiron in the mix, it's going to feel completely overwhelming and confusing at times, but don't worry, your ruler is very strongly placed. And the TNO Quaoar is going to come in to help you.

The trust is the 8th house of joint assets, with Uranus exalted in the 8th as your dispositor. Your stepmom is Taurus/the 10th house cusp/Venus at a critical degree just separating from Algol's reach, and T-squaring the Sun and Moon. Your stepmom is Venus in Cap in the 5th house of real estate proceeds (since it's the 2nd house from the 4th), squaring and mutually recepted with the debilitated Saturn in your house of $$. This is really about negotiation, rather than emotional drama/histrionics. Deriving the 10th cusp/stepmom to the first, her ruler Venus is in detriment by house in the house of joint assets/trusts (derived 8th) and squaring debilitated Saturn in the derived 5th of real estate sale proceeds.

Your significators, Merc and Moon, make no aspect to her or her dispositors—combined with Aquarius, this means the more amicable and detached you remain in your dealings/communications with her, and the more contract-specific details you can stick to, the better off you'll be.

So let the lawyers slug it out if need be. Saturn Rx and Via Combust in the 2nd shows the money coming to you will be delayed due to the skirmish with her; I think the still-early ASC shows the beginning of the end of the process. Pluto as ruler of the 4th and in the 4th with the Node, semi-square your ruler Mercury, and angles changing from mutable to fixed show a permanent change and complicated ending to the situation, at some cost.

But don't let any of that scare you. Why? Quaoar, the benefic TNO at 22 Sadge, is connected to everything, trining your Moon and sextiling Saturn, Mars and Mercury, shows that despite the sturm and drang of the sitch, you'll make it through and come out smelling like a rose, with a whole new, happier way of life ahead of you and available to you once this whole thing is over. The boat anchor will finally be removed from around your neck. Quaoar and Pluto in her derived 7th shows that what your stepmom's "fight" really is has absolutely NOTHING to do with you—it's about what we talked about at the beginning of this whole discussion: She finally has to let go of the last thing that connects her to her deceased husband, and the memories of that way of life. It's going to vanish, forever, once this settles. Uranus at the end of Pisces mutually recepted with Neptune at the end of Aquarius means it's the end of that era for her and she will be forced to finally let it go. It will be her crucifixion prior to her resurrection and it's her ordeal, not yours, though some of the debris will be flung your way. Duck it, stay detached and don't take it personally. Have faith (Quaoar in Sadge, Uranus in Pisces) even though there's going to be times when it will seem like there's no reason to have any.

Quaoar is bringing full circle and to completion all the long-buried issues for both of you that we talked about at the very beginning, so you can begin anew. The chart is really about the finality and end of the matter (and ordeal) for both of you, so you can finally bury your dead so to speak, and start over.

QUERENT: Well shoot with the cazimi, but that's okay. I just saw all the red and it reminded me of junior high when the teacher would return an assignment with red ink chicken scratches. Usually not a good sign!

You really did bring up a great point with my stepmom and what she is most likely going through with moving out of the house—the house being her last link to my father. I feel bad that I didn't consider that and since she's lived in the house all this time, she hasn't been able to cope and detach like I have. That is something I will definitely be more aware of and also know that if she upset not to take it personally. I'll try to be more empathetic.

I haven't even brought up the money issue yet since she's going nuts trying to get everything out of the house. The couple of times I've spoken with her briefly I can tell she's stressed to the limits and I feel it's better to let her ride that storm. She does have help and a moving team ready to go, so I know she has support at least.

Oh, sigh. I am so ready for this to be done, but thank you for your encouragement. I feel like Frodo carrying the ring to Mordor, so I'm ready to be rid of it. I've been patient this long, so I *can* wait a bit longer for the issue to be closed. Starting over sounds so nice.

Thanks again for taking the time to stay with this wild and crazy ride, I really do appreciate it beyond any words I can type!

206 Open Source Modern Horary Astrology

Case Study #13: A Big Change Looms at 29 Degrees

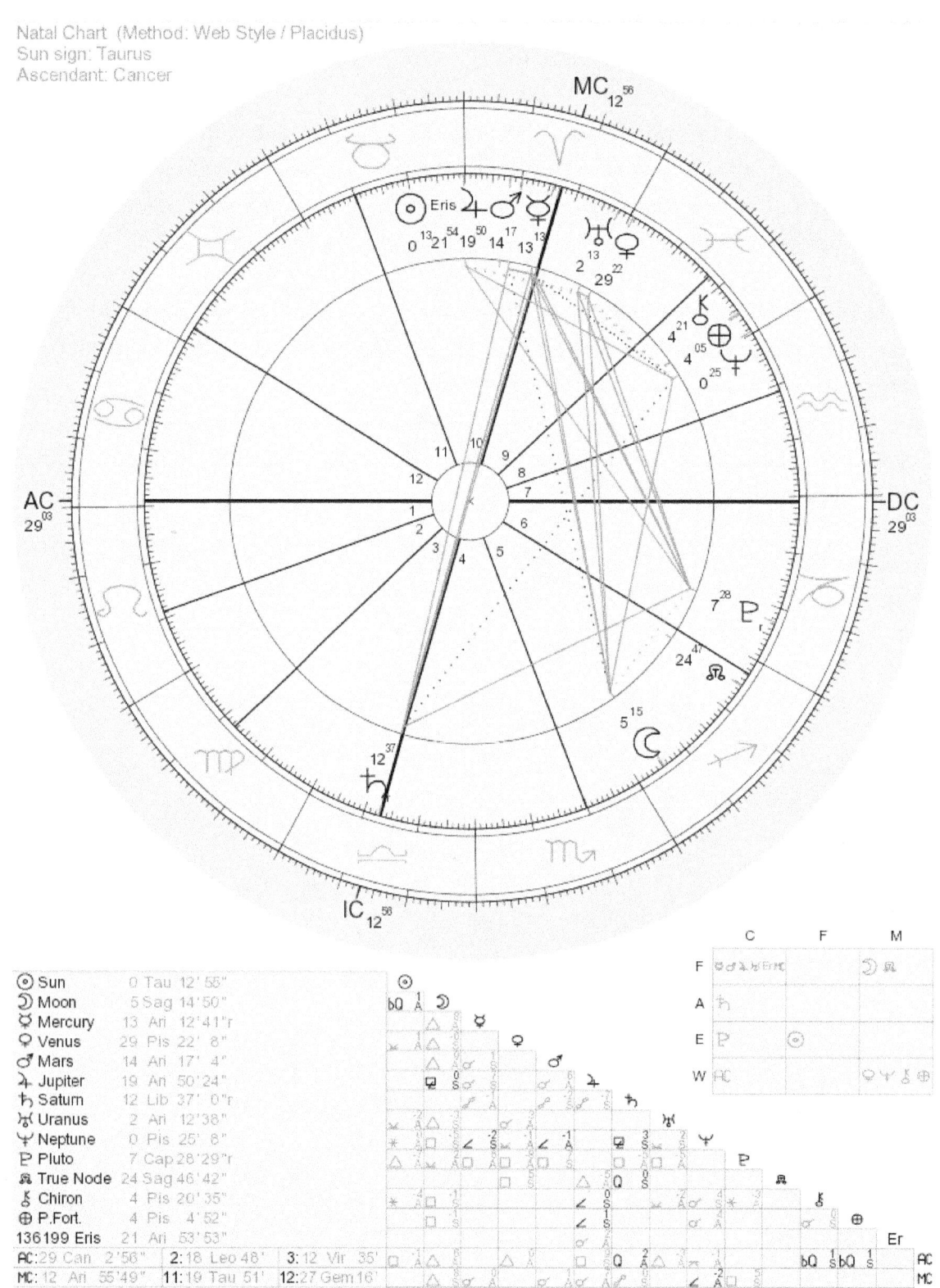

QUERENT: For the past two years, my situation with finding decent employment has been so poor! Have had situations with layoffs, not getting paid for work, harassment, and in general situations where it has been a poor fit in terms of what the work consists of, what these jobs pay, etc.

In the past couple of months, I was one of two people considered for positions that I was very excited about, but did not get them. So I made this chart to see if/when something that I can see myself in with long term and happy prospects. Some things I am not clear with though. First, the chart has a very late ASC. This usually means the matter has been decided, but obviously my explanation shows that it is not!

Also, there is an approaching trine, from me (Moon) to Mars, 10th house ruler, in approximately 9 units, which I hope would mean days since the angles are cardinal? Is this correct? It looks as if Mars has got something going for it here! BUT, before this occurs, I will meet a trine with Mercury retro, which is right on top of the 10th house. I'm looking to see what Mercury represents, but cannot draw any conclusions. It also appears that I will sextile Saturn which opposes Mercury, although the aspect grid does not show this. I'm really feeling down in the dumps about this, some light at the end of this would be great! Thanks!

R.K. ALEXANDER: Your Moon/Ruler of the ASC and 12th house is besieged between Rx Saturn and Rx Pluto, so no wonder you're feeling depressed (along with Moon square the Neptune-Chiron conjunction=self doubt). But don't worry—there are very blue skies ahead. They say the final furlong is always the hardest (Saturn Rx on the 12th house side of the 4th house cusp), but with the critical degree ASC, the chart is saying that the sitch is about to change—bigtime.

QUERENT: Just had another thought about what was mentioned about the ASC in late degree—I have a small grasp on understanding timing with planets, but does timing also apply when dealing with something like the ASC, DSC, MC, IC ? If so, how is this determined in actual units? For example, one degree with a planet can mean day, week, month and so on, depending on the modality, yes? How does this work in the example above?

R.K. ALEXANDER: There are four types of timing in horary: modal/degree timing, ephemeris timing, lunar timing and significator progression timing. I use ephemeris and progressed timing because they actually work consistently. In this case, having the speedy Moon as your significator seems great, but the problem is it's intercepted, a debilitation that "traps" it or inhibits it from acting. So what has to happen is that Mars (MC ruler and most powerful planet in the chart and skies right now) and Jupiter (Moon's dispositor) have to conjoin, with both applying to conjoin the MC, with the Moon moving up to trine it all. Since the Moon is just getting established in early degrees Sadge, it's going to take little while to hit the early 20's of degrees where Mars/Jupiter/MC will be.

There are also other niggling details pooling in the background, because you're emerging from a horary triple-whammy, in the same way a victim staggers away from a car crash:

1) A double quindecile (now separating) to Saturn involving Venus and the Sun. So you've been obsessing over the whole thing (moneyandsecuritymoneyandsecuritymoneyandsecurity) rather than taking action. The lack of action was due to the Moon square Neptune-Chiron with the Part of Fortune, making you feel a lack of direction, loss of faith, and no hope of a lucky break. Double quindeciles are a high enough degree of difficulty in horary, so to compound it with the Moon's problems, well, no wonder you were depressed and discouraged. Luckily, you're separating from both.

2) The Saturn-Pluto-Merc/Mars T-square in your 4th/10th/6th houses, with the outlet leg in the 12th and Cancer/you on the 12th. This is especially problematic, because Mercury Rx is conjunct the Mars/MC midpoint, with both opposing Saturn Rx in the 3rd. Mercury Rx is also beseiged between Mars and Uranus—Talk about a dearth of valid leads/opportunities! Jupiter is separating from the T-square now, but when it was part of it, no wonder things were weighing heavily on you.

3) Eris. I love her dearly, but God she is a pain in the ass. Jupiter, your co-significator, is conjunct Eris and beseiged between her and Mars at 21 degrees. And guess what? Mars and Jupiter will conjoin at 22 degrees Aries. There will still be some continued angst and sturm and drang around the new forthcoming opportunity, as your Moon will trine Eris, too.

Okay, so you're emerging from all that and now for the good news:

With the Sun sextiling Neptune (and Uranus-Venus conjunct its midpoint), keep the faith and expect the unexpected. The Sun is dispositing to Venus trining the ASC at her dead degree of exaltation (another indicator that things are going to change). The Sun and Moon are in applying biquintile, so you have the chops to hang in there, though with the Sun squaring the ASC you don't think so sometimes.

Timing: Take advantage of Mercury direct this weekend by getting the ball rolling now, and then by the end of the month at the Mars-Jupiter conjunction, you should have something to go on.

QUERENT: Thank you so much for the effort you put into this explanation! It pretty much describes my situation—the lack of direction, loss of faith, etc. I have to say I have been holding off up until lately. I used to enjoy a situation where I had great opportunities, and very strong work experience. Due to the slide things have taken over this past period of time, my confidence has been shattered, and frequently psych myself out of going after more suitable positions. Just this past week, I've sent my resume off to about 20 potential employers. Had three interviews so far, one of which is the one I've just mentioned where I came so close. I have two more at the beginning of next week, in a city about 1.5 hours away where I used to work for quite some time. I really do not like the prospect of the whole searching/packing/moving/unpacking, but I feel as if my options will become even more limited than they already are. I sure hope that by the end of the month something with potential does make an appearance!

[SEVEN DAYS LATER, 3 DAYS BEFORE THE END OF THE MONTH]

QUERENT: Just an update—Just spent a couple of days in the city for some interviews. This was for two different spots, both are part of large companies and each has a multiple step process—first interview, then a second, then a background and reference check, then a one day on-site performance interview, and then on to getting an offer, or not.

One place called me back within hours to complete the second part, the other I am awaiting word from. Then a third place called me, who I already interviewed for, and wants me in tomorrow to speak a bit more to them and spend some time in there to get a glimpse of the place in action.

Not sure what will come of any of this, and will keep sending applications out when the opportunities arise.

R.K. ALEXANDER: The focus of the chart is clearly on the 10th, and beginning anew (Aries) in your career. The Sun will trine Pluto and give you the strength to tough it out and endure while you slowly get back on your feet financially (Sun 0° Taurus ruling the 2nd).

Remember first and foremost that the T-square outlet leg is in the 12th, ruled by Moon in Sadge and in the 5th it means your fears are exaggerated. Your best days are ahead of you, not behind you—when outer planets tussle, it takes awhile to see that. When Sadge is involved, you have to go on faith. The fact that you are getting interviews is a GREAT sign! You're sooooooooooooo close. Soooooooooooooooooooooo close.

[THREE DAYS LATER ON THE LAST DAY OF THE MONTH; TEN DAYS AFTER TIME OF QUESTION]

QUERENT: You are my hero! Thanks so much for that response! The latest: Things are moving quickly, and getting a little complicated! The third option I mentioned above has made an offer, is near where I live, and this means I would not have to move to a new place, BUT I'm tempted to pass on it because it is pretty much a seasonal position, with little, if any, opportunity for growth, AND BECAUSE...one of the two positions with the larger companies (and the one who has my interest most) is looking quite positive!

I've completed the succession of interviews—even one from the right hand of the Big Guy, who during our conversation said all three people in the company who I've previously interviewed with had great things to say.

Now we're awaiting the results of the background/reference check, I do the drug test tomorrow, and finally on to a practical test of sorts to test my skill set. A long process, but a really great company with work that is engaging, great package, and numerous growth opportunities.

It may seems nuts to pass on the existing offer in today's climate, but this job puts me where I want to be! In the midst of this, I got a call from another spot as well, and we are currently trying to line up an interview time. That's all I got for now!

R.K. ALEXANDER: Oh my God, that's an embarrassment of riches! From nowheresville to everyone falling at your feet in a little over a week! I am so happy for you!!!

QUERENT: Thanks!!! Again, while none of these positions are bad, and I've yet to hear back from all except the two I've mentioned, I'm really holding out for this particular one. Hope this is not a mistake! Interestingly enough, after looking at my natal chart, my 6th house is packed with the stellium going on in Aries. Somehow, I thought the Mars-Jupiter conjunction would have brought something on!

OUTCOME

[FOUR DAYS LATER; 14 DAYS AFTER TIME OF QUESTION]

QUERENT: I GOT IT!!! It was the one I was holding out for! I start tomorrow with all the preliminary orientation, etc.

One of the crazy things about all this is that two days before the offer was officially on, I got a text from a former co-worker friend of mine, who is in the loop up there, asking me how the new job was going. I asked him what he meant by this, and apparently the manager happened to be chatting with him and another former co-worker and mentioned that he hired me. This was even before the results of the background check, tests, etc. were complete. Was the last to know, but hey, better late than never!

R.K. ALEXANDER: I love it when a chart comes together. Glad I could help. Good luck to you!

[TIMING NOTE: One day after the end of the month, on the 1st day of the month following the time of the question, the hiring manager told the co-worker friend of the querent that the querent had been hired. The querent didn't find out until two days later, likely awaiting the results of the drug-testing, etc., before making a formal offer to the querent.]

APPENDIX B – Horary Cheat Sheets

BASIC HORARY FORMULA — Use With Chapter 6 Guidelines

$$
\begin{array}{rl}
& S = \text{Significators} \\
+ & A = \text{Aspects} \\
+ & M = \text{Moon} \\
+ & E = \text{Extras} \\
\hline
= & \text{Conclusion}
\end{array}
$$

S	• Cast chart, note significators of relevant houses, any co-significators, and current transits • Look at strengths and weaknesses of significators by house, sign, disposition, reception, early/late degrees, debilitation (retrograde, combustion, Via Combust, interception, etc.) • Look at strengths and weaknesses (dignity/debility) of planet that naturally rules the matter • Connections to and reception of a) significators to each other; b) significators to relevant house ruler; c) significators to Moon; d) planet that naturally rules the matter • Asteroids and TNOs by house placement
+A	• Aspects between significators: harsh, easy, mixed or none • Aspects between significators and the planet ruling the relevant house (e.g., ruler of the 3rd cusp for communication questions between querent/1st house and quesited/7th significant other) • Aspects between the Moon and significators: harsh or benign • Aspects between the Moon and the planet ruling the matter and the relevant house • Aspects between significators and asteroids and TNOs • Aspects to significator/co-significator midpoints • Dispositors of significators/co-significators • Nodes by house axis and aspect to significators and the Moon
+M	• Early or late degrees • Void-of-course, Via Combust, eclipsed, new, full, or occulting another planet • Strong or weak by sign or house • Aspecting significator midpoints • Aspecting asteroid or TNO midpoints • Past, current and future aspects, particularly with significators and planet ruling matter • Last Ptolemaic aspect and last true aspect before void-of-course
+E	• Part of Fortune by house, sign, dispositor • Fixed stars • Other Arabic parts in addition to Part of Fortune
=C	• Never judge a chart based on one isolated factor • How well connected and fortified are the significators, or estranged and weakened? • Benefic, harmonious and well-aspected significators and Moon = Yes • Afflictions and debilitations to significators and Moon = No • Mixed significators and Moon; a mix or combination of good and harsh aspects and connections = matter can come to pass with difficulty or dissatisfaction with result, *or* not come to pass to the querent's overall benefit.

ASPECTS

Aspect	Symbol	Degrees Apart	Meaning
Conjunction	☌	0	Bringing together or culmination, prominence, emphasis, reinforcement. Harmonious, depending on nature of planets involved
Semi-sextile	⚺	30	Harmony, growth. 12th house-sided semi-sextiles bad for health, 2nd house-sided semi-sextiles good for financial matters. Midpoint of a sextile
Semisquare	∠	45	A difficult circumstance. Friction and irritation, minor difficulty. Midpoint of a square
Sextile	✶	60	Harmony, ease and opportunity. Midpoint of a trine
Quintile	Q	72	Easy, fortunate, accomplishment. Midpoint of a biquintile
Square	□	90	Conflict, obstacle, stress, frustration. Midpoint of an opposition
Trine	△	120	Luck, ease, flow, talent, knack, harmony
Sesquiquadrate or Sesquisquare	⚼	135	Stressful condition. Friction, conflict, aggravation and agitation. Midpoint is 67.5 degrees
Biquintile	Bq	144	Subtle, benefic, harmony
Inconjunct or Quincunx	⚻	150	Adjustment and strain. Midpoint is 75 degrees
Quindecile	Ⓓ	165	Obsession-compulsion causing upheaval or instability. Overly preoccupied by a matter; nags until issue is resolved. Midpoint of a quincunx and opposition
Opposition	☍	180	Separation, divergence, tension
Parallel (same declination)	∥	n/a	Amplification with the essence of a conjunction; an extra connection between the two planets involved
Contra-Parallel (opp. declination)	⚯	n/a	Amplification with the essence of an opposition; an extra connection between the two planets involved

HOUSES - BASIC MEANINGS

1st	Personal self, appearance, temperament, talent, self-image, body, self-potential. Signifies the querent, the person asking the question
2nd	Possessions, values, finances, material stability and wealth, portable goods or objects of the 1st house person
3rd	Communications, short trips, siblings, neighbors, facts of the matter, thinking processes, dissemination of info, primary or elementary schooling
4th	Home and family environment, the mother, real estate, antiques, endings
5th	Children, romance, love, speculation, entertainment, gambling, creativity, dating, pleasure, performing arts, artistic talent
6th	Health, occupation/jobs, small animals, employees, service, labor, craft or trade, health industry, work
7th	Yoked/committed partnerships, professionals consulted, open enemies, marriage, the public, contracts, relationships personal and public
8th	Death, taxes, insurance, finances and possessions of 7th house persons, mortgages, inheritances, debt, pensions, loss, legacy, wills, obsessions, retirement income, surgery, sex, mortality
9th	Foreign travel, publishing, philosophy/religion/faith, college/higher education, lawyers, long distance travel, higher mind
10th	Career, profession, employer, the father, professional reputation or standing, government, judges, business, public life, public reputation
11th	Friends, hopes and wishes, large groups and organizations, humanity, internet, goals, colleagues, societies, profit from 10th house business
12th	Self-undoing, sorrow, privacy, confinement, large animals, hospitals and institutions, secret enemies, secrets, drug or alcohol addiction, spirituality or spiritual life, selfless service, self-destruction, jails

BASIC PLANETARY NOUN & VERB KEYWORDS

SUN - Self expression, men, head of a group, employer. Vitality, individuality, will, power, leadership, vigor, ego, masculine principle, creativeness, authority.

MOON - Personality and subconscious self. Mothers, wives, females, the public. Fluctuation, change, domestic, instinctual, impressionable, nourishing, receptivity, feminine principle, responsiveness.

MERCURY - Objective awareness of self, mind, young people, messenger. Communication, expression, adaptability, intellect, perception, spoken and written expression, alertness, thought, skill, dexterity.

VENUS-Females, loved ones, artists. Social association, harmony, attraction, cohesion, ease, love, pleasure, affection, mildness, decoration, beauty.

MARS - Males, soldiers, surgeons, mechanics. Energy, initiative, action, aggression, assertion, courage, construction and destruction, passion, independence.

JUPITER - Professional men, judges, lawyers, clergymen, lawgivers, sportsmen/athletes, mature men of benefic nature. Expansion, benevolence, vision, abundance, devotion, protection, optimism, justice, prosperity, generosity.

SATURN - Older males in authority, older people, statesmen, administrators, teachers, government. Contraction, systems, limitation, restriction, tradition, prudence, framework, crystallization, persistence, discipline.

URANUS - Inventors, reformers, altruists, rebels, psychologists, humanitarians. Uniqueness, disruption, originality, unexpected, eccentric, altruism, renunciation, non-conformity, progressive, invention.

NEPTUNE - Mystics, prophets, promoters, actors, motion picture industry, seafaring men, recluses. Visionaries, utopians, mystics, idealists, illusions, confusion, mediumistic, imaginative, vague, inspiration, indecisiveness.

PLUTO - Groups, organizations, spiritual leader, gangsters, monopolies, plutocracies. Alien or foreign things, regimes, regeneration, mutation, transformation, annihilation, complication, integration, collectivity, coercion, inversion, anonymity, domination, alteration of a permanent nature.

Planetary Rulerships/Dignities and Debilitations

Planet	Rulership	Exaltation	Detriment	Fall
Moon	Cancer/4th house	Taurus/2nd house	Capricorn/10th house	Scorpio/8th house
Sun	Leo/5th house	Aries/1st house	Aquarius/11th house	Libra/7th house
Mercury	Gemini/Virgo/3rd & 6th houses	Aquarius/11th house	Sagittarius/Pisces/9th &12th houses	Leo/5th house
Venus	Taurus/Libra/2nd & 7th houses	Pisces/12th house	Aries/Scorpio/1st & 8th houses	Virgo/6th house
Mars	Aries/1st house	Capricorn/10th house	Taurus/Libra/2nd & 7th houses	Cancer/4th house
Jupiter	Sagittarius/ 9th house	Cancer/4th house	Gemini/Virgo/3rd & 6th houses	Capricorn/10th house
Saturn	Capricorn/10th house	Libra/7th house	Cancer/4th house	Aries/1st house
Uranus	Aquarius/11th house	Scorpio/8th house	Leo/5th house	Taurus/2nd house
Neptune	Pisces/12th house	Cancer/4th house	Virgo/6th house	Capricorn/10th house
Pluto	Scorpio/8th house	Aries/1st house	Taurus/2nd house	Libra/7th house

ASTEROIDS & TNOs

ASTEROIDS		
Chiron	⚷	Pain prior to healing or transformation. Also represents teachers and mentors
Lilith	⚸	Personal revolt as a result of personal injustice; not always conscious
Pallas	⚴	Wisdom and strategic application and execution. Shows the wise course of action; if afflicted, what's preventing it
Juno	⚵	Committed personal relationships and marriages, and struggles in them especially due to inequality or injustice
Vesta	⚶	Steadfast focus, devotion and dedication
Ceres	⚳	Nurturing, caring, empathy, nourishment; what feeds the querent in life
TNOs		
Eris	⯰ (proposed glyph)	Heavily malefic; where you'll find strife, discord and trouble in a chart; hassle
Varuna	No glyph	Symbolizes truth, integrity and validity
Quaoar	No glyph	Benefic; beginnings and endings, often simultaneously; sunset clause; "when one door closes, another opens"; doing good in secret
Sedna	No glyph	Malefic; damage at the hands of others; bitterness, aloneness, outcast
Orcus	No glyph	Anti-Pluto; use together to determine intent and outcome; power struggles
Haumea	No glyph	Benefic; splintered, fragmented, to create something new; quirky; controversy over beginning of something; Hawaii significator
Makemake	No glyph	Incubation period prior to new start; fragile and delicate situations; denuded where something once thrived

REGIONS OF THE BODY

Aries	Head and face	Libra	Kidneys, ovaries, lower back
Taurus	Neck, throat and ears	Scorpio	Organs of generation and elimination
Gemini	Arms, hands, lungs	Sagittarius	Hips and thighs
Cancer	Stomach and breasts	Capricorn	Knees, bones, teeth
Leo	Heart and upper back	Aquarius	Lower legs, calves, ankles
Virgo	Intestines	Pisces	Feet

FIXED STARS

Caput Algol (26° Taurus)	More of a message than a malefic. Losing one's head in a matter to the extent that things aren't being seen clearly or rationally. Over-attached or over-invested to where a person can't think straight, to their own detriment.
Pleiades/Alcyone (0° Gemini)	The Weeping Sisters constellation; a significator here will give you something to cry about.
Aldebaran (10° Gemini)	Related to Mars with its energy and drive, but considered volatile.
Sirius (14° Cancer)	Success through your own efforts. Benign action and results. A flourishing.
22° Leo	Not a fixed star but a malefic fixed degree. One's own worst enemy in a more overt way than the 12th house meaning. A no-win degree. Not free to act on your own behalf.
Regulus (0° Virgo)	The most benefic fixed star. Enhances or glorifies a significator, but can also exaggerate or create grandiose hopes.
Spica/Arcturus (Spica 24° Libra, Arcturus 25° Libra)	Benefic oasis in the otherwise fiery and turbulent Via Combust zone. Helps matters.
Serpentis (19° Scorpio)	Also not a fixed star, but a malefic fixed degree. Considered the worst place in the zodiac.
Antares (10° Sagittarius)	The need to defend or fight back in a given situation. Valorous at best, vengeful at worst. Conflict.
Fomalhaut (3° Pisces)	Considered to bestow great and lasting honors. A benefic influence if conjunct a significator.

APPENDIX C – Practice Chart Answers

Here are the answers to the practice charts in Chapter 8.

Chart 1: Should the querent move her residence to city X?

Short order can be made of this chart. Mercury is in fall by sign, but rulership by house and conjunct Saturn, the planet of limitation. Mercury disposits to the Sun in rulership in the fourth house of the current residence. The Moon, natural ruler of home and residence, is in detriment in the 7th house (the house of removal, or where the querent would move to) with Pluto retrograde, promising complications compounded. The Moon is going to square the ruler of the 7th house, and quincunx the Sun, ruler of the 4th house, before going void-of-course.

The outcome? The querent remained in the city she was living in.

Chart 2: Should the querent pursue screenwriting?

The querent recently left his job in computer programming to try to find something more glamorous. He took a couple of screenwriting courses and enjoyed them, but with no contacts in the industry, was skeptical of his chances for success.

Mercury rules the ascendant and the 5th house of screenwriting. Mercury is retrograde, combust the Sun and in early degrees, which overwhelms and debilitates its rulership. The Moon is void-of-course, intercepted, and in fall at a dead degree of Scorpio. The pursuit was literally over before it began, as the querent returned to a "normal" day job (ruler of 6th house in the 2nd house) in his field, content to be bored but secure.

Chart 3: Will the querent get the job with the evil megacorporation?

(Hint: Use the 10th house for this, not the 6th, as it's a career position. Also, she is seeking placement with the evil megacorp via a recruiter.)

Saturn, ruler of the ascendant is combust the Sun in the 6th house, and both are opposing Pluto in the 12th house. Something is definitely not on the level here. Neptune is retrograde in the 1st house and rules the 3rd house of the facts in the matter. Mars is opposing the ascendant, and the exalted Moon, ruling the recruiter, is smack dab on top of malefic fixed star Caput Algol, mitigating the exaltation. Clearly, the recruiter is making promises he can't keep and giving her false hope with Jupiter in the 7th house ruling the twelfth.

Neptune in the 1st house and retrograde shows the querent is somewhat unrealistic about her chances, probably due to the line of bull the recruiter is feeding her. This was a case where I really had to stick to my guns and the facts in the chart, as the querent kept trying to lobby me to side with her wishful thinking. "But the recruiter told me it's a done deal," she said. "They are going to figure out salary and make an offer tomorrow."

"Um, no," I said, noting that Venus, Moon and Saturn make no applying aspects to each other. In fact, Venus is making a mutually applying quincunx to retrograde Uranus in the 2nd house, where Uranus is in fall. Further, the Moon's last aspect is a big fat square to Uranus while the Moon is at the Pleiades, giving the querent something to weep about on top of a rude awakening.

The recruiter called her the following day to tell her the evil megacorp was no longer interested and would continue interviewing other candidates. The 12th house shows the recruiter was misleading her all along about her chances, and she probably was never a serious contender to begin with.

Chart 4: Should the querent rent a craft booth at the city's 4th of July event?

The querent is a crafter and she wanted to know if she should rent a booth at her city's annual Fourth of July celebration that attracts thousands of people from the surrounding area into her small town. After the parade, held during midday, the visitors head to a nearby park to visit the food and crafts booths. The booth fee was affordable and she wouldn't have to sell unreasonable quantities of her crafts to make a profit.

Saturn retrograde in the 1st house, ruling the 5th house of crafts, is pretty much all you need to see to know this is a bad idea and the rest of the chart would have to be spectacular to overcome it. Saturn is also sitting right on the 2nd house cusp of money—another deal-killer. Saturn is opposing Jupiter in the 7th house, ouch, let's stop looking at Saturn for a minute, it's too painful.

Mercury, ruler of the querent, is in fall by house but mutually recepted with Venus in Gemini in the 10th house. Venus is T-squaring Saturn and Uranus as well as Jupiter, which rules the 4th house of outcome. So the mutual reception can't help her because of the T-square.

The Part of Fortune is unfortunate in the 12th house, and disposits back to the Sun, ruler of creativity and crafts, applying to Caput Algol.

So this isn't a great chart by any stretch. The querent didn't rent the booth. It turned out that attendance at the event was its lowest ever, and vendors reported abysmal sales, perhaps due to a stock market "flash crash" at the time, and the overall lousy economy.

APPENDIX D – Sources Used for Planetary Names

Gazetteer of Planetary Nomenclature
International Astronomical Union (IAU)
Working Group for Planetary System Nomenclature (WGPSN)
Reprinted in its entirety with permission from: http://planetarynames.wr.usgs.gov/References

Sources of Planetary Names

1. Larousse Encyclopedia of Mythology, translated by R. Aldington and D. Ames; Hamlyn Publishing Group Ltd., New York, 1976.
2. Hawaiian Folk Tales: A Collection of Native Legends, by Thomas G. Thrum; AMS Printing Inc., New York, 1907.
3. Oceanic Mythology, by Roslyn Poignant; Paul Hamlyn Ltd., London, 1967.
4. Australian Legendary Tales, collected by K. Langloh Parker; Angus & Robertson, Brighton, 1963.
5. Aboriginal Myths and Legends, selected by Roland Robinson; Hamlyn Pub. Group Ltd., London, 1969.
6. Dreamtime: Australian Aboriginal Myths, text by Charles Mountford; Rigby Ltd., Adelaide, 1965.
7. Nomads and Empire Builders: Native Peoples and Cultures of South America, by Carleton Beals; Citadel, Secaucus, New Jersey, 1965.
8. The Indian Background of Colonial Yucatan, by R. L. Roys; Gordon Press, New York, 1976.
9. Kiowa Tales, by Elsie W. Parsons; The American Folklore Society, vol. XXII, New York, 1929.
10. Myths and Tales of the Jicarilla Apache, by Morris Edward Opler; The American Folklore Society, G. E. Stechert & Co., New York, 1938.
11. The Book of the Navajo, by Raymond Friday Locke; Mankind Pub. Co., Los Angeles, Calif., 1976.
12. Indian Mythology, by Veronica Ions; Paul Hamlyn Ltd., London, 1967.
13. African Mythology, by Geoffrey Parrinder; Paul Hamlyn Ltd., London, 1967.
14. South American Mythology, by Harold Osborne; Paul Hamlyn Ltd., London, 1968.
15. Chinese Mythology, by Anthony Christie; Paul Hamlyn Ltd., London, 1968.
16. Japanese Mythology, by Juliet Piggott; Paul Hamlyn Ltd., London, 1969.
17. Norse mythology; lists provided by Kaare Aksnes.

18. List compiled by V. G. Teifel.
19. The Greek Myths (2 vols.), by Robert Graves; Penguin Books Ltd., Harmondsworth, Middlesex, England, 1974.
20. American Men and Women of Science; R.R. Bowker, New York, 1982, 1989, 1994.
21. Handbook of Greek Mythology, by H. J. Rose; E. P. Dutton & Co., Inc., New York, 1959.
22. Gilgamesh: A Verse Narrative, by Herbert Mason; Houghton Mifflin Company, Boston, Mass., 1971.
23. The Lost Gods of England, by Brian Branston; Thames & Hudson Ltd., London, 1957.
24. Orisha: The Gods of Yorubaland, by Judith Gleason; Atheneum, New York, 1971.
25. Ainu Creed and Cult, by Neil Gordon Munro; Columbia University Press, New York, 1963.
26. North American Indian Mythology, by Cottie Burland; Paul Hamlyn Pub. Group Ltd., London, 1968.
27. The Mythology of All Races (13 vols.), edited by John Arnott MacCulloch and George Foot Moore; Cooper Square Publishers, Inc., New York, 1964.
28. The Odyssey, by Homer, translated by W. H. D. Rouse; Thomas Nelson and Sons, Ltd., Edinburgh, 1934. or 28b. The Odyssey of Homer, translated by Herbert Bates; Harper Brothers, New York, 1929
29. Song of Roland, translated by Dorothy L. Sayers; Penguin Books Ltd., Harmondsworth, Middlesex, England, 1967.
30. Comparative Cultures; Human Relations Area File Inc., New Haven, Conn.
31. Gods, Heroes, and Men of Ancient Greece, translated by W. H. D. Rouse; The New American Library of World Literature, Inc., New York, 1957.
32. Myths of the Greeks and Romans, by Michael Grant; World Publishing Company, New York, 1962.
33. Mythology: Timeless Tales of Gods and Heros, by Edith Hamilton; Little, Brown and Company, Boston, Mass., 1942.
34. African Myths and Tales, edited by Susan Feldmann; Dell Publishing Co., Inc., New York, 1970.
35. Gods and Myths of Northern Europe, by H. R. Ellis Davidson; Penguin Books Ltd., Harmondsworth, Middlesex, England, 1974.
36. National Geographic Atlas of the World: National Geographic Society, Washington, D.C., 1970 (and other editions).
37. Malory's Le Morte d'Arthur, by Keith Baines; Clarkson N. Potter, Inc., New York, 1962.
38. Njal's Saga, by Magnus Magnusson and Hermann Paulsson; Penguin Books Ltd., Harmondsworth, Middlesex, England, 1975.
39. The Age of Fable, by Thomas Bulfinch; The Heritage Press, New York, 1942.
40. Primal Myths: Creating the World, by Barbara C. Sproul; Harper & Row, New York, 1979.

41. The Iliad of Homer, translated by Benjamin Smith and Walter Miller; MacMillan & Co., New York, 1944.
42. Beowulf, translated by Burton Raffel; The New American Library of World Literature, Inc., New York, 1963.
43. Dictionary of Classical Mythology, by J. E. Zimmerman; Harper and Row, New York, 1971.
44. The Aeneid of Virgil, translated by Allen Mandelbaum; Bantam Books, Inc., New York, 1971.
45. Tales of Yoruba Gods and Heroes, by Harold Courlander; Crown Publishers, Inc., New York, 1973.
46. List of famous women provided by the National Organization for Women.
47. Giants, by David Larkin and Sarah Teale; Harry Abrams, Inc., New York, 1979.
48. Letter from G. H. Pettengill to Venus Task Group, April 27, 1977.
49. Letter from M. Ya. Marov to G. H. Pettengill, September 8, 1977.
50. List compiled by N. P. Erpylev; includes names from various Russian legends.
51. Letter from M. Ya. Marov to G. H. Pettengill, January 3, 1981.
52. Alf Laylah Wa Laylah, The Book of the Thousand Nights and a Night, by Richard F. Burton; Larsen-Harper, Colo. Press, Denver, Colo., 1900.
53. Myths and Folklore of the Temiskaming Algonquin, and Timagami Ojibwa, by F. G. Speck; Canada Department of Mines Memoir 71, Ottawa, 1915.
54. The New Century Handbook of Classical Geography, edited by Catherine B. Avery; Meredith Corp., New York, 1972.
55. Webster's New Geographical Dictionary; G. & C. Merriam Co., Springfield, Mass., 1972, 1977.
56. Everymans Classical Atlas, by J. Oliver Thomson; J. M. Dent and Sons Ltd., London, 1963.
57. Map of albedo features of Mars, (plates 2-5), in La Planéte Mars, by E.M. Antoniadi; Librairie Scientifique, Hermann et Cie., Paris, 1930.
58. Letter from M. Ya. Marov to Harold Masursky, March 19, 1979.
59. The New Encyclopaedia Britannica; Encyclopaedia Britannica Inc., Chicago, 1974, 1993.
60. Proceedings of the General Assembly in Transactions of the International Astronomical Union, vol. XIVB, 1971, through XIXB, 1986 , Reidel & Co., Dordrecht, Holland, 1971, 1974, 1977, 1980, 1983, 1986.
61. List of radar scientists provided by G. H. Pettengill.
62. List of names for Mars in various languages provided by Carl Sagan.
63. List supplied by N. P. Erpylev.
64. Soviet Encyclopedia (30 volumes, in Russian).
65. Myths of the Peoples of the World (two volumes, in Russian).

66. Named Lunar Formations, by Mary A. Blagg and K. Müller; Percy Lund, Humphries and Co. Ltd., London, 1935.
67. The System of Lunar Craters, Quadrants I, II, III, IV; by D. W. G. Arthur and others; Communications of the Lunar and Planetary Laboratory, vol. 2, no. 30, 1963; vol. 3, no. 40, 1964; vol. 3, no. 50, 1965; vol. 5, no. 70, 1966.
68. World Who's Who in Science, edited by Allen G. Debus; Western Publishing Company, Hannibal, Mo., 1968; New York, 1973.
69. World Mythology, edited by Roy Willis; Henry Holt & Co., New York, 1993.
70. Letter from V. Straizys (Lithuanian Astronomical Council, Vilnius, Lithuania) to G. Burba, October 7, 1991.
71. Mars and its Satellites, A Detailed Commentary on the Nomenclature, 2nd edition, by Jürgen Blunck; Exposition Press, Smithtown, New York, 1982.
72. Soviet Men of Science, by John Turkevich; Van Nostrand Company, Princeton, New Jersey, 1963.
73. McGraw-Hill International Atlas; McGraw-Hill Book Co., New York, 1963.
74. The Times Atlas of the World, Comprehensive Edition; The Times of London in collaboration with John Bartholomew & Son Ltd., Edinburgh, 1971 (and other editions).
75. Webster's Biographical Dictionary; G. & C. Merriam Company, Springfield, Mass., 1974 (and other editions).
76. Who's Who; St. Martin's Press, New York, 1974.
77. Observatories of the World, by Siegfried Marx and Werner Pfau; Van Nostrand, Reinhold Co., New York, 1982.
78. The Oxford Companion to Art; Oxford University Press, London, 1970.
79. Cassel's Encyclopaedia of World Literature; William Morrow & Company Inc., New York, 1973.
80. Lists of names for Mercury nomenclature, provided by David Morrison.
81. Kodansha Encyclopedia of Japan; Kodansha Ltd., New York, 1983.
82. Information supplied by V.V. Shevchenko, Sternberg Astronomical Institute, Moscow.
83. Dictionary of Mythology, Folklore, and Symbols (in 3 vols.), by Gertrude Jobes; Scarecrow Press, Inc., New York, 1962.
84. Ancient Mirrors of Womanhood, by Merlin Stone; Beacon Press, Boston, Mass., 1984.
85. The Complete Works of William Shakespeare, Illustrated; Avenel Books, a division of Crown Publishers, Inc., New York, 1975.
86. The World Guide to Gnomes, Fairies, Elves and other Little People, by Thomas Keightley, Avenel Books, New York, 1978.
87. Italo Calvino, by Martin McLaughlin; Edinburgh University Press, Edinburgh, 1998.

88. Astronauts and Cosmonautics Biographical and Statistical Data, revised June 28, 1985, prepared by the Congressional Research Service, Library of Congress; U.S. Government Printing Office, Washington, D.C., 1985.
89. Dictionary of Scientific Biography, Charles Coulston Gillispie, editor in chief, vol. 9; Charles Scribner's Sons, New York, 1981.
90. Encyclopedia Americana, International Edition; Grolier Inc., Danbury, Conn., 1984, 1996.
91. The Rand McNally International Atlas; Rand McNally and Co., New York, 1980.
92. Fairies, by Brian Froud and Alan Lee; Harry N. Abrams, Inc., New York, 1978.
93. Funk and Wagnalls Standard Dictionary of Folklore, Mythology, and Legend, edited by Maria Leach; Harper and Row, Inc., New York, 1984.
94. List of names supplied by T. C. Owen.
95. Poem "Rape of the Lock" by Alexander Pope.
96. Green Mansions, by W. H. Hudson; AMS Press Inc., New York, 1923.
97. The Blue Bird (printed with The Betrothal), by Maurice Maeterlinck; Philosophical Pub. Co., Quakertown, Penn., 1987.
98. Female first names supplied by Russian members of WGPSN and task groups.
99. Index to Women of the World, by N.O. Ireland; F.W. Faxon Co., Westwood, Mass., 1988 (and other editions).
100. List provided by Women's Study Program, Brown University, Providence, R.I.
101. An Account of the Polynesian Race, by A. Fernandez; Tuttle Press, 1969.
102. List provided by V.G. Suriquez, University of Hawaii at Manoa.
103. Macmillan Illustrated Encyclopedia of Myths and Legends, A. Cotterell; Macmillan Publishing Co., New York, 1989.
104. Great North American Indians, by F. Dockstader; Van Nostrand Reinhold Co., New York, 1977.
105. List provided by S.V. Meschel, University of Chicago.
106. List provided by The Age (newspaper), Melbourne, Australia.
107. List provided by George Burba, Vernadsky Institute, Moscow.
108. List provided by Mikhail Ya. Marov, Academy of Science, Moscow.
109. Dictionary of First Names, by Alfred J. Kolatch; Putnam Publishing Group, New York, 1990.
110. Asimov's Biographical Encyclopedia of Science and Technology, by I. Asimov; Doubleday & Co., Garden City, New York, 1972.
111. The Book of Goddesses and Heroines, by P. Monaghan; Llewellyn Publications, St. Paul, Minn., 1990.
112. Great Folk Tales of Old Ireland, by Mary McGarry; Bell Publishing, New York, 1972.

113. Atlas of the Great Caves of the World, by P. Courbon, C. Chabert, P. Bosted, K. Lindsley; Cave Books, St. Louis, 1989.
114. Bulletin Volcanologique, by A. Atkinson, T.J. Griffin, P.J. Stephenson, 1975.
115. Exploration and Geology of Some Lava Tube Caves on the Hawaiian Volcanoes, by C. Wood; Trans. British Cave Res. Assoc., 1981.
116. Kartchner Cavern: Arizona's Newest State Park, by B.R. Tufts; Arizona Highways, vol. 65, 1989.
117. The Galileo Solid-State Imaging Experiment, by Michael J.S. Belton and others; Space Science Reviews, vol. 60, 1992.
118. The Blue Guides, Southern Italy, by L.V. Bertarelli; Macmillan & Co., London, 1925.
119. Guida D'Italia del Touring Club Italiano, by Abruzzo e Molise; Milano, 1965.
120. The Cave of Postojna and Other Marvels of the Karst, by Dr. A. Serko; Zavod Potojnske jame, Yugoslavia, 1958.
121. Memoirs of a Speleologist, The Adventurous Life of a Famous French Cave Explorer, by Robert deJoly; Zephyrus Press, New Jersey, 1975.
122. Viaggio in Italia, by Guido Piovene and Arnoldo Mondadori; Milano, 1966.
123. Pueblo Gods and Myths, by Hamilton A. Tyler; University of Oklahoma Press, Norman, Oklahoma, 1964.
124. Cathy Please Don't Move, by H.J. Bender; Make-A-Wish Foundation, Winchester, VA, 1989.
125. Women in Chemistry and Physics: A Bibliographic Source Book, eds.: L.S. Grinstein, R.K. Rose, M.H. Rafailovich; Greenwood Press, Westport, CT, 1993.
126. The Astronomy of the Australian Aborigines, by Roslynn D. Haynes; in The Astronomy Quarterly, vol. 7, Pergamon Press, 1990.
127. Goddesses in World Mythology, by Martha Ann and Dorothy Myers Imel; ABC-CLIO, Inc., Santa Barbara, CA 1993.
128. Celtic Myth and Legend, by Charles Squire; Newcastle Publishing Co., Hollywood, CA 1975.
129. Hammond Atlas of the World; Hammond Incorporated, Maplewood, NJ, 1999.
130. Women in Myth and Legend, by Patricia Monaghan; Junction Books, London, 1981.
131. Zhenshchina v mifakh i legendakh (Woman in mythes and legends); Encyclopedic Dictionary, Komus Publishing, Tashkent, 1992 (in Russian).
132. Letter from Jouko Raitala (University of Oulu, Finland) to G. Burba, February 26, 1991.
133. List of Estonian first names by Uku Hanni (Tartu University, Estonia) provided to G. Burba, June, 1986.
134. Almanac of Famous People, edited by Beverly Baer and Neil E. Walker; Gale Research Inc., Detroit, 1994.

135. Macmillan Illustrated Encyclopedia of Myths and Legends, by Arthur Cotterell; Macmillan Publishing, New York, 1989.
136. Norse Mythology: Legends of Gods and Heroes, by Peter Andreas Munch; The American-Scandinavian Foundation, New York, 1942.
137. The Gods and Symbols of Ancient Mexico and the Maya, by Mary Miller and Karl Taube; Thames and Hudson, New York, 1993.
138. Commemoration of Prof. Andre Cailleux, by E. Dudich; International Union of the History and Philosophy of Sciences, International Commission of the History of the Geological Sciences (INHIGEO), 1987.
139. International Who's Who 1992-93; Europa Publications Limited, London, 1992 (and other editions).
140. National Atlas of the United States of America; U.S. Department of the Interior Geological Survey, Washington, D.C., 1970.
141. Discovery, by Eric Flaum; Gallery Books, New York, 1990.
142. From Carnac to Callanish, by A. Burl; Yale University Press, New Haven, 1993.
143. The Gods of the Egyptians, by E.A. Wallis Budge; Dover Publications, Inc., New York, 1969.
144. Myths of the North American Indians, by C. Taylor; Barnes & Noble, New York, 1995.
145. Springs of Florida, by Jack C. Rosenau, Glen L. Faulkner, Charles W. Hendry, and Robert W. Hull; U.S. Geological Survey Bulletin No. 31, 1977.
146. The Healing Gods of Ancient Civilizations, by Walter Addison Jayne, M.D.; University Books, Inc., New York, 1962.
147. Hawaiian Mythology, by Martha Beckwith; University of Hawaii Press, Honolulu, 1970.
148. Priklyucheniya v Okeanii [Adventures in Oceania, in Russian], by M. Stingl; Pravda Publishers, Moscow, 1986.
149. A Dictionary of World Mythology, by Arthur Cotterell; Oxford University Press, Oxford/Melbourne, 1986.
150. Concise Guide to World Coalfields, compiled by World Coal Resources and Reserves Data Bank Services; International Energy Agency, London, 1983.
151. Coal: Availability, Mining, and Preparation, by James C. Hower, et al., in Encyclopedia of Energy Technology and the Environment, John Wiley & Sons, Inc., New York, 1995.
152. Dictionary of Irish Mythology, by Peter Berresford Ellis; Oxford University Press, New York, 1987.
153. Slovar' slavyanskoy mifologii [Dictionary of the Slavic mythology]. - Nizhniy Novgorod, 1995 (in Russian).
154. Letter from Lisa Leghorn (Rigdzin Ling, Junction City, CA, USA) to Merton and Louise Davies, May 15, 1990.
155. G:otter in Planeten und Monden, by J. Blunck; Verlag Harri Deutsch, Frankfort a/M, Thun, 1987.

156. The Inferno, by Dante Alighieri; Mentor Books, New York, 1954.
157. Great Figures of Mythology, by Peter Clayton; Crescent Books, New York, 1990.
158. Kakadu, Looking After the Country-the Gagudju Way, by S. Breeden and B. Wright; Prentice Hall, Paramus, New Jersey, 1990.
159. Random House Webster's Dictionary of Scientists; Random House, New York, 1996.
160. Dictionary of Celtic Mythology, by Peter Berresford Ellis; Oxford University Press, Oxford, 1992.
161. Who's Who in the Moon; B.A.A. Historical Section Memoir #1, London, 1938.
162. Article by F. Fischer, Prague, 1937.
163. Email message from Cacique Pedro Guanikeyu Torres, Principal Tribal Chief and Elder of the Jatibonicu' Taino Tribe of Puerto Rico (NJ-USA Taino Tribal Affairs Office, Vineland, NJ) of the Jatibonicu' Taino Tribal Nation of Boriken to J. Blue, October, 1999.
164. Madame Bovary, by Gustave Flaubert; Random House Publications, New York, 1957.
165. Galileo's Daughter, by Dava Sobel; Chivers Press, Bath, England, 2000.
166. The New Grove Dictionary of Opera, edited by Stanley Sadie; Macmillan Press, London, 1992.
167. Astronomiche Nachrichten, vol. 276, page 192, 1948.
168. Sky & Telescope, New Track Media LLC, Cambridge, MA.
169. Palanga, Svarbiausois Zintos, by S. Markelyte; Mintis, Vilnius, pages 23-29, 1987.
170. Myths and Legends of the Ancient Slavs (in Russian), by A. Asov; Nauka i Religiya Publications, Moscow, 1998.
171. Divine Horsemen: Voodoo Gods of Haiti, by Maya Deren; Chelsea House Publishers, New York, 1970.
172. Notable Women in the Physical Sciences: A Biographical Dictionary, edited by Benjamin F. Shearer and Barbara S. Shearer, Greenwood Press, Westport CT & London, 1997.
173. The Columbia Gazetteer of the World, edited by Saul B. Cohen; Columbia University Press, New York, 1998.
174. Guide to the Gods, by Majorie Leach; ABC-CLIO, Santa Barbara, 1992.
175. The Encyclopeadia of Islam, edited by H.A.R. Gibb et al., E.J. Brill Academic Publishers; The Netherlands,1960 (and other editions).
176. The Great Soviet Encyclopedia; Translation of the Third Edition; Macmillan, Inc., New York, 1975.
177. The Argonautica, by Valerius Flaccus (with an English translation by J.H. Mozley); The Loeb Classical Library, Cambridge (Mass.), 1934.
178. Hyginus: Fabulae, edited by Peter K. Marshall; Stuttgart, 1993.
179. Reader's Digest Wide World Atlas; Reader's Digest Association, New York, 1979.
180. Atlas SSSR, 2nd edition, Moscow, GUGK, 1983 (in Russian).

181. Samuel Taylor Coleridge, The Major Works, by Samuel Taylor Coleridge; Oxford University Press, Oxford, 1983.

182. Oxford Classical Dictionary; Oxford University Press, London, 1968.

183. The Discovery of the Correct Birth Date for Selenographer Thomas Gwyn Empy Elger, by Robert A. Garfinkle; Journal of the British Astronomical Association, April, 2006.

184. NIH Record (National Institute of Health newsletter), March 8, 1988, page 7.

185. Astrid Lindgren, by Eva-Marie Metcalf; Twayne Publishers, New York, 1995.

186. Alaska Atlas and Gazetteer; DeLorme, Yarmouth, Maine, 1998.

187. Asteroids III, edited by William F. Bottke, Jr., Alberto Cellino, Paolo Paolicchi, and Richard P. Binzel; University of Arizona Press, Tucson, 2002.

188. Wilhelmine Wittes Präzisionsrelief des Mondes. Eine Pionierarbeit im Urteil der Wissenschaft, by Jürgen Blunck, in Beiträge zur Astronomiegeschichte, Bd.8, Frankfurt a.M. 2006, Acta Historica Astronomiae, vol.29, pp.150-180.

189. Who's Who on the Moon, by Elijah E. Cocks and Josiah C. Cocks; Tudor Publishers, Greensboro, 1995.

190. Laurent Cassegrain Commemorated at Chaudon, by P.D. Hingley; Astronomy & Geophysics, vol. 40, number 1, February 1999.

191. Gulliver's Travels, by Jonathan Swift; Holt, Rinehart, and Winston, New York, 1967.

192. Publications of the Astronomical Society of the Pacific, by Robert S. Richardson; volume 55, number 324, pages 136-144.

193. Men of Space, by Shirley Thomas; Chilton Company, Philadelphia, 1961

194. EOS, Transactions, American Geophysical Union; 80, No. 25, June 22, 1999; pp 283-284.

195. Astronomy & Geophysics, Volume 43, Issue 3, pp. 3.35-3.38, 06/2002.

196. Who Was Who in American History-Science and Technology, Marquis Who's Who Inc., Chicago, 1975.

197. American Mineralogist, vol. 55, March-April 1970, page 569.

198. Quarterly Journal of the Royal Astronomical Society, Vol. 21, February, 1980 (and other editions).

199. Icarus, Vol. 12, No. 3, May 1970, pp. 498-499.

200. Discovery of the Real Person Behind the Name of the Lunar Crater Kinau, by Robert A. Garfinkle and Bernd Pfeiffer, Journal of the British Astronomical Association, vol. 117, April, 2007.

201. Obituary for William M. Sinton, by John Spencer, Bulletin of the American Astronomical Society, 2004, p. 1685-1686.

202. Mapping Mars, by Oliver Morton; Picador USA, New York, 2002.

203. Planetary and Space Science, Vol. 52, 2004, p. 1231-1232.

204. Collins Malay gem dictionary, by Abdul Rahman bin Yusop, Haji; Collins, London, 1976.
205. In the Celtic Past, by Ethna Carbery; Gill and Son, Ltd. Dublin, 1904.
206. Collection of Shotaro Miyamoto's Scientific Papers, Kyoto School of Computer Sciences, Kyoto, Japan, 1993.
207. The Journal of the Association of Lunar and Planetary Observers, Charles F. Capen Memorial Issue, Volume 31, Numbers 11-12, San Francisco, 1986.
208. Monthly Notices of the Royal Astronomical Society, Vol. 84, p. 226, 1924.
209. African Authors: A Companion to Black African Writing, Vol. 1: 1300-1973, by Donald E. Herdeck; Black Orpheus Press, Washington, D.C., 1973.
210. Dictionary of Women Artists, edited by Delia Gaze; Fitzroy Dearborn Publishers, Chicago/London, 1997.
211. The Dictionary of Art, Vols. 1-33, edited by Jane Turne; Macmillan Publishers, New York, 1996.
212. The Work of Atget: Vol. 1, Old France, by Szarkowski and Hambourg; Museum of Modern Art, New York, 1981.
213. Legendary Islands of the Atlantic; A Study in Medieval Geography, by William Henry Babcock; Ayer Publishing, 1975.
214. St. James Guide to Black Artists, edited by Thomas Riggs; St. James Press, Detroit, 1997.
215. Finding Paradise, Island Art in Private Collections, by D.R. Severson; University of Hawaii Press, 2002.
216. Dictionary of Literary Biography, Vol. 175: Native American Writers of the United States, edited by Kenneth M. Roemer; Gale Research Inc., Detroit, 1997.
217. The Paintings of Xugu and Qi Baishi, by Jung Ying Tsao, edited by Carol Ann Bardoff; Far East Fine Arts, Inc., 1993.
218. Icarus, vol. 194, issue 2, April 2008, p. 399-400.
219. The Geochemical News, April 2005, Issue 123, p. 8-9.
220. Astronomer's Encyclopedia, Naukova Dumka, Kiev, 1986.
221. The History of Cartography, by Leo Bagrow; Transaction Publishers, New Jersey, 1985.
222. Who's Who of British Scientists; Longman, London, 1970
223. Radiophysics and Quantum Electronics, Volume 46, Numbers 8-9, Springer, New York, August 2003.
224. Lost Horizon, by James Hilton; HarperCollins, New York, 2004.
225. Kahlil Gibran Man and Poet: A New Biography, by S. Bushrui and J. Jenkins; Oneworld Publications, 1998.
226. Hungary and the Hungarians, by Bart István; Corvina Kaidó, Budapest, 2002.
227. Larousse Dictionary of Writers, edited by Rosemary Goring; Larousse, New York, 1994.

228. History of Modern Art, by H.H. Arnason and M.F. Prather; Harry N. Abrams, New York, 1998.
229. Dune, by Frank Herbert; Chilton Book Company, Radnor, Pennsylvania, 1965.
230. Foreign names in Russian Text, 3rd edition, by R.S. Gilyarevsky and B.A. Starostin; Moscow, 1985.
231. Bulletin of the American Astronomical Society ; vol. 29, no. 4, p. 1477-1478.
232. New York Times obituary; June 4, 2005.
233. Collier's Encyclopedia, P.F. Collier, Inc., New York, 1993.
234. New York Times obituary; August 9, 1998.
235. Pacific Mythology, by Jan Knappert; Diamond Books, 1995.
236. Dictionary of Creation Myths, by David Adams Leeming and Margaret Adams Leeming; Oxford University Press, Oxford, 1994.
237. The Chinook Indians: Traders of the Lower Columbia River, by Robert H. Ruby and John A. Brown; Univ. Oklahoma Press, 1976.
238. The Gods and Symbols of Ancient Mexico and the Maya: An Illustrated Dictionary of Mesoamerican Religion, by Mary Miller and Karl Taube; Thanes & Hudson, London, 1993.
239. Chinese Mythology, by Anthony Christie; Hamlyn Publishing, NY, 1996.
240. Creation Myths of the World: An Encyclopedia, by David Adams Leeming; ABC_CLIO, 2009.
241. The Encyclopedia of Science Fiction, by John Clute and Peter Nicholls; St Martin's Press, NY, 1993.
242. Quarterly Journal of the Royal Astronomical Society, v. 4, p. 450, 1963.
243. Biographical Dictionary of the History of Technology, edited by Lance Day and Ian McNeil; Routledge, London, 1996.
244. Suppl. Acta Astron. Sin. 27 (1986).
245. Sun Songs: Creation Myths from around the World, by Raymond Van Over; Mentor Books, New York, 1980.
246. Myths and Legends of the Pacific Northwest, 2nd Ed., by Katharine B. Judson; A.C. McClurg & Co., Chicago, 1912.
247. Quarterly Journal of the Royal Astronomical Society, v. 23, p. 629, 1982.
248. Māori Religion and Mythology, by Edward Shortland; Longmans, Green and Co., London, 1882 (reprint by Kiwi Publishers, Christchurch, 1998).
249. Death Valley Geology: Rocks and Faults, Fans and Salts, by Wes Hildreth; Death Valley Natural History Association, 1976.
250. Barrington Atlas of the Greek and Roman World, edited by Richard J.A. Talbert; Princeton University Press, Princeton, 2000.
251. Lexicon Novinum Locorum, by Caroli Egger; Officina Libaria Vaticana, 1977

252. News and Comments: Phobos, Nature of Acceleration, by E.J. Öpik; Irish Astronomical Journal, 6: 40, March, 1963.

253. Universe, Life, Intelligence, by I.S. Shklovsky; USSR Academy of Sciences Publisher, Moscow, 1962 (in Russian).

254. History of the Vestal Virgins of Rome, by T. Cato Worsfold; Kessinger Publishing, 1997.

255. Rome's Vestal Virgins: A study of Rome's Vestal priestesses in the late Republic and early Empire, by Robin Lorsch Wildfang; Routledge, 2006.

256. A Dictionary of Greek and Roman Biography and Mythology, by Sir William Smith; I.B. Tauris, 2007.

257. Roman Festival Calendar of Numa Pompilius, by Michael York; Lang, Peter Publishing, Inc., 1986.

APPENDIX E – IAU Resolutions B5 & B6

Copyright International Astronomical Union, 2006; reprinted with permission from 'Proceedings of the twenty-sixth General Assembly, Prague 2006, Transactions of the International Astronomical Union Volume XXVIB, Cambridge University Press, 2008'. Used with permission.
<http://www.iau.org/static/resolutions/Resolution_GA26-5-6.pdf >

RESOLUTION B5
Definition of a Planet in the Solar System

Contemporary observations are changing our understanding of planetary systems, and it is important that our nomenclature for objects reflect our current understanding. This applies, in particular, to the designation "planets". The word "planet" originally described "wanderers" that were known only as moving lights in the sky. Recent discoveries lead us to create a new definition, which we can make using currently available scientific information.

The IAU therefore resolves that planets and other bodies, except satellites, in our Solar System be defined into three distinct categories in the following way:

(1) A planet[1] is a celestial body that
   (a) is in orbit around the Sun,
   (b) has sufficient mass for its self-gravity to overcome rigid body forces so that it assumes a hydrostatic equilibrium (nearly round) shape, and
   (c) has cleared the neighbourhood around its orbit.

(2) A "dwarf planet" is a celestial body that
   (a) is in orbit around the Sun,
   (b) has sufficient mass for its self-gravity to overcome rigid body forces so that it assumes a hydrostatic equilibrium (nearly round) shape[2],
   (c) has not cleared the neighbourhood around its orbit, and
   (d) is not a satellite.

(3) All other objects[3], except satellites, orbiting the Sun shall be referred to collectively as "Small Solar System Bodies".

---

[1] The eight planets are: Mercury, Venus, Earth, Mars, Jupiter, Saturn, Uranus, and Neptune.

[2] An IAU process will be established to assign borderline objects to the dwarf planet or to another category.

[3] These currently include most of the Solar System asteroids, most Trans-Neptunian Objects (TNOs), comets, and other small bodies.

RESOLUTION B6
Pluto

The IAU further resolves:

Pluto is a "dwarf planet" by the above definition and is recognized as the prototype of a new category of Trans-Neptunian Objects[1].

---

[1] An IAU process will be established to select a name for this category.

APPENDIX F – Astronomica

Part I - Sedna Discovery White Paper

DISCOVERY OF A CANDIDATE INNER OORT CLOUD PLANETOID

The Astrophysical Journal, 617:645–649, 2004 December 10
Copyright © 2004. The American Astronomical Society. All rights reserved.

http://www.gps.caltech.edu/classes/ge133/reading/sedna.pdf
OR
http://bit.ly/q4VEtY

Part II - History of the Asteroids as Minor Planets

US NAVAL OBSERVATORY (USNO)
WHEN DID THE ASTEROIDS BECOME MINOR PLANETS?

http://www.usno.navy.mil/USNO/astronomical-applications/astronomical-information-center/minor-planets/?searchterm=minor%20planets
OR
http://1.usa.gov/mYpXPB

Part III - The New Horizons Mission 2015-2020

NEW HORIZONS: NASA's Pluto-Kuiper Belt Mission

http://pluto.jhuapl.edu/
and
http://www.nasa.gov/mission_pages/newhorizons/main/index.html

APPENDIX G – TNOs for Recovery Data & Further Study

Recovery of objects is the only time in astrology where 20/20 hindsight can be used to your advantage. Below is the list of named TNOs for further study and integration. The quick and immediate nature of horary astrology, with its relatively rapid resolution of outcomes, makes it a prime research bed. Help advance the astrological body of knowledge by recovering and integrating them in your horary charts, and sharing your findings.

Don't try to learn everything at once. Pick an object, study it, get used to it, integrate it, and then once you're comfortable using it, move on to another object to study and repeat the process with.

Number	Name	Type	Number	Name	Type
148780	Altjira	TNO	10370	Hylonome	Centaur
55576	Amycus	Centaur	28978	Ixion	TNO
8405	Asbolus	Centaur	58534	Logos	TNO
54598	Bienor	Centaur	136472	Makemake	TNO
66652	Borasisi	TNO	7066	Nessus	Centaur
65489	Ceto	SDO	52872	Okyrhoe	Centaur
19521	Chaos	TNO	90482	Orcus	TNO
10199	Chariklo	Centaur	49036	Pelion	Centaur
2060	Chiron	Centaur	5145	Pholus	Centaur
83982	Crantor	Centaur	134340	Pluto	TNO
52975	Cyllarus	Centaur	50000	Quaoar	TNO
53311	Deucalion	TNO	38083	Rhadamanthus	TNO
60558	Echeclus	Centaur	90377	Sedna	SDO
31824	Elatus	Centaur	88611	Teharonhiawako	TNO
136199	Eris	SDO	32532	Thereus	Centaur
136108	Haumea	TNO	42355	Typhon	SDO
38628	Huya	TNO	20000	Varuna	TNO

Data above courtesy of Distant EKOs: The Kuiper Belt Electronic Newsletter: http://bitly.com/eeRTXo
and IAU Minor Planet Center: http://bit.ly/f0fFwf

Part I - How to Recover Newly Discovered Astronomical Objects in Horary Charts

1. Study the object's mythological symbolism to familiarize yourself with its basic characteristics. (See Appendix D for some primary sources.) Look online and in libraries for astronomical discovery publications, news articles or notes. Then check for astrological research backed by case studies and data, not opinion or speculation.
2. Place the object in old horary charts where the outcome is already known. (See below for instructions on how to generate a recovery chart.) You can use historical event charts as well. You don't have to use only your own data; you can use other astrologers' case study data as well. Do this for *at least* 100-200 charts. Study the objects' house placement and interactions within the whole chart. Observe any effect on events leading up to the question as well as the outcome.
3. Apply the object to new horary charts and observe for awhile. Take your time. See if the symbolism and characteristics you learned and observed apply consistently to the new charts. Go back and note discrepancies if not. Adopt a mindset of "What is this object doing, and why is it (or is it not) relevant?"
4. Integrate and use the objects in all future horary charts. Write up your case studies and share them with other astrologers.

The office space chart in Chapter 8 (Fig. 8.1) is an example of object recovery in a horary chart. The following Triangle Shirtwaist Factory Fire analysis in Part III is an example of object recovery in an historical event chart.

Part II - How to Generate Charts for Object Recovery

Objects can be recovered using the free online chart generation software at Astro.com, as they have all of the Minor Planet Center data for TNOs integrated with their chart calculation program. Most major astrology software packages don't yet have this capability.

1. Choose "Free Horoscopes" from the upper right menu bar.
2. In the column on the right, scroll down to the bottom to "Extended Chart Selection" and click on it.
3. Scroll down to the bottom of the page to the "Additional Objects" section. On the left side is a box already containing some of the TNOs and Centaurs. You can select some of them from there, or you can enter the TNOs permanent number (left column, above)

in the empty box next to the words "Additional Asteroids." You can also look up TNOs alphabetically by clicking on the "Asteroid Name/Number List" link below the box.[1] When you have finished selecting, in the bottom right corner is the "Click Here to Show the Chart." button. It will take you to a link to the data entry page.

4. Enter the data and then click "Continue." The chart will be generated with the TNOs you have entered.

Part III - The Triangle Shirtwaist Factory Fire: Recovering Pluto, Chiron, Sedna & Eris

On March 25, 1911, in New York City, 146 garment workers died when the factory where they manufactured blouses caught fire. The doors had been locked by the factory managers to deter theft, and prevented the workers' escape. Those who did not burn to death jumped out of the building's eighth, ninth and tenth-story windows, plunging to their deaths on the pavement 100 feet below. The public outrage in the aftermath of the fire led to key labor reforms and improved safety standards for factory workers in the U.S.[2]

Neither Pluto, Chiron, Sedna, or Eris had been discovered at the time of the fire, and all of them play significant roles in the event chart. Pluto in particular has a profoundly devastating impact in the chart via all of the connections it makes to significators and midpoints.

Mercury is the significator of both the women (Ascendant) and the company and its management team (10th house). Mercury is combust the Sun and conjunct Sedna, which is lurking on the 12th house side of the 8th house cusp of death. Both Mercury and Sedna disposit to Mars, ruler of the 8th house.

---

[1] The IAU Minor Planet Center (MPC) data is updated more frequently than the Astrodienst data. You can find the MPC alphabetical list here: http://www.minorplanetcenter.org/iau/lists/MPNames.html

[2] Wikipedia Contributors. "Triangle Shirtwaist Factory Fire." *Wikipedia, The Free Encyclopedia.* <http://en.wikipedia.org/wiki/Triangle_Shirtwaist_Factory_fire > Photo courtesy of Wikipedia.

244 Open Source Modern Horary Astrology

Name: Triangle Shirtwaist Factory Fire
born on: Sa, 25 March 1911
in: Manhattan, NY (US)
73w59, 40n46

Time: 4:40 pm
Univ.Time: 21:40
Sid. Time: 4:52:58

ASTRO DIENST
www.astro.com
Type: 2.GW 0.0-1 4-Mai-2011

Natal Chart (Method: Web Style / Placidus)
Sun sign: Aries
Ascendant: Virgo

☉ Sun	4 Ari 7'17"	
☽ Moon	6 Aqu 30'20"	
☿ Mercury	9 Ari 35'37"	
♀ Venus	2 Tau 20'35"	
♂ Mars	8 Aqu 48'44"	
♃ Jupiter	13 Sco 37'42"r	
♄ Saturn	5 Tau 13'35"	
♅ Uranus	28 Cap 41'44"	
♆ Neptune	18 Can 46'20"r	
♇ Pluto	25 Gem 55'58"	
☊ True Node	10 Tau 37'56"	
⚷ Chiron	4 Pis 26'54"	
⊕ P.Fort.	19 Can 6'11"	
⚸ Lilith	11 Sag 8'26"	
⚳ Ceres	8 Tau 8'36"	
⚴ Pallas	1 Ari 50'39"	
⚵ Juno	17 Lib 48'50"r	
⚶ Vesta	22 Tau 7'48"	
136199 Eris	26 Pis 1'0"	
90377 Sedna	10 Ari 54'22"	

AC: 16 Vir 43' 9"   2: 11 Lib 32'   3: 11 Sco 10'
MC: 14 Gem 33'26" 11: 18 Can 33' 12: 19 Leo 41'

The Moon is besieged and under duress between Uranus and Mars, with Mars ruling fire dispositing to Uranus in Capricorn. Uranus rules the 6th house of the women's workplace, and it is quincunxing Pluto in the 10th house, with Pluto co-signifying the company and its management. The Moon is applying to conjoin Mars, and squaring retrograde Jupiter in Scorpio, in detriment by house and disposited by Pluto. Jupiter is also quincunxing the Midheaven, assuring bad publicity (3rd house) in a big way (Jupiter) over the terrible destructiveness of the incident (Scorpio; with dispositor Pluto opposing the Moon-Jupiter and Mars-Jupiter midpoints). Pluto is in the angular 10th, representing destruction and death in a business environment, with devastating public visibility. Pluto disposits to Mercury. The final dispositor of the entire chart (Mercury→, and Moon-Mars→Uranus→Saturn→) is Mars.

If you use wide orbs, there is a T-square between Jupiter, Uranus-Moon-Mars, and Ceres-Saturn-Venus, with the outlet leg in the 11th house. That's really the whole story right there. The limitation of the locked factory (Jupiter opposing Saturn as part of the larger T-square, with Mars conjunct the Jupiter-Saturn midpoint and squaring both planets) by management led to the worker's deaths, which would cause widespread public outrage and demand for accountability and reform. Pluto is squaring the midpoint of the Ceres-Saturn-Venus square to Uranus-Moon-Mars. Pluto is also opposing the Jupiter-Mars square's midpoint. Saturn is conjunct dignified Venus, which is in the 8th house of her detriment. The catalyst is the Moon-Mars conjunction that is squaring the Saturn-Venus conjunction. Eris is squaring Pluto; so far there is nothing but malefics, trouble and mayhem involved in a big way in the chart.

Sedna is about women who suffer at the hands of others, particularly men (their management and employer in this case), so the Sedna-Mercury conjunction as ruler of the Ascendant amplifies that these women were sitting ducks—literally because they couldn't escape (Mercury) due to a lack of freedom (Moon in Aquarius besieged by Uranus and Mars) and were quickly overwhelmed (Mercury-Sun combustion in the sign of the Sun's exaltation, Aries, dispositing to Mars, making it that much more overpowering). Interestingly, the Sun rules the 12th house of confinement (they were locked inside the factory), and as mentioned above, it is combusting Mercury, the ruler of the Ascendant.

Planets in the same degree as the Nodes signify a catastrophe, and the Nodes are in the same degree as Sedna, co-signifying the women. Sedna is also conjunct the Moon/MC and Mars/MC midpoints. Pluto is semi-square the North Node. It was definitely, absolutely a bad day to show up for work.

Chiron in Pisces in the 6th house of working conditions disposits back to the 11th house exalted Neptune conjunct the Part of Fortune, showing a sacrifice (Pisces) for the greater good (11th house). Chiron is the pain and suffering prior to a great transformation, and it may have set the stage for the 11th house ideas for workplace reforms (Uranus, ruler of the 6th quincunxing Pluto in the 10th). Unfortunately, Neptune is retrograde, so the reforms would take awhile. This is affirmed by Uranus quintiling Sedna, with Uranus in the "dead degrees" of Capricorn, before its ingress into its home sign of Aquarius (mass protests to create workplace safety changes).

The Moon's last aspects are a trine to Pluto and a semi-sextile to Eris and Uranus, conjoining their midpoint in the 6th house, before going void-of-course. The incident captivated the entire country (Moon ruling the 11th, Neptune in the 11th) and led to policy changes (Pluto in the 10th) that improved safety standards. It also increased labor union participation and employee agitation for better working conditions (Eris-Uranus).

APPENDIX H – The Future of Astrology as Mirrored in Astronomy

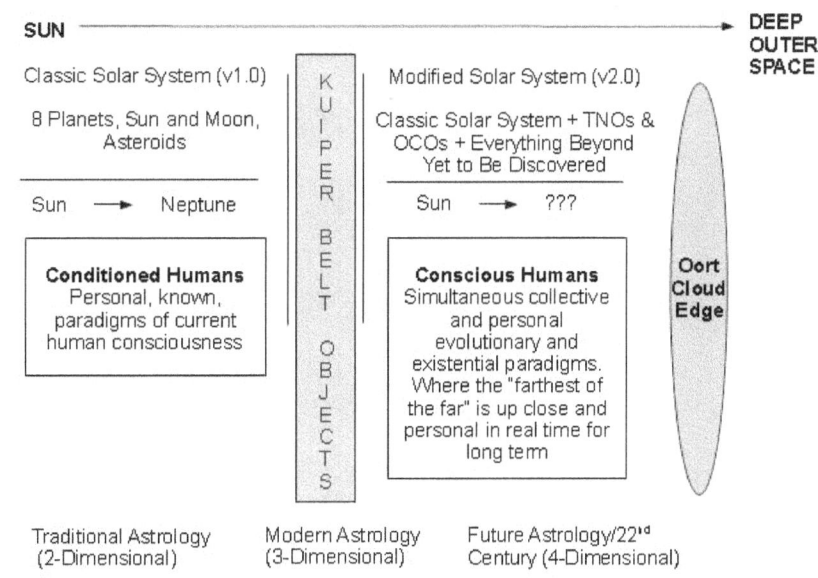

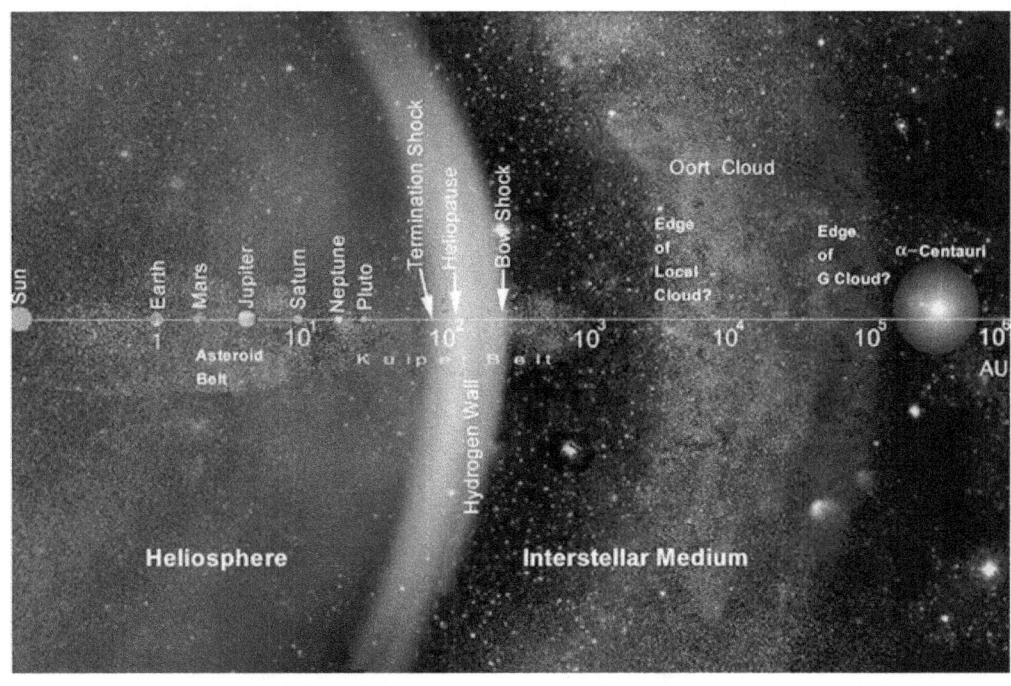

Image: NASA/JPL <http://interstellar.jpl.nasa.gov/interstellar/probe/introduction/scale.html>
http://bit.ly/vtFb3J

BIBLIOGRAPHY

Bertucelli, Penelope. *Phoenix Workshop: Uranian Astrology Manual, Cosmobiology Conference.* Weston, Florida: Penelope Publications, 1995.

Bills, Rex E. *The Rulership Book; A Directory of Astrological Correspondences.* Richmond: Macoy Pub. & Masonic Supply Co., 1971.

Brown, Mike. *How I Killed Pluto and Why It Had It Coming.* New York: Spiegel & Grau, 2010.

Cunningham, Donna. *Sky Writer: Donna Cunningham's Blog on Astrology, Healing and Writing.* April 17, 2010.

Hampar, Joann. *Electional Astrology: The Art of Timing.* St. Paul, Minn.: Llewellyn Publications, 2005.

Jacobson-Goldstein, Ivy M. *Simplified Horary Astrology.* Alhambra, Calif.: Frank Severy Publishing, 1960.

Jones, Barrie W. *Pluto: Sentinel of the Solar System.* New York: Cambridge University Press, 2010.

Louis, Anthony. *Horary Astrology: The History and Practice of Astro-Divination: The Venerable Art of Answering Pressing Personal Questions Based on the Planets Positions at the Time of Inquiry.* St. Paul, Minn.: Llewellyn, 1991.

———. *Horary Astrology Plain & Simple: Fast & Accurate Answers to Real World Questions.* St. Paul, Minn.: Llewellyn, 1998.

Lutin, Michael. *Made in Heaven: The Astrology of Relationships: Ideal and Real.* New York: Ballantine, 1987.

———. *Sunshines: The Astrology of Being Happy.* New York: Simon & Schuster, 2007.

March, Marion & McEvers, Joan. *The Only Way to Learn About Horary & Electional Astrology, Vol VI.* San Diego, California: ACS Publications, 1994.

Matrix Software. *Win*Star Express Astrology Software.* Big Rapids, Michigan: http://www.astrologysoftware.com. 2006.

McBroom, Don. *Midpoints: Identify & Integrate Midpoints Into Horoscope Synthesis.* Woodbury, Minnesota: Llewellyn, 2007.

Mlodinow, Leonard. *The Drunkard's Walk: How Randomness Rules Our Lives.* New York: Pantheon Books, 2008.

Osho. *Being in Love: How to Love With Awareness and Relate Without Fear.* New York: Harmony Books, 2008.

———. *Destiny, Freedom, and the Soul: What is the Meaning of Life?* New York: St. Martin's Griffin, 2010.

———. *Fame, Fortune, and Ambition: What is the Real Meaning of Success?* New York: St. Martin's Griffin, 2010.

Rostant, Beverley. *An Astrological Comparison of Planets in Medical Diagnosis.* Victoria, B.C.: Trafford, 2002.

Sullivan, Erin. *The Astrology of Midlife and Aging.* New York: J.P. Tarcher/Penguin, 2005.

Tyson, Neil deGrasse. *The Pluto Files: The Rise and Fall of America's Favorite Planet.* New York: W. W. Norton, 2008.

ACKNOWLEDGEMENTS

"No man is an Island, entire of itself; every man is
a piece of the Continent, a part of the main..."[1]

John Donne, *Meditation XVII*
English clergyman & poet (1572 - 1631)

Dr. Mike Brown	International Astronomical Union (I.A.U.)
Diana Stone	NASA
Michael Lutin	Kathy Svitil
Beverley Rostant	Jennifer Blue, U.S. Geological Survey
Mitch Horowitz	Carolyn Greenough
Erin Sullivan	Mark Velez
Don McBroom	Klaus at Osho International
Donna Cunningham	Susan Daily
Dr. Alois Treindl (& his Astrodienst.com team)	Juan Revilla
Sally Heuer at Llewellyn Publications	Judy McGuire
Sue Ward	Joseph C. Crane
Alexander A. Gurshtein (I.A.U. ret.)	D. Martinez
Anthony Louis	Debbie Pasquotto
Henry Seltzer	Dan Poynter
Harvey Craft	

---

[1] http://www.quotationspage.com/quote/29901.html

ENDNOTES

1. Brown, Mike. "I [Heart] Astrologers". Mike Brown's Planets. Jan. 26, 2008. <http://www.mikebrownsplanets.com/2008/01/i-heart-astrologers.html >. Used with permission.
2. Seltzer, Henry. Seltzer's article on the astrology of Eris appeared in The Mountain Astrologer in October 2007. Excerpt used with permission. Full text of the article can be viewed at <http://www.astrograph.com/learning-astrology/Eris.php

Introduction

1. "Open Source." Dictionary.com. © Encyclopedia Britannica, Inc. <http://dictionary.reference.com/browse/open source>

Chapter 1 - Horary Builds on Natal Astrology's Foundation

1. Lutin, Michael. "The Horoscope of Japan." Mar. 30, 2011. <http://www.michaellutin.com>

Chapter 2 - Astrology & Astronomy Reunite from Pluto's Ashes

1. Svitil, Kathy A. "Beyond Pluto." *Discover*. Nov. 25, 2004. <http://discovermagazine.com/2004/nov/cover/article_view?b_start:int=2&-C=_>
2. Brown, Mike. "I do not love pseudo-science." Mike Brown's Planets. Feb. 2, 2008. <http://www.mikebrownsplanets.com/2008/02/i-do-not-pseudo-science.html >
3. Brown, Mike. <http://www.mikebrownsplanets.com/2008/02/i-do-not-pseudo-science.html >
4. Brown, Mike. "I do not love pseudo-science." Mike Brown's Planets. Feb. 2, 2008. <http://www.mikebrownsplanets.com/2008/02/i-do-not-pseudo-science.html >
5. Svitil, Kathy A. "Beyond Pluto." *Discover*. Nov. 25, 2004. <http://discovermagazine.com/2004/nov/cover/article_view?b_start:int=2&-C=>
6. Svitil, Kathy A. "Beyond Pluto." *Discover*. Nov. 25, 2004. <http://discovermagazine.com/2004/nov/cover/article_view?b_start:int=2&-C= >

Chapter 3 - Philosophical Differences Between Modern & Traditional Horary

1. Osho. *Destiny, Freedom and the Soul: What is the Meaning of Life?* New York: St. Martin's Griffin, 2010. Pg. 20. Used with permission by Osho International.
2. Svitil, Kathy. "Beyond Pluto", *Discover Magazine*, November 2004 issue, published online November 25, 2004. <http://discovermagazine.com/2004/nov/cover > Pg. 8.
3. Greene, Liz. "Astrologer's Agendas: How We View Life is How We Read Charts." Lecture by Liz Greene at the Astrological Association Conference, Sept. 2008. <http://www.astro.com/astrology/in_lifeview_e.htm>
4. Ruperti Alexander, 'Dane Rudhyar: Seed-Man for the New Era' in *The Astrological Journal*, Vol. 32, No. 2 (Spring 1986), p. 57.
5. Louis, pg. 103.
6. Louis, pg. 102.
7. Louis email to author. Sept. 4, 2010.
8. March, Marion & McEvers, Joan. "*The Only Way to Learn About Horary & Electional Astrology, Vol VI.*" ACS Publications, 1994. Pg. 1.
9. Spencer, Jane. "Pluto's Demotion Divides Astrologers, Troubles Scorpios." *Wall Street Journal Online*. Aug. 25, 2006. <http://www.planetwaves.net/contents/wsj.html>.
10. See: http://www.skyscript.co.uk/frawley.html and http://www.skyscript.co.uk/horary1b.html

11. Louis, Anthony. Email to author. September 4, 2010.
12. Stone phone call with the author, Nov. 5, 2010.
13. Ward, Susan. "An Introduction to the Planets and Houses in Traditional Astrology." February 22, 1996. "The New Planets." <http://www.horary.com/sward/sward4.html> See also: < http://www.sue-ward.co.uk >
14. Sullivan, Erin. *The Astrology of Midlife & Aging*. New York: Tarcher/Penguin, 2005. Pgs. 121-122.
15. Sullivan, Erin. "*The Astrology of Midlife & Aging: The Significance of Saturn and Uranus in the Midlife Transition.*" Astrodienst.com website. <http://www.astro.com/astrology/in_midlife_e.htm >
16. Stone, Diana. "The 22-year Old Chart." The Fraser Valley Astrological Guild. 2003. <http://www.astrologyguild.com/horary6.htm >
17. Deusner, Stephen. "Planet Killer: Mike Brown, 'How I Killed Pluto and Why It Had It Coming' at National Air & Space Museum." *Express Night Out*. Jan. 6, 2011. <http://www.expressnightout.com/content/2011/01/mike-brown-how-i-killed-pluto-why-it-had-it-coming-national-air-space-museum.php >
18. Hitchens, Christopher. "Less than Miraculous," *Free Inquiry* magazine (February/March 2004), Volume 24. See also: <http://en.wikiquote.org/wiki/Christopher_Hitchens >
19. "How Facts Backfire." Boston Globe. July 11, 2010. <http://www.boston.com/bostonglobe/ideas/articles/2010/07/11/ how_facts_backfire/>.
20. Kuklinski, James H. "The Limits of Facts In Decision-making." From *Extensions: A Journal of the Carl Albert Congressional Research and Studies Center*. Fall 2007. <http://www.ou.edu/carlalbertcenter/extensions/fall2007/Kuklinski.pdf >
21. Brown, Mike. "I do not love pseudo-science." Mike Brown's Planets. Feb. 2, 2008. <http://www.mikebrownsplanets.com/2008/02/i-do-not-pseudo-science.html>.
22. Louis, p. 102.
23. Louis, p. 102.
24. Wikipedia contributors, "Inquisition," *Wikipedia, The Free Encyclopedia*, <http://en.wikipedia.org/w/index.php?title=Inquisition&oldid=398174354>.
25. Louis, p. 552.
26. Brown, Mike. "I do not love pseudo-science." Mike Brown's Planets. Feb. 2, 2008. <http://www.mikebrownsplanets.com/2008/02/i-do-not-pseudo-science.html >
27. Brown, Mike. "I do not love pseudo-science." Mike Brown's Planets. Feb. 2, 2008. <http://www.mikebrownsplanets.com/2008/02/i-do-not-pseudo-science.html >
28. Brown, Mike. "I do not love pseudo-science." Mike Brown's Planets. Feb. 2, 2008. <http://www.mikebrownsplanets.com/2008/02/i-do-not-pseudo-science.html >
29. Cunningham, Donna. "Real World Astrology - Continuing Ed for Professionals." *Skywriter* blog. Apr. 17, 2010. <http://skywriter.wordpress.com/2010/04/17/real-world-astrology%E2%80%94continuing-ed-for-professionals/ > and <http://skywriter.wordpress.com/ >.
30. Stone, Diana. Phone call with author. Nov. 5, 2010.
31. Lutin, Michael. "The Horoscope of Japan." Mar. 30, 2011. <http://www.michaellutin.com>
32. Lutin, Michael. Lecture in Portland, Oregon. Jan. 13, 2007.

Chapter 4 - Technical Differences Between Modern & Traditional Horary

1. Louis, Anthony. *Horary Astrology: The History and Practice of Astro-Divination*. Minnesota: Llewellyn Publications, 1991., pg. 69.
2. March, Marion & McEvers, Joan. "The Only Way to Learn About Horary & Electional Astrology, Vol VI." ACS Publications, 1994. Pg. 2.
3. Louis, pg. 66.
4. Stone phone call. Nov. 5, 2010.
5. Houlding, Deborah. "Learning Horary Astrology: Traditional Sign Rulerships." Skyscript website. <http://www.skyscript.co.uk/horary1b.html>
6. Cunningham, Donna. "Mining the Minor Aspects: Research in the Blogosphere." *The Mountain Astrologer*. December 2010/January 2011 issue. Pgs. 18-21.

7. Navarro, Gilbert. "What is Horary Astrology?" Horary Astrology with Gilbert Navarro. <http://www.navarroastrology.com/horary-astrology/> Story verified by Diana Stone via phone conversation with the author.
8. Louis email. Sept. 4, 2010.
9. Houlding, Deborah. "Learning Horary Astrology: Traditional Sign Rulerships." Skyscript website. <http://www.skyscript.co.uk/horary1b.html>
10. March, Marion & McEvers, Joan. *"The Only Way to Learn About Horary & Electional Astrology, Vol VI."* ACS Publications, 1994. Pg. 133.
11. Houlding, Deborah. "Learning Horary Astrology: Traditional Sign Rulerships." Skyscript website. <http://www.skyscript.co.uk/horary1b.html>
12. Louis. *Horary Astrology.* Pg. 161.
13. Louis. *Horary Astrology.* Pg. 161.
14. Houlding, Deborah. "Learning Horary Astrology: Traditional Sign Rulerships." Skyscript website. <http://www.skyscript.co.uk/horary1b.html>
15. Houlding, Deborah. "Learning Horary Astrology: Traditional Sign Rulerships." Skyscript website. <http://www.skyscript.co.uk/horary1b.html>
16. Louis. *Horary Astrology.* Pg. 161.
17. Louis. *Horary Astrology.* Pg. 61.
18. Lutin, Michael. "This Shit Works." Feb. 23, 2011. <www.michaellutin.com>.
19. Mlodinow, Leonard. *Drunkard's Walk: How Randomness Rules Our Lives.* New York: Pantheon Books, 2008.
20. Louis email. Sept. 4, 2010.

Chapter 5 - The Modern Horary Toolbox

1. Quote Garden. Quotations About Astrology. <http://www.quotegarden.com/astrology.html>
2. Keim, Brandon. "Waterboarding Doesn't Work, Scientists Say." Wired Magazine. Sept. 21, 2009. <http://www.wired.com/wiredscience/2009/09/badintelligence/>. See also: <http://thinkprogress.org/why-enhanced-interrogation-failed/#Ia> and <http://www.washingtonpost.com/wp-dyn/content/article/2007/01/15/AR2007011501204.html> and <http://judiciary.senate.gov/hearings/testimony.cfm?id=3399&wit_id=7228>
3. Cunningham, Donna. "Aspect Analysis: Mining the Minor Aspects–Research in the Blogosphere." *The Mountain Astrologer.* Dec. 2010/Jan. 2011 issue. Pgs. 18-21.
4. Stone, Diana. "Wanna See a Reeeeally Bad Chart? Or, What Happens If You Don't Listen to the Astrologer?" The Fraser Valley Astrological Guild. 2003. http://www.astrologyguild.com/horary3.htm
5. Brown, Mike. *How I Killed Pluto & Why It Had It Coming.* New York: Spiegel and Grau, 2010. Pgs. 24-6.
6. Williams, David R. "Chiron Fact Sheet." NASA. Sept. 4, 2004. <http://nssdc.gsfc.nasa.gov/planetary/factsheet/chironfact.html>
7. Lutin, Michael. "Chiron Premium Message." Nov. 15, 2007. http://www.michaellutin.com/dailyfix.htm.
8. Revilla, Juan Antonio. As quoted in Wikipedia Wikipedia contributors, "Astrological symbols," Wikipedia, The Free Encyclopedia, <http://en.wikipedia.org/w/index.php?title=Astrological_symbols&oldid=396378398>. See also Revilla, Juan Antonio. "The Astronomical Variants of the Lunar Apogee-Black Moon". <http://www.expreso.co.cr/centaurs/blackmoon/barycentric.html>
9. Wikipedia contributors, "Formation and evolution of the Solar System," Wikipedia, The Free Encyclopedia, <http://en.wikipedia.org/w/index.php?title=Formation_and_evolution_of_the_Solar_System&oldid=404637868>.
10. Jacobson-Goldstein, Ivy M. *Simplified Horary Astrology.* Alhambra, Calif.: Frank Severy Publishing, 1960.
11. Robson, Vivian. *Fixed Stars and Constellations in Astrology.* 1923, pg. 136. As quoted in <http://www.constellationsofwords.com/stars/Antares.html>
12. Ebertin, Elsbeth. *Fixed Stars and Their Interpretation.* 1928, p.70-71. As quoted in <http://www.constellationsofwords.com/stars/Antares.html>

13. Crane, Joseph C. "Fixed Star Lessons: Number Three Aldebaran and Antares, Two Other Royal Stars of the Persians." Astrology Institute. 2002. <http://www.astrologyinstitute.com/Fixed_star_lessons/lesson_three.htm >
14. Stone, Diana. "The Client Who Found Out More Than He Wanted to Know." The Fraser Valley Astrological Guild. 2003. <http://www.astrologyguild.com/horary2.htm >.
15. Stone, Diana. "A Medical Case." The Fraser Valley Astrological Guild. 2003. <http://www.astrologyguild.com/horary5.htm >
16. Louis, Anthony. *Horary Astrology Plain and Simple*. Pg. 110
17. See <http://www.aquamoonlight.co.uk/midpoints.html > and <http://www.cafeastrology.com/astrologytopics/midpoints.html > for explanations of the origin and use of midpoints, as well as <http://www.noendpress.com/pvachier/midpoints/index.php > for a midpoint calculator.
18. Wikipedia contributors, "Astrological Aspect," Wikipedia, The Free Encyclopedia. <http://en.wikipedia.org/wiki/Astrological_aspect>.
19. Louis, Anthony. *Horary Astrology*. Pg. 173.
20. Stone, Diana. "Horary Astrology Case Studies: Woman Client Asks: 'Should I Wait to Sell My House In 2006?'" The Meta Arts. August 2005. <http://www.themetaarts.com/2005august/diana.html >
21. Stone, Diana. "Man Asks: Where Is My Missing Bid Book?" The Fraser Valley Astrological Guild. 2003. <http://www.astrologyguild.com/horary7.htm >
22. Navarro, Gilbert. "Gilbert Navarro's Rules of Horary." The Ancient Sky website. <http://ancientsky.com/index.php?option=com_content&task=view&id=9&Itemid=88 >.
23. Navarro, Gilbert. "Gilbert Navarro's Rules of Horary." The Ancient Sky website. <http://ancientsky.com/index.php?option=com_content&task=view&id=9&Itemid=88 >.
24. Navarro, Gilbert. "Gilbert Navarro's Rules of Horary." The Ancient Sky website. <http://ancientsky.com/index.php?option=com_content&task=view&id=9&Itemid=88 >.
25. Stone, Diana. "Horary Astrology Case Studies: Woman Client Asks: 'Should I Wait to Sell My House In 2006?'" The Meta Arts. August 2005. <http://www.themetaarts.com/2005august/diana.html >
26. Stone, Diana. "Woman Asks: Should I Accept the Job Offer?" Diana Stone website. 2003. <http://www.dianastone.com/horaryz.html >
27. Lutin, Michael. *Sunshines: The Astrology of Being Happy*. New York: Simon & Schuster. 2007. Pg. 478
28. Stone, Diana. "The 22-year Old Chart" The Fraser Valley Astrological Guild. 2003. <http://www.astrologyguild.com/horary6.htm >
29. Lutin, Michael. Lecture in Portland, Oregon. Jan. 13, 2007.
30. Stone, Diana. "'A Twist in a Twist Fate' or How the universe tricked me into doing my first Horary chart." Horary Astrology Case Study. 2008. <http://www.dianastone.com/firsthorary.html >
31. Rostant, Beverley. "Horary Astrology Lecture Series: Part 5, Retrograde Motion in Horary Astrology." <http://www.astrologicalpredictions.ca/news/horaryseries.htm >
32. Stone, Diana. "Woman Asks: Should I Accept the Job Offer?" Diana Stone's website. 2003. <http://www.dianastone.com/horary1.html >
33. Stone, Diana. "David asks: Should I pursue a business relationship with XYZ Co.?" The Fraser Valley Astrological Guild. 2003.<http://www.astrologyguild.com/horary1.htm >
34. Louis, Anthony. *Horary Astrology*. Pg. 528.
35. Louis, Anthony. *Horary Astrology*. Pg. 131.
36. Louis, Anthony. *Horary Astrology*. Pg. 528.
37. Lutin, Michael. "This Sh*t Works: An Astrology Class." Feb. 23, 2011. Where's the Moon website. <http://www.michaellutin.com>
38. Brown, Mike. "Quaoar & the Edge of the Solar System." Caltech Watson Lecture. May 21, 2003. < http://www.gps.caltech.edu/~mbrown/appearances.html >
39. Russell, Randy. "The Kuiper Belt." Windows to the Universe website. National Earth Science Teacher's Assoc. Jan. 31, 2006. <http://www.windows2universe.org/comets/Kuiper_belt.html >.
40. Svitil, Kathy. "Beyond Pluto", Discover Magazine, November 2004 issue, published online November 25, 2004. <http://discovermagazine.com/2004/nov/cover >pg. 8.
41. Louis, Anthony. *Horary Astrology*. Pg. 528.
42. Louis, Anthony. *Horary Astrology*. Pg. 530.

43 Stone, Diana. "Helen asks: At some appropriate time, should I use Jane Doe to train Sunny?" The Fraser Valley Astrological Guild. 2003. <http://www.astrologyguild.com/horary14.htm > Stone, Diana. "Horary Letters." 2002. <http://www.astrologyguild.com/horaryletters.htm >
44 Louis, Anthony. *Horary Astrology*. Pg. 141.

Chapter 6 - Modern Horary Interpretation, Step-By-Step

1 Stone, Diana. "Woman Asks: Should I Sell My House?" The Fraser Valley Astrological Guild. 2003. <http://www.astrologyguild.com/horary22.htm >
2 Stone, Diana. "You Don't Always Know Why a Chart Says Yes." The Fraser Valley Astrological Guild. 2003. <http://www.astrologyguild.com/horary8.htm >
3 Stone, Diana. "The 22-year Old Chart." The Fraser Valley Astrological Guild. 2003. <http://www.astrologyguild.com/horary6.htm >
4 Stone, Diana. "Sometimes Things Are Over Before They Start." The Fraser Valley Astrological Guild. 2003.<http://www.astrologyguild.com/horary11.htm >
5 Stone, Diana. "You Don't Always Know Why a Chart Says Yes." The Fraser Valley Astrological Guild. 2003. <http://www.astrologyguild.com/horary8.htm >
6 Stone, Diana. "Sometimes Things Are Over Before They Start." The Fraser Valley Astrological Guild. 2003.<http://www.astrologyguild.com/horary11.htm >

Chapter 7 - Electional Astrology & Event Charts

1 "Other Presidents Looked to the Stars." *San Jose Mercury News*. May 3, 1988.
2 Stone, Diana. "It's All a Matter of Time(ing)." The Meta Arts. 2003. <http://www.themetaarts.com/archives/200308/diana.html >
3 Stone, Diana. "It's All a Matter of Time(ing)." The Meta Arts. 2003. <http://www.themetaarts.com/archives/200308/diana.html >
4 Stone, Diana. "It's All a Matter of Time(ing)." The Meta Arts. 2003. <http://www.themetaarts.com/archives/200308/diana.html >
5 Stone, Diana. "It's All a Matter of Time(ing)." The Meta Arts. 2003. <http://www.themetaarts.com/archives/200308/diana.html >
6 Read, Piers Paul. *Alive: The Story of the Andes Survivors*. Philadelphia: J.B. Lippincott Company: 1974.
7 Read, Piers Paul. *Alive: The Story of the Andes Survivors*. Philadelphia: J.B. Lippincott Company: 1974. Pgs. 344-5

Chapter 8 - Modern Horary In Action

1 Zibel, Alan. "Bank of America Starts Thaw in Foreclosure Freeze." Yahoo News. October 18, 2010. <http://news.yahoo.com/s/ap/20101018/ap_on_bi_ge/us_bank_of_america_foreclosures >. See also: <http://www.walletpop.com/2010/10/25/foreclosure-freezes-end-but-there-are-lingering-after-effects/ >.
2 "Bank of America Lifts Freeze on Foreclosures." *Modesto Bee*. Dec. 10, 2010. <http://www.modbee.com/2010/12/10/1466795/buzz-on-business.html > (It's the 2nd story on the page.)

Chapter 9 - Best Practices

1 McBroom, Don. "Essential Traits for Astrologers—Being Objective & Having an Objective." Monthly Astrology Articles from Don McBroom's Website. Feb. 2003. <http://www.donmc.com/objectivity.htm>
2 Lutin, Michael. Lecture in Portland, Oregon. Jan. 13, 2007.

3 Osho. "Destiny, Freedom and the Soul: What is the Meaning of Life?" New York: St. Martin's Griffin, 2010. Pg. 30. Used with permission by Osho International.
4 McBroom, Don. "Essential Traits for Astrologers—Being Objective & Having an Objective." Monthly Astrology Articles from Don McBroom's Website. Feb. 2003. <http://www.donmc.com/objectivity.htm>
5 Stone, Diana. A Twist in a Twist of Fate, or How the Universe Tricked Me into Doing My First Horary." Horary Astrology Case Study. 2008. <http://www.dianastone.com/firsthorary.html>
6 Louis. Pg. 118.
7 Wikiquote contributors, "History," Wikiquote, <http://en.wikiquote.org/wiki/History >
8 Louis. *Horary Astrology*. Pg. 115.
9 Louis. *Horary Astrology*. Pg. 118.
10 March, Marion & McEvers, Joan. *The Only Way to Learn About Horary & Electional Astrology - Vol. VI*. ACS Publications, 1994. Pg. 4.
11 Stone, Diana. "You Don't Always Know Why a Chart Says Yes." The Fraser Valley Astrological Guild. 2003. <http://www.astrologyguild.com/horary8.htm>

Chapter 10 - Top Ten Horary Mistakes & How To Avoid Them

1 Lutin, Michael. Lecture in Portland, Oregon. Jan. 13, 2007.
2 Louis email. Sept. 4, 2010.
3 Stone, Diana. "It's All a Matter of Time(ing)." The Meta Arts. 2003. <http://www.themetaarts.com/archives/200308/diana.html >
4 Louis, Anthony. *Horary Astrology*. Pg. 173.
5 Stone. Diana. "Sometimes Astrologers Are the WORST Horary Clients." Exploring Horary Astrology (website page). <http://www.dianastone.com/horary.html >

Chapter 11 - Relationship-Oriented Horary Questions

1 Lutin, Michael. Saturn in Libra 2010 Premium Message for Aries.
2 McGuire, Judy. "How Many Dates to Decide?" Seattle Weekly. December 15-21, 2010. Vol 35, No. 50. Pg. 51. <http://www.seattleweekly.com/2010-12-15/diversions/rules-to-click-by/ >
3 Louis, Anthony. *Horary Astrology*. Pgs 242-3.
4 Louis, Anthony. *Horary Astrology*. Pg. 252.
5 Lutin, Michael. "Daily Fix." Dec. 18, 2009. <http://www.michaellutin.com>
6 Lutin, Michael. *Sunshines: The Astrology of Being Happy*. New York: Simon & Schuster. 2007. Pg. 342.
7 Lutin, Michael. Phone conversation with the author. May 2005. See also: Made in Heaven, 1987.
8 Lutin, Michael. "Relationships." Entry on website May 16, 2011. <http://www.michaellutin.com>
9 Lutin, Michael. "Relationships." Entry on website May 16, 2011. <http://www.michaellutin.com>
10 Lutin, Michael. "Relationships." Entry on website May 16, 2011. <http://www.michaellutin.com>
11 Lutin, Michael. "Relationships." Entry on website May 16, 2011. <http://www.michaellutin.com>

Chapter 12 - An Evolving Body of Work

1 Svitil, Kathy A. "Beyond Pluto." *Discover*. Nov. 25, 2004. <http://discovermagazine.com/2004/nov/cover/article_view?b_start:int=2&-C= >
2 Craft, Harvey. "Is Chiron an Asteroid or a Comet or a Mystery? This Strange Object has Scientists Scratching Their Heads." Suite101.com. Feb. 1, 2010. <http://www.suite101.com/content/is-chiron-an-asteroid-or-a-comet-or-a-mystery-a196500#ixzz15lPhW9Pm >
3 Svitil, Kathy A. "Beyond Pluto." *Discover*. Nov. 25, 2004. <http://discovermagazine.com/2004/nov/cover/article_view?b_start:int=2&-C= >

4. Noll, Keith. "Naming the Worlds Beyond Neptune" from Binaries (and More) in the Kuiper Belt. Hubblesite. Hubble Discoveries: Science Year in Review: Hubble 2006. Pg. 46. <http://hubblesite.org/hubble_discoveries/science_year_in_review/pdf/2006/binaries_and_more_in_the_kupier_belt.pdf >
5. Brown, Mike."S/1 (90482) 2005 Needs Your Help." March 23, 2009. Mike Brown's Planets. <http://www.mikebrownsplanets.com/2009/03/s1-90482-2005-needs-your-help.html>
6. Horowitz, Mitch. "Unlocking the Mysteries of Sedna: A New Planet Discovered; An Ancient Myth Revived." *Venture Inward* magazine. March/April 2005 issue. See also: <http://www.mitchhorowitz.com/sedna.html >
7. Brown, Mike. "Snow White Needs a Bailout." Mike Brown's Planets (blog). March 10, 2009. <http://www.mikebrownsplanets.com/2009/03/snow-white-needs-bailout.html >
8. Brown, Mike. "What's in a Name — Part 2". Mike Brown's Planets (blog). July 13, 2008. <http://www.mikebrownsplanets.com/2008/07/whats-in-name-part-2.html >
9. Brown, Mike. "Dwarf Planets Are Crazy." Mike Brown's Planets. Nov. 12, 2010. <http://www.mikebrownsplanets.com/2010/11/dwarf-planets-are-crazy.html>
10. Brown, Mike. "There Is Something Out There - Part 1." Mike Brown's Planets. Oct. 20, 2010. <http://www.mikebrownsplanets.com/2010/10/there-is-something-out-there.html >
11. Brown, Mike. "Dwarf Planets Are Crazy." Mike Brown's Planets. Nov. 12, 2010. <http://www.mikebrownsplanets.com/2010/11/dwarf-planets-are-crazy.html>
12. Various sources: http://en.wikipedia.org/wiki/20000_Varuna#cite_note-MPC41805-12 , http://en.wikipedia.org/wiki/Varuna , http://www.csuchico.edu/~cheinz/syllabi/asst001/fall97/chissuc.htm
13. Wikipedia contributors, "From a Distance," Wikipedia, The Free Encyclopedia. <http://en.wikipedia.org/w/index.php?title=From_a_Distance&oldid=424521687>
14. Wikipedia contributors, "50000 Quaoar," Wikipedia, The Free Encyclopedia, <http://en.wikipedia.org/w/index.php?title=50000_Quaoar&oldid=410478372>. See also: Chad Trujillo's site (co-discoverer) <http://www.chadtrujillo.com/quaoar/ > <http://www.chadtrujillo.com/quaoar/quaoarorbit.gif > and the Tongva tribe site: <http://www.tongva.com/ >
15. NASA. "Hubble Spots an Icy World Far Beyond Pluto." Hubblesite Newscenter. News Release Number: STScI-2002-17. Oct. 7, 2002. <http://hubblesite.org/newscenter/archive/releases/2002/17/text/ >
16. NASA. "Hubble Observes Planetoid Sedna, Mystery Deepens." Hubblesite Newscenter. News Release Number: STScI-2004-14. Apr. 14, 2004. <http://hubblesite.org/newscenter/archive/releases/2004/14/ >
17. Horowitz, Mitch. "Unlocking the Mysteries of Sedna: A New Planet Discovered; An Ancient Myth Revived." *Venture Inward* magazine. March/April 2005 issue. See also: <http://www.mitchhorowitz.com/sedna.html > See also: Stacey Dresner; "Yale Researcher Helps to Discover New Planet;" Jewish Ledger: 4/16/04.
18. Horowitz, Mitch. "Unlocking the Mysteries of Sedna: A New Planet Discovered; An Ancient Myth Revived." *Venture Inward* magazine. March/April 2005 issue. See also: <http://www.mitchhorowitz.com/sedna.html > See also: Stacey Dresner; "Yale Researcher Helps to Discover New Planet;" Jewish Ledger: 4/16/04.
19. Horowitz, Mitch. "Unlocking the Mysteries of Sedna: A New Planet Discovered; An Ancient Myth Revived." *Venture Inward* magazine. March/April 2005 issue. See also: <http://www.mitchhorowitz.com/sedna.html >
20. Brown, Mike. "There's Something Out There—Part 2" Mike Brown's Planets. Oct. 28, 2010. <http://www.mikebrownsplanets.com/2010/10/theres-something-out-there-part-2.html >
21. Brown, Mike."S/1 (90482) 2005 Needs Your Help." March 23, 2009. Mike Brown's Planets. <http://www.mikebrownsplanets.com/2009/03/s1-90482-2005-needs-your-help.html>
22. Brown, Mike."S/1 (90482) 2005 Needs Your Help." March 23, 2009. Mike Brown's Planets. <http://www.mikebrownsplanets.com/2009/03/s1-90482-2005-needs-your-help.html>
23. Brown, Mike."S/1 (90482) 2005 Needs Your Help." March 23, 2009. Mike Brown's Planets. <http://www.mikebrownsplanets.com/2009/03/s1-90482-2005-needs-your-help.html>

24 Wikipedia contributors, "Moons of Haumea." *Wikipedia, The Free Encyclopedia"* <http://en.wikipedia.org/w/index.php?title=Moons_of_Haumea&oldid=398105859>
25 Wikipedia contributors, "Haumea (dwarf planet)." *Wikipedia, The Free Encyclopedia.* <http://en.wikipedia.org/wiki/Haumea_(dwarf_planet)#Discovery_controversy >
26 Brown, Mike. *How I Killed Pluto & Why It Had It Coming.* New York: Spiegel and Grau, 2010. Pg. 249.
27 Wikipedia contributors, "Makemake (dwarf planet)," Wikipedia, The Free Encyclopedia. <http://en.wikipedia.org/w/index.php?title=Makemake_(dwarf_planet)&oldid=406575394 >
28 Sullivan, Erin. *The Astrology of Midlife & Aging.* New York: Tarcher/Penguin, 2005. Pgs. 121-122.
29 Brown, Mike. "A Ghost of Christmas Past." Mike Brown's Planets. Dec. 29, 2009. <http://www.mikebrownsplanets.com/2009/12/ghost-of-christmas-past.html >
30 Lutin, Michael. "Daily Fix." Nov. 2, 2010. <http://www.michaellutin.com>
31 Mlodinow, Leonard. *Drunkard's Walk: How Randomness Rules Our Lives.* New York: Pantheon Books, 2008.

EPILOGUE - Beyond Astrology

1 Osho. *"Destiny, Freedom and the Soul: What is the Meaning of Life?"* New York: St. Martin's Griffin, 2010. Pg. 145. Used with permission by Osho International. <http://books.google.com/books?id=cS_m8ixeM3UC&pg=PA191&lpg=PA191&dq=osho+destiny+freedom+and+the+soul+gurdjieff&source=bl&ots=duYfViUigE&sig=Q5wOhre_rwthBNFFcKWtZe54_DU&hl=en&ei=RE83TZDXDomosQP-p5H_Ag&sa=X&oi=book_result&ct=result&resnum=1&ved=0CB0Q6AEwAA#v=onepage&q=astrologer&f=false >
2 Osho. *"Destiny, Freedom and the Soul: What is the Meaning of Life?"* New York: St. Martin's Griffin, 2010. Pg. 147. Used with permission by Osho International.

ABOUT THE AUTHOR

R.K. Alexander is a former journalist who has logged more than a quarter century on the astrological rockpile—including 18 of those years practicing modern horary astrology in addition to natal, transits and progressions. Instead of continued individual interpretation, this work endeavors to bring the beauty, simplicity, and accuracy of the art to a much wider audience. It's time to bypass and go beyond the blind, cult-like followings of <insert name of famous astrologer>.com, and faith- and belief-based mystical mumbo-jumbo. It's time for a mature, humanistic, democratic, do-it-yourself, science- and reality-based horary astrology that is infinitely more substantive, helpful, and useful to querents and practitioners alike.

www.ingramcontent.com/pod-product-compliance
Lightning Source LLC
Chambersburg PA
CBHW081219170426
43198CB00017B/2655